ENGLAND AND THE ENGLISH

FROM

AN AMERICAN POINT OF VIEW

BY

PRICE COLLIER

CHARLES SCRIBNER'S SONS
NEW YORK : : : : 1911

To
MY WIFE KATHARINE

CONTENTS

MISCELLANEOUS POEMS AND SONNETS

Page

ENGLAND AND THE ENGLISH
FROM AN AMERICAN POINT OF VIEW

I

FIRST IMPRESSIONS

LEAVING New York on a steamer officered and manned by Englishmen your impressions may begin from the moment you put foot on board. The change from the restless volubility of the Irish cab driver to the icy servility of the Englishman of the servant class is soothing, depressing, irritating or amusing as the case may be. The chattering, waving, gesticulating high-voiced travellers, and good-byers, are apparently of no interest to the stolid stewards, who move about at slower speed, speak in lower tones, do what they have to do with as little unnecessary expenditure of nerve, and muscle, and speech power, as possible. Even before the ship moves you have moved from the exhilarating, bracing, bright air of inland and upland plains, to the heavier and more

1

moist climate of an island. Movement, speech, feature and bulk are different. They are all, movement, speech, feature and bulk, different in a way that is easily and definitely expressed by one word: heavy. Later one finds that this word is used accurately. The English men, women, horses, vehicles, machinery, houses, furniture, food, are all heavier in proportion than ours.

What will you have for breakfast, if, alas, you will have any breakfast the first morning out? Something very light perhaps. These islanders, you soon find, have little regard for lightness. A light dish of eggs in some form, a light roll, fresh butter, coffee and hot milk? Yes, of a sort, but none of them light. You soon forswear coffee for tea, and ere long the passive bulwark of resistance wearies you into eggs and bacon, and cold meat, and jams, for your first meal of the day. Little things are typical. What you want is not refused you, but what they have and like is gradually forced upon you. Thus they govern their colonies. No raising of voices, no useless and prolonged discussion, no heat generated, no ridicule of your habits, or eulogy of their own, none of these, but just slow-moving, unchanging, confident bulk!

The monotonous and solemn "yes, sir,"

"thank you, sir," of the servants, may lead you to suppose that at any rate this class of English man and woman is servile, is lacking in the national trait of confidence, is perhaps amenable to suggestions of a change. On the contrary, this class less even than others. The manner and speech are merely mechanical. The unblushing demands, either frankly open, or awkwardly surreptitious, for tips are part of the day's work. They are servants, they know it, they have no objection to your knowing it, and most of them have little ambition to be anything else. They are not in that position in the meantime, but permanently; they are not serving, while waiting for something else; service is their career. The American may "sling hash" at Coney Island, or in a western frontier town, until he can escape to become something else, but as a vocation he does not recognize it. At first, therefore, these people are puzzling, we shall see later that they are a factor in the civilization we are about to explore. They have their pride, their rules of precedence, their code; they are fixed, immovable, unconcerned about other careers, undisturbed by hazy ambitions, and insistent upon their privileges, as are all other Englishmen. They will not overstep the boundary lines of your personal position, and they jealously guard the boundaries of their own.

When we come to know them better we find that, although they are of all the laboring classes completely unorganized, without unions or societies, they are the one class which has kept up and increased the standard of wages. As a class they have made no claims, they have not appealed to the public, or to the politician, but they have, none the less, increased their demands, and obtained their demands. This is rather a curious commentary upon organized labor. The servant class numbers something like one in forty of the total population. My only explanation is that, as they are the class coming most closely in contact with the ruling class, they have absorbed and used the methods of that class. They hold themselves at a high value, assert that value, and wherever and whenever possible, take all they can get. It is done quietly, as a matter of right, and with a sort of subdued air of sanctity. This is the British way, an impressive and an eminently successful way. At any rate, so far as the servants themselves are concerned, they may well laugh in their sleeves at the troubles of the trades unions and other societies, which, with much noise, turmoil, strikes and boycotts, have not succeeded as well as they have in bettering their condition. The wages of servants have increased out of all proportion to the increase of wages in other occupations in the last fifteen years.

Though I have written that they are unorganized as a class, in the sense in which the miners or the spinners are organized, they maintain among themselves distinctions and gradations as sharp as those of a Court. The house-keeper, the butler, the head coachman, the master's valet, and the mistress's maid, are the nobility and gentry of the servants' hall, while footmen, grooms, maids and the like are commoners. To the average American these distinctions may be merely laughable. Let him come to England and keep house for a year and he will find them adamant. He can no more ignore them or override them than he can alter the procedure in the House of Lords. If he accepts them, well and good; if not, he will have no servants. The butler and the house-keeper are spoken of by the other servants as "Mr." Jones and "Mrs." Brown, and the mistress's maid is "Miss," and woe be to the unlucky underling who forgets these prefixes! At a large house party where there are many men servants and maids, they take the precedence of their particular master and mistress. You smile at first, and then you realize that underlying the snobbishness, the petty dignities, is the national love of orderliness, the desire for a cut-and-dried routine, the British contentment in having a fixed personal status. Those who have read Thackeray's novels, and his Yellowplush papers, have a not inaccurate, though a brightly colored picture of the English servant class. Above all things, do not forget the most important factor of all,— they are all English, they are all of the same race as their masters. This explains, if not everything, almost everything.

But, like all good Americans, let us be moving, let us get on. Here we are at last in London! That yellow ball above the horizon, seen through this bituminous haze, is the sun — the sun sadly tarnished. Those little toy coaches and engines, are cars and locomotives. The noiseless gliding out, and gliding into the station, is the English way of running things. No shouting, no nervous snapping of watches, no shriek of whistle, no clanging of bell; a scarcely audible whistle, and the thing is done. These people must know their business or somebody would be left behind, somebody would get into the wrong train; they do know their business. We are soon to find that this is the country of personal freedom, and also personal responsibility. You may do as you please unmolested, uncriticised, unreported, unphotographed, unheralded, unnoticed even, as in no other country in the world, but the moment you do what you ought not to please to do, from the policeman to the court, and thence to the jail, is a shorter road here than anywhere else. So much personal liberty is only possible where justice is swift, unprejudiced impartial and sure. The lord, the millionaire, the drunkard and the snatch thief are treated the same — within the same six months a great financial schemer and the son of a great nobleman were ushered behind the bars with almost as little ceremony and as little delay as are required for the trial of a wife-beater or a burglar. Personal freedom has this serious responsibility: its misuse is promptly punished, and there is no escape,— they even behead a king on occasion.

When we are in England we do, so far as our temperamental limitations permit, as the English do. We go to a private hotel, small, with a front door always locked and only opened on demand, and we are ushered into our own apartment. For a week now, not another guest has revealed himself. Meals are served to each in his own rooms, and though there is a coffee-room, no one, apparently, uses it. The Englishman brings his home to his hotel. It is not a meeting-place, but, quite on the contrary, a place for personal privacy and seclusion. There are, of course, now in London, great caravansaries, but they are for the stranger and for the modernized Englishman, the real John Bull abhors them. The rooms are damp, a small grate-fire mitigates the gloom of the sitting-room, but bedroom and dressing-room retain their damp-blanket atmosphere throughout our stay. A tin tub is brought in in the morning and evening, and you bathe as a protection from the cold. A sound rubbing with a coarse towel takes the place of a fire, or steam heat. No doubt many people die in becoming accustomed to this method of keeping warm, but those who survive have conquered for themselves the greatest empire extant.

The first days in the streets of London bring so many impressions that it is as confusing to remember them as to recall, in their proper order, the changes of a kaleidoscope. It is apparent that the men are heavier here than with us; apparent, too, that this is a land of men, ruled by men, obedient to the ways and comforts and prejudices of men, not women. Here the male bird has the brilliant plumage. The best of them, as one sees them in Piccadilly, in Bond

Street, in St. James's Street, in the clubs, in the park on a Sunday after church, are fine-looking fellows, well set up and scrupulously well groomed and turned out. But the women! What hats, what clothes, what shoes, what colors, what amorphous figures! One hears of English economies, evidently they begin with the dress-maker's bill. Who permits that nice-looking girl to wear a white flannel skirt, a purple jacket, and a fur hat with a bunch of small feathers sticking out of it at right angles? Here is another with an embroidered linen coat, and a bit of ermine fur, and a straw hat with flowers on it! The grotesque costumes of the women would make one stop to stare, were it not that they are so common one ceases at last to notice them. But their taste in dress is nothing new. When Queen Victoria came to the throne their tasteless vagaries of costume were noticeable. A well-dressed lady is described as wearing, in those days, "a blue satin robe, a black-violet mantlet lined with blue satin and trimmed with black lace, and an emerald-green hat, trimmed with blonde and roses, as well as ribbon and feathers"!

The complexions of the English have often been exploited for our benefit. The damp climate and the exercise out-of-doors produce the red, they say. But on examination it proves to

be not the red of the rose, but the red of raw
beef, and often streaky and fibrous at that.
The features are large and the faces high-col-
ored, but it is not a delicate pink, it is a coarse
red. At a distance, the effect is charming, bright,
refreshing, but close to, often rather unpleasant.
Here the features of the women, even the features of the beautiful women, are moulded; while
the features of our beautiful American women
are chiselled.

The shops wear the colors, so to speak, of the
dominant sex. Those that most attract you
have in their windows the paraphernalia of the
male bird. Shops with guns, and folding seats
to carry about when shooting, and everything
pertaining to the sport in profusion; shops with
windows draped with haberdashery; shops filled
with leather and silver conveniences for men;
shops with all sorts of hats for all sorts of climates
for men's wear; shops with harness, shops with
whips, shops with saddles, shops with tobacco,
endless shops with potables of all kinds from
those vintages of '47, '64, '84, '99, and 1900, for
the particular imbiber, to those with the ever-
lasting "Bitter" and "Gin," enjoyed by the nomadic drinker with only pennies on his person
and no credit. Should you take the trouble to
count you would find that the purveyors to

masculine taste largely predominate. The men dress, the women are clothed, and the shops are provided accordingly.

The Englishwoman pretends that the French-woman and the American woman are over-dressed, inappropriately dressed. This, how-ever, is only a salve to her feelings, and is acqui-esced in by her lord for reasons of economy. In the country, in stout boots, nondescript hats, and cheap flannel and tweed, the Englishwoman is properly clothed because such costumes are cheap; but in town she is awkwardly clothed because well-fitting clothes of fine material are expensive, and the Englishwoman is not given her appropriate share of the income for purposes of personal adornment. That is the truth of the matter, that and the national all-pervasive lack of taste, which accounts for the odd, often comi-cal appearance of women in London.

It might imperil the faith of the reader in these impressions, were one to give facts in this connection; if one, that is to say, were to give the figures of amounts allowed to certain women, wives, sisters, daughters, in certain families to dress on. Just as our women are so often wick-edly and grotesquely extravagant in their ex-penditure, so, here, such matters are on a scale that can only be called mean. Very often facts.

statements from real life are flouted as isolated, exaggerated and hence untrue to life. Often enough, therefore, a general impression carries more weight, and is, in truth, more valuable. This is the case in this particular instance as in many others. After an experience of England and the English covering some thirty odd years, I could easily quote example after example of the pittances allowed Englishwomen for their personal expenditure. Is it not, perhaps, easier and surer, after all, to develop particular instances from general lines of civilization? This England has become the great Empire she is because she is a man's country; this fact at any rate will protrude itself, make itself unmistakable at every turn as we go on, and the expenditures permitted to the women are merely one of the minor results of this.

To those who have given some attention to gastronomics either for the stomach's or the pocket's sake, the food provided here is almost more than a first impression, it is a daily, thrice daily, bugbear. Here, again, it is surely the masculine stomach that dictates. Meat, meat, meat, and no alleviation. The vegetables are few, and even they, as Heine — how Heine must have suffered in England — phrased it, "are boiled in water, and then put upon the table just

as God made them!" It is true that one may
go to the expensive restaurants, the Ritz, the
Carlton, the Savoy and others, and live daintily
enough, but that is not England, that is a foreign
country with which we have nothing to do.
During the past two weeks, I have dined at our
own private hotel, — which, by the way, it is fair
to the student to say, is a first-rate one in the
fashionable West End district — at the country
house of a distinguished peer of the realm and
at a middle-class restaurant in the Strand. At
all of these meat predominated. At his lordship's it is needless to say, there were fruits, and
salads, and vegetables from his own gardens,
and there was such variety that a guest might
please himself, and must have been over-critical
not to dine well whatever his tastes; but the
eternal round of eggs, bacon, sole, beef, mutton, ham, tongue and chicken, with potatoes,
and cabbage, and cheese, is the familiar diet of
the Englishman. Nor does he complain. He
wants nothing else. He demands just this bill-
of-fare. I have heard at Julien's in Paris, where,
when Julien himself presides over your meal,
you dine completely, the Englishman sighing for
some good plain beef or mutton. He likes it,
it agrees with him, he sighs for it when he has
been separated from it, and those who survive

this sanguinary flesh diet are, it must be admitted, splendid animals indeed.

> "Was ever Tartar fierce or cruel,
>   Upon the strength of water gruel?
> But who can stand his raging force,
>   When first he rides then eats his horse!"

This damp, cool climate, where, as King Charles said, one can be out-of-doors and enjoy being out-of-doors more days in the year than in any other country in the world, is a climate where the warmly dressed, agreeably exercising, comfortably housed male flourishes like a green bay tree. Let it be borne in mind constantly that these pages are not written in criticism — that is poor business for any man, most of all for a happy man who numbers many Englishmen among his friends — but as a study. Who is this Englishman? what is he? why is he? where and how does he live? above all, why has he conquered the world? how much longer will he be supreme? — those are the questions of interest. We are noting facts not because they are pleasant or unpleasant, not because they fit in with some theory of our own, but because they are to light the road we propose to travel among these people.

It is this climate, seldom very hot, seldom very

cold, rarely very bright, which lends itself better than any other to exercise out-of-doors, which makes fuel of a bulky and beefy sort necessary. No man in America, not even a coal heaver could live the year round on the food and drink which are the daily dietary of many men here; mostly men, it is true, who spend much time out-of-doors, shooting, fishing, hunting, golfing and the like. Eggs and bacon and sole with tea or coffee for breakfast. A hot dish of meat and potatoes, vegetable marrow, cabbage, celery, all boiled, or cold meat, salad and cheese, with beer or whiskey and soda, and a glass of port to follow for luncheon. Soup, generally very poor, fish, meat, an entrée often of meat, a sweet, cheese and fruit for dinner, with champagne, whiskey and soda or a light wine according to taste, again with port to follow, this bill-of-fare is a fair average diet. Added to by the rich, subtracted from by the poor, until it is the best of good living at the table of a Rothschild, because there is nothing so difficult in all the realm of cookery as plain cooking; or the most awfully unwholesome fodder at the table of the poor man, because these elements that lend themselves to the most wholesome diet, lend themselves also to the most unwholesome.

Look at the people who swarm the streets to

see the Lord Mayor's Show, and where will you see a more pitiable sight. These beef-eating port-drinking fellows in Piccadilly, exercised, scrubbed, groomed, they are well enough to be sure; but this other side of the shield is distressing to look at. Poor, stunted, bad-complexioned, shabbily dressed, ill-featured are these pork-eating, gin-drinking denizens of the East End. Crowds I have seen in America, in Mexico, and in most of the great cities of Europe— of India and China I know nothing. Nowhere is there such squalor, such pinching poverty, so many undersized, so many plainly and revoltingly diseased, so much human rottenness as here. This is what the climate, the food, and the drink, and man's rule of the weaker to the wall, accomplish for the weak.

> "The good old rule, the ancient plan,
>   That he should take who has the power,
>   And he should keep who can."

But more of this at another time. It is one of England's ugly problems and deserves a chapter to itself.

What an orderly crowd it is! Call it by all the bad names you will, and there remains this characteristic of law-abidingness which has been to me for many years, and is still, a ceaseless source of wonder. See them at the great race on the Epsom Downs on Derby Day. As you look from your coach top you see a black mass of people. No sign of a track, no sign of a race. A bell rings, two or three policemen on horseback, half a dozen more on foot, begin moving along the track, and this enormous crowd melts aside, makes a lane; the horses come out, dash away, the race is run, and back the people swarm again. The same at the Lord Mayor's Show. A few policemen begin clearing the middle of Fleet Street — a narrow street at best. Then mounted police, four abreast, not a word said, scarcely a gesture; no clubs, no noise, a lane is made through these people packed together, without shoving, pushing, elbowing, cursing or angry words, and here comes the procession. I have walked these streets now, on and off, for many years and at all hours of the day and night, and I cannot remember being pushed, shoved, shouldered, or elbowed. It is marvellous. So, too, I have driven through these streets, one, two and four horses, many and many a time, and each time with renewed admiration, not only for the admirable driving but for the good humor, the give and take, the fair play, the intuitive and universal willingness to give every fellow his fair chance and his rights. If that crowd in the

City is incomparably and uncompromisingly unpleasant to look at, it is none the less permeated with the national gift for law and order and fair play.

It is not a dull crowd. There are wags amongst them, and much appreciation of their humor. In this particular procession the various King Edwards appeared in appropriate costume, and with attendants in the trappings of their time. As Edward the Confessor appears some one says: "'Ello Eddie, you don't seem to 'ave changed much!" and there is a roar of appreciation at this chaff, and Eddie looks embarrassed enough in spite of his big horse, and his magnificent followers. "Oh, Oi soi, 'is beard and 'air don't match!" greets the appearance of another Edward, and again the crowd laughs good-naturedly. But for forty minutes, while the procession passes, and for hours before and hours after, this enormous crowd manages itself. Indeed, it is to be doubted, whether, were there no policemen in the streets, these people would not of themselves have made way and given the new Lord Mayor fair play and a clear passage.

There is one police patrolman to every 496 inhabitants of London; one to every 547 in New York; one to every 485 in Washington; one to every 509 in Boston; one to every 449 in Liverpool; one to every 330 in Dublin; one to every 340 in Berlin; one to every 184 in St. Petersburg; one to every 175 in Lisbon. When one considers the enormous area of London, and the universally acknowledged success of their daily dealings with crowds and with the traffic, and the comparative comfort and safety of people in this town, so large that it is almost a nation in itself, one is driven to the conclusion that the people themselves have the root of orderliness and fair play in them.

How is it in quite another social sphere? At Newmarket in the members' stand, walking from the stand to the paddock, I see a short, heavily built man of sixty odd, with gray beard and moustache, a fine aquiline nose, clear eyes, a cigar in his mouth, dressed in a brown bowler hat and a formless brown overcoat. It is the King. The King of that crowd in Fleet Street. The King of that crowd at Epsom. The King of these quiet people here in the paddock at Newmarket. No one stares, points, whispers, no one even looks. He, too, is given fair play, a chance with other English gentlemen to enjoy himself. He does not meddle with them, they do not meddle with him. If it is necessary to have a row, as has happened when there was undue meddling on either side, it is fought out and settled. In the meantime, fair play, and give every fellow a chance, from the King to the coster-monger. As an American I take off my hat. I should take off my hat to this King, any way. He is the cheapest investment and the most valuable asset England has to-day. Whenever he has taken a part in national affairs it has been for the glory, the peace and prosperity of his country. When he meddles it is not to advertise himself, not for the humiliation and undoing of his country, but for her honor.

When one remembers that there is no written constitution here, no infallible or inviolable body of law, but that each emergency is met by common-sense and solved by the application of a kind of working worldly wisdom, one admires the more the calm way in which each, from the highest to the lowest, submits, is satisfied, and goes his way. The House of Lords is the highest court of appeal, and though nowadays law lords are created who do the legal work of the House of Lords, this was not always the case. These hereditary rulers were supposed by instinct, or divine grace, or what not, to be capable of passing judgment upon the most intricate legal questions. One sees how they have been trained for centuries to meet and settle disputes, big and little, between themselves as Englishmen, and between themselves as a nation, and other nations, along these same lines.

Sitting on the bench at Bow Street with the Magistrate, I listened all one morning to his disposal of the cases that came before him. It seemed to me when I left that I had known beforehand what would happen. Quarrelsome women and men, mostly through drink; men and children accused of begging; a few cases of assault or resistance to the constable; all of them, hour after hour, dealt with in a good-tempered paternal sort of way, with appeals to their own sense of what was right. Only the cases where there had been resistance to the constable, the constable who represents British law and order, then hard labor and wholesome punishment. Always the same from the King to Bow Street. How can we live together amicably, with the utmost freedom for each one? that is the problem. The practical result is—you see it, if you have eyes, everywhere you go—a success. The machinery that brings it about seems from a theoretical point of view ill adapted to its purpose, but somehow there is a quality in the people themselves that permits a working basis.

I have never forgotten an almost grotesque example of this method of depending upon the people themselves to take care of themselves and to play fair. It was at a cricket match. My daughter and I walked round to the entrance to the reserved seats stand. I asked for two seats. "Where would you like them, sir?" asked the attendant. He saw that I hesitated, and said, "Go in and see where you would like to sit, come back and tell me the numbers of the seats you have chosen, and I will give them to you!" I accordingly went in and chose my seats and walked back and received and paid for my tickets. This was an important cricket match. There were some thirty or forty people behind me waiting to buy tickets, there were perhaps half a dozen inside choosing their seats, and the attendant was calmly running over his book of tickets, pulling out the numbers called for by those, myself among the number, who had found the numbers of the seats they wanted. There was no excitement or haste on the part of anybody; nobody grumbled, nobody seemed dissatisfied with this ridiculously slow and cumbersome machinery. On the contrary, because it *did work* with these law-abiding people everybody was the better off. This incident remains fixed in my memory as unique. Imagine a crowd at a race-course in France treated in this way. Picture the preposterousness of treating an American crowd at a base-ball game in this way. In either case there would be pushing and crowding, bad language and appeals to Heaven or to other lower powers to blast and destroy a management which sanctioned such methods. There is much talk and writing these days of the danger to this Empire from Germany and other powers. Much is written of English decadence along certain lines. I expect to show in other pages that there are legitimate reasons for such statements, but if I were their enemy I should always be cautious in attacking the English for that one reason, if for no other. They know how to take care of themselves as do no other people; and they seem to muddle along with the old stage-coach methods about as fast as do others with the latest thing in locomotive engines.

I have watched for hours at a time the crowds which came by the hundred thousand to support or to protest against the Licensing Bill — the imperturbable policeman, the docility of the people, the coming and going through the streets, the assembling in Hyde Park, all with a smoothness and lack of trouble of a trained army. Coming from Mars — or from Paris, the spectator would say: these people have been trained for months to march in procession, to assemble, to disperse, to re-assemble and depart. But they have not been so trained. It is the outstanding characteristic of the race. No wonder the average Englishman cannot be terrified, or even aroused, to take decent precautions against invasion. They do not need the training of other peoples. They are already trained. When I see this quality of the race I smile to think what would become of a hundred or two hundred thousand Germans landed on these shores, with their machine-like methods, their lack of initiative, and their dependence upon a bureaucracy. They would be swallowed up, or dispersed like chaff. These Saxons would dispose of them as they disposed of the Danes. The old street song of the Jingo days was not mere bluster. It had the heart of the philosophy of the race in it:

> " We don't want to fight
> But, by Jingo, if we do,"

etc., etc. This is true. They are not quarrelsome, not oversensitive, not inclined to carry chips on their shoulders, or to call attention to the length of their coat tails as offering an opportunity to any who dare to tread upon them, but they are a nasty lot to deal with once the row is on. Perhaps it is because they realize, as Hobbes has said, that the people do not flourish in a monarchy because one man has a right to rule them, but because they obey him; or perhaps it is because they are not a mixed race, but of that at another time.

The newspapers, being the eyes and ears of the nation, are apparently unduly impressed by disorderliness in other countries, particularly in America. Each morning and evening the American news consists largely of the chronicling of murders, railway disasters, divorces, fires, strikes, suicides, trials in the law courts, and the like. No doubt there are still people in provincial English towns who look upon the American as half horse, half alligator, with a dash of earthquake. But in the last two weeks in England, I note a bad railway accident, eighteen killed and injured; a disaster in a mine, seven men killed; two women kidnapped right here in London; three murders in broad daylight; a noble lord killed in the hunting field; a noble lord throws himself out of a window and kills himself; another noble lord appears as corespondent in the divorce court, and is found guilty; fog so dense one evening that there are several accidents to the traffic; a distinguished naval officer signals a humorous but none the less discourteous message to one of his ships which brings down upon him a severe reprimand from the admiral of the fleet, and so on, and so on.

I note these merely to reassure myself. Evi·
dently things go wrong here sometimes as elsewhere in the world, but less is made of them.
The newspapers pass over these incidents lightly,
and with little comment. They are not even a
nine days' wonder as with us. The profound
sense of personal freedom, and the jealousy with
which it is guarded and protected, does not permit the interference of newspaper reporters in
private affairs. Hence these matters cannot be
exploited, and dramatized, in epigrammatic paragraphs. There are fewer journals dedicated to
the putrid of the upper circles, wherein, as Mere-
dith says, "initials raise sewer lamps, and Asmodeus lifts a roof, leering hideously." There
would be too much horse-whipping here to make
blackmail journalism profitable. There is, too,
among the best people, an almost morbid dislike
of publicity. This is due to the fact that, for centuries, only mountebanks, quacks, people with
something to sell, public mummers, and the
like, advertised themselves, or for that matter,
do so now. Most of the advertising of people
in America, putting their photographs in the
papers and the like, is bought and paid for in
more or less roundabout ways, by the people
themselves. So I am told by journalists who
ought to know. We deem it necessary to be

known, to keep ourselves before the public; the men think it good business and pay for it as for any other advertising; the women from Eve-old vanity think the same, and we are only just beginning to realize that this is letting Asmodeus in at the front door.

But this ample protection of each one in his personal liberty of action and speech has its dark side. Where a sense of propriety on the one hand, and the punishment, ready to hand, of social ostracism on the other, prevail, things go well enough. There are, however, millions who care nothing for propriety, and who already have no social status, and consequently the traffic in women and drink goes on in London in an unblushing, embarrassing, and revolting manner. Only here in London does one see, or rather is it held under your nose, the most shameless parading of harlotry. The streets of the West End after dusk, and some of the restaurants at supper time, are simply overrun with hawkers of their own daubed but tarnished charms. New York, Paris, Vienna, Madrid, Berlin, City of Mexico, I know them all. In them all vice is more or less secluded, abashed, kept to one side by the police, not so here. It may parade itself, walk the streets, flaunt itself, to receive the same protection as any other pedestrian. So, too, may one drink—men, women, and even children—at almost every corner. What the rich man does, the poor man may do as well; what the virtuous woman does, the strumpet may do, too, so long as the law is not violated. Protection for all alike, liberty for all alike, and, be it said, punishment and the cold neutrality of impartial justice, for all alike.

In this damp, chill climate, in these gloomy streets, the poor and the vicious seem more sodden and more brutal, and vice more unappetizing than elsewhere. The gloom and ponderousness of this huge grimy city of London are reflected in the faces and the manners of the submerged and semi-submerged part of the population. One gets here, more than elsewhere, an early and indelible impression of the fearful struggle to survive. It would seem that one must be more fit here to keep out the damp and the cold, to eat the heavy food, to struggle against, and to keep oneself against, the huge mass of people centred here. The very bulk of the place looms the larger, and is the more terrifying because it is so much of the time in semi-darkness; and to the weak and unarmed it must appeal as a great crushing, dark, amorphous monster.

Nor am I altogether wrong in supposing that these people merely look weak and uncared for.

They are, as a matter of fact, of anything but a robust type. The following table, covering the twelvemonth ended September 30, 1907, gives us a commentary upon the physical condition of the men offering themselves as recruits for the regular army:

TOWN	OFFERED FOR ENLISTMENT	REJECTED FOR PHYSICAL REASONS
London	20,975	8,806
Birmingham	1,858	1,084
Manchester	2,523	1,821
Sheffield	1,031	363
Leeds	791	452
Newcastle	1,493	1,046
Sunderland.	776	282
Glasgow	2,905	1,135
Dundee.	956	680
Edinburgh.	1,500	628

These men were young men, and men with a taste for outdoor life. Nor is the standard itself very high which they are called upon to pass.

On the other hand, those who survive, those who are well armed and in control, are the more confident and proud. Those who are in the saddle in England ride a very fine horse, there is no doubt of that. England and the English have been dominant in the affairs of men for just about a century, or since the Napoleonic wars. It is hardly to be expected that having been so long dominant they should not be domineering.

This expresses itself in the best Englishmen by an easy and natural attitude of confidence and repose; but in the second and third rate Englishman, by an attitude of provincial bumptiousness and impudence unequalled in the world. This is what has made the Englishman the most unpopular, one may say, the most generally disliked, of men. The Germans and the Irish hate him; the French ridicule and distrust him; the average American takes his awkwardness, or what Carlyle once called "his pot-bellied equanimity," for patronage, giving him little credit for what is often mere shyness, and is forever irritated by him, now that he is too big to be bothered by him as a bully. His power, his stability, his honesty have won him allies and make allies for him to-day, but he has no friends. It would be a sad day for the Lion if he lost his teeth and claws. The real attitude of other nations toward him would surprise him. It is hard to be dominant and not to be domineering, and only the very first-rate Englishmen escape the temptation; and here, as everywhere else, the first-rate are in a large minority. It is the mass of men who make the composite photograph's main lineaments for the English nation's likeness, as must be the case with other peoples. And the mass of English people do not make themselves agreeable to other people; oftener than not they seem to pride themselves upon a studied erinaceous attitude toward all the world. The result of such behavior needs no chronicling by me. It is evident enough. It is noted here as an impression, deserving a place amongst first impressions, because it is accountable for much that is to follow.

It is fair, however, to add in this connection, that there are two reasons for this fish-like social attitude of the Englishman. In the first place, his nerves are not on the surface, as with us, and as is the case with all the Latin races. He is not intentionally, but constitutionally, stolid. His food and his climate have much to do with this. He is not effusive, not sympathetic, because he is not made that way. Here the mind frets not the body. He is not easily disturbed or moved. This is not a pose, it is a fact. He does not shrink from display or warmth of manner, so much as that they are lacking in his composition. I dined on one occasion with a party of gentlemen met to say good-bye to a friend of all of them, who was off for a long journey in the East. His health was drunk, each one shook him by the hand, and wished him a pleasant journey; they were not to see him for a year or two, but had I not known, I should not have guessed that he was leaving these dozen friends for a long absence. Doubtless his friends were as hearty in their good wishes and as loath to lose him as other men in other climes would have been, but there was little evidence of it. That is their way.

Another reason for the seeming lack of spontaneity in their manner is their grounded horror of interfering in other people's business. This is carried to a point almost beyond belief. Men who have belonged to the same club for years know nothing of one another's private affairs.

"I didn't know he was married!" said a friend to me one night at dinner, of a common friend, whom we had both known for years. A man's intimate friends for years, men he has known at school, at the club, in the army, are often quite unknown to, or by, his wife. Not that any man, anywhere, cares to introduce all his acquaintances into his home; but here the arrangement of a man's life, quite apart from his home-life is often carried to an extreme.

They avoid the smallest suspicion of even curiosity about one another's affairs or private concerns. It is considered a monstrous indiscretion even to show any interest in the affairs of a man who has not first invited you to an interest therein. The result is a delightful freedom from prying, or questioning, but at the same time there is, in consequence, an entire lack of ease and vivacity. It is necessarily only the bare surface of things that one may touch upon, where each one is wrapping himself in a mantle of mental aloofness. Hence the English are much given to the *axiomata media* in conversation, and much given to talking not at all when they do not feel like it. They feel under no obligation to be entertainers or entertaining.

England, as a whole, has little patience with the virtues not easily recognized by the community as a whole. Originality is neither sought nor commended. The man who expresses and represents the community is the valued man. The Mills and Spencers, and Merediths and Bagehots, of whom the great mass of the English even now know nothing and care less, the Byrons and Shelleys, they willingly let die. England treats her men of wayward genius as a hen treats the unexpectedly hatched duckling. She is amazed to find herself responsible for an animal which prefers the water to the land; but once it actually takes to the water, her responsibility ceases. If the hen were English, and could talk, it would say: "Well, that fellow is an awful ass, and too clever by half!" When, therefore, they come in contact with French, Germans, Americans, Italians, Irish, or even their own breed from Canada or Australia, they have nothing to say to them, no sympathy with them, no comprehension of them, and not the least wish in the world to understand them, unless there is something tangible and valuable to be got out of it.

If I have heard it once from my compatriots I have heard it an hundred times, this dissatisfaction and even irritation at the Englishman's indifference. The American cannot understand that this chilliness is not in the least assumed. It is just as much a part of the Englishman as his speech. He does not care for strangers, particularly foreigners, and he very seldom pretends to. Our enthusiastic and indiscriminating hospitality to foreigners, especially to Englishmen and Englishwomen, is simply looked upon by them as an acknowledgment of their superiority. Some day we shall realize this, and become more careful, but it is wonderful that an intelligent race like the Americans should take the cuffing and snubbing they get for their pains, whether at home or as Americans domiciled in England, not even now realizing that the Englishmen care nothing about them unless they come bearing gifts. But there is no hypocrisy about it. The Englishman does not treat foreigners that way, and he does not in the least understand why we do so.

There is never an international boat-race or affair of any kind but what there are heart-burnings on the part of the Americans; while the Englishman, who has been hospitable in his fashion, remains serenely unconscious that he has not done all that was expected of him. He simply does not understand our enthusiastic hospitality—and, be it said, if he is a "bounder," laughs at us for it behind our backs — and would not dream of practising it if he did. In the case of the Englishman it is not a theory, it is a condition of mind and body, a heritage of social training, for which he is in no sense to be blamed. If we do not like it, we can leave it alone, but it is absurd to be irritated. Americans who have become domiciled in England, who give lavishly to charities, who entertain luxuriously, would be surprised to know the attitude of mind of the average Englishman in regard to them. He looks upon them first as people who have recognized his superiority and therefore prefer his society; but secondly, and always, as renegades, as people who have shirked their duty as Americans. This is typical of the Englishman's make-up; he is complacently sure of himself, he is condescendingly generous in the acceptance of all forms of sport, amusement, and hospitality offered by his American host, but he believes

religiously in doing one's duty, and he knows
very well that runaways cannot be doing their
duty, even if it take the form of providing entertainment for his adopted countrymen.   I
should be sorry in closing this chapter if I have
not made it clear that I am offering explanations
not criticisms. Few criticisms, and no superficial
criticisms, are of the least value; while, perhaps,
an explanation, especially if it is by way of being
a discovery, may soothe, even if it does not entirely satisfy. Nor should the last word on this
particular subject go without the personal testi-
mony of the writer, which, no doubt, is shared
by many others, that there is no kindlier, no more
hospitable and no pleasanter comrade than the
Englishman, once one is upon a footing of inti-
macy with him. Then he accepts you just as
naturally as he does not accept the stranger.

II

WHO ARE THE ENGLISH ?

IF this question: Who are the English ? were asked, either of the average Englishman, or of the average American visitor to England, the answer would probably be both inaccurate and confusing. The average Englishman knows little of the origins of his race, and is not of the mental make-up that sets much store by such matters in any case; and the American pays little heed to anything except to what comes directly under his notice as he travels about to and from London as his centre.

London itself is a city of some seven million six hundred odd thousand inhabitants. It is a small nation in itself. The total population of the Kingdom of Great Britain and Ireland is only 43,660,000 (1906). But London is not England. The United Kingdom of Great Britain and Ireland is not England, with its total area of 121,000 square miles. No, what the world knows as England is the British Empire, which includes the above, and, in addition, some 11,400,000 square miles, and a population of about 410,000,000. The known surface of the globe is estimated at about 55,000,000 square miles — its total population is believed to be about 1,800,000,000. The British Empire, therefore, occupies more than one-fifth of the earth's surface, and its population is also more than one-fifth, or about twenty-two per cent. of the inhabitants of the globe.

That is England! In Asia they have a population of some 237,000,000; in Africa, a population of some 31,000,000; in America, a population of some 60,000,000; in the West Indies, some 2,000,000; in Australasia, some 5,500,000, and so on. When you walk the streets of London, therefore, you are in the capital of something over one-fifth of the world. These gentlemen in clubs, and offices, and in the streets, are the masters of the world. There must be a great many of them, and they must be very wonderful men, one says to oneself. No, the population of Great Britain and Ireland is, as we have seen, only about 43,500,000, and what of them?

It is stated on trustworthy authority that the aggregate income of these 43,000,000 of people is $8,550,000,000. Of this total, 1,250,000 peo-

ple have $2,925,000,000, these are the rich;
3,750,000 people have $1,225,000,000, these are
the comfortable class; the other 38,000,000
have $4,400,000,000, to divide, and if we do
the dividing for them, we see that these 38,000,-
000 have nearly one hundred and sixteen dollars
apiece. Not a large income by any means.
But we are not Socialists, these figures are not
put down here to bolster any argument for or
against the distribution of wealth, but to call
attention to quite another matter. It is evident
from these figures that we may deduct 38,000,-
000 from the 43,000,000 of population and still
have in the 5,000,000 that remain the sum total
of those who do the real governing, the real ruling, of this enormous Empire. The other 38,-
000,000, with their average income of $116,
have in all probability neither leisure nor ability
to look after anybody but themselves, and they
even do that precariously. We may go still further, and say that out of these 5,000,000 certainly not more than 1,000,000 are male adults.
I know very well the admirable phrase of Walter
Bagehot that "there are lies, damned lies, and
statistics"; but I may claim for this analysis that
it is a matter of facts, and not of statistics. It
requires no juggling with figures, no poetic exaggeration for the petty purpose of making a

point, to arrive at this rather startling conclusion: that about 1,000,000 Englishmen of the ruling class control one-fifth of the known surface of the globe, and one in every five of all the inhabitants thereof.

Out of the various wars and invasions of the island of Great Britain, from the time of Cæsar's first landing in 55 B.C., there have percolated down a million men who rule the world.

This is sufficiently interesting to make it worth while to find out who these Englishmen are. We can, any and all of us, make our notes about them as we see them, here and now. According as our eyes differ, our tastes differ, our education and experience differ, we come to different conclusions. Personally, I am inclined to think that the Englishman is an acquired taste, but for the moment that is neither here nor there. When any comparatively small number of men come to play such a rôle as this in the world, one must begin further back to study them. This is not a sociological or psychological freak, this maintenance of superiority over the world — not a matter that can be explained by snippity chapters written at short range about the Englishman's religion, his Parliament, his clubs, his home life, his sports, his clothes, and so on, indefinitely. These are merely the outside trap-

pings, which are interesting enough in their way
and well worthy of the reporter and his camera,
because there are plenty of people about who
only want to know what the great man looks
like, and what he smokes, and what he drinks,
and whether he wears a turned-down collar or
not — and some of them, perchance, will make
themselves great in his likeness by copying his
wardrobe, his diet, and his potables.

But we are so superficial as to believe that in
these two thousand years, since Cæsar's day,
there must be, here and there, interesting and
important documents dealing with the origins,
the ancestry, the lineage, and training of this
superb band of a million men who hold the
world in their hands.

We know the misty moist island in which they
have lived all this time. We know that even
Tacitus wrote that its climate was repulsive because of its rains and continual mists. Cæsar
and his Romans did not go there for a holiday
on account of the charms of the climate. No
Roman, of those days, or these, would choose
this island as a place of residence. The Roman
invasion was merely to control the resident
Britons, and to prevent their sending aid to the
Gauls who were fighting Rome. The Romans
stayed there for three hundred and fifty years.

They built two great walls across the land to check the invasions of the Britons; they built roads for the passage of the legions; they constructed intrenched camps, which are the origin of many of the names of places ending in *cester*, or *chester*, from the Latin word *castrum*, and when the legions were called away in 408 A.D. to check the invasion of the Barbarians on the Continent, they left the island as British as it was before, with no trace of their language, their customs, or their laws. Though both English and American jurisprudence is based upon Roman law, this came later. England is not, therefore, in any sense Roman.

These Britons of Cæsar's time were a mixed race of Iberian stock—Iberian meaning south-western Europe—at the present time the Basque is the last and best representative. But as there is no Roman, so there is no Briton, or very little, in the English ancestry. From north-western Germany came Saxons, Engles and Jutes who, from time to time, invaded the England of the Briton, and finally crowded him out. By 829 the Germanic tribes had poured in, and completely invested England, or what we now know as England. But of these tribes the one that really made the England of to-day, the one from which England, and the English, get their chief characteristics, was the tribe of the Saxons. Sussex, Essex, Middlesex, the familiar names of English counties, are nothing more nor less than South Saxony, East Saxony and Middle Saxony. They were not of the marauding or piratical type. They came in the first instance as companions of their neighbors the Jutes. But while the Jutes came for adventure and for booty, the Saxons came because they wanted land to settle on. They came because their own country was becoming overcrowded. They were an agricultural people of the peasant class. There was no trace of feudalism amongst them. They were landowners with equal rights, who gradually pushed their way over the land, taking more and more territory; beating back the Britons, and securely occupying the territory they had won. The conquered Britons finally fled to the Welsh mountains where some of them remained, while others passed over in large numbers to the other side of the Channel to Armorica, and the Brittany of to-day is the land of this body of exiles from England.

These Saxons were independent farmers; they acknowledged no chief, no king, and when they were called upon to fight together, they answered the call of the leader or answered it not as they chose. When King Alfred called upon

them the first time to join him in driving out the
Danes, they refused to aid him. Finally they
came to his aid, but at a time of their own choosing. When they came together to discuss questions of common and general interest, their
meeting or assembly was not one of subjects, or
followers, but of freemen. They had apparently
little taste for public meetings, and those of
them who were much occupied with their own
estates and their own affairs, got into the way of
staying away altogether. Those who had leisure,
or talent for such matters, went. Finally what
was then known as the *Witenagemot*, or the
Meeting of Wise Men, and what has since become the English Parliament, took over the settlement of these questions, and left the farmers
free to attend to their own affairs. Even in
matters of justice and punishment each group
appointed one of their number richer or more
expert in such matters to choose juries and to
preside over such cases. Finally the sovereign
got into the habit of naming such persons, already marked out as fit for such duties by their
neighbors, as magistrates, and in this, as we
should call it, free and easy fashion, the business
of government was carried on. You may go to
the Bow Street Police Court and see the business of the day carried on in much the same

fashion now. The magistrate is a wise gentleman dealing with the problems of his less fortunate neighbors. That is all. They were people with little aptitude for public affairs, and with a rooted distaste for overmuch government, and so law-abiding, and naturally industrious and peaceable, that they needed and need less machinery of government than other peoples. They wanted independence on their own estates, and they wanted not to be meddled with.

It is not my intention to provide origins for the English people in order to trace later, and thus easily from my own hypothesis, the development of their present characteristics.

"They are the finest of all the German tribes, and strive more than the rest to found their greatness upon equity." "A passionless, firm and quiet people, they live a solitary life, and do not stir up wars or harass the country by plunder and theft." "And yet they are always ready to a man to take up arms and even to form an army if the case demands it." Thus writes Tacitus of them.

This tribe of Saxons had, by accident or wise leadership, happened upon the very country best suited to them. A fertile island, cut off from the rest of the world, and with room for all so that each one might with his family have a kingdom of his own. This with as little machinery of government as possible, and yet all ready to combine as equals in self-defence. But as they made their land productive, as they became rich, they became the prey of other peoples from north-western Germany and what is now the Scandinavian peninsula, and were forced to defend their possessions and their customs against Angles, Danes, and Normans.

It is a curious feature of the abiding, unrelenting purpose of these Saxons to govern themselves, and to be let alone, that though they were conquered in turn by Angles, Danes and Normans, they swallowed up all three in the end, and imposed their customs, their language, their habit of mind, and their institutions upon each of the invaders in turn. They would have nothing to do with the half-developed feudalism of Angles and Danes, or with the fully developed feudalism of William the Conqueror and his followers. The Conqueror claimed that the land was his and that every holder of land owed fealty to him personally. It took just about an hundred years for the Saxon idea to prevail over this feudalistic notion, and the result was Magna Charta. The Magna Charta, wrested from King John by the Norman barons, was in reality the shaking off of personal allegiance to a chief-

tain by the Norman barons, *aided by the Saxon
gentry*, who had finally imbued them also with
their own love of independence and a free government. They insisted then, and have maintained ever since, that they derived their rights,
their liberties, and their laws, not from a king,
but from themselves. In the days of William
the Conqueror their king was elective, though
chosen from the reigning house. As late as 1689
the Commons voted that King James had abdi-
cated and that the throne was vacant! They
chose their own rulers, and no doubt would do
so again to-day if necessary. It is much too long
a story to go, step by step, through the recital of
this development. It concerns us here only to
note these unchanging characteristics of the
race, maintained and strengthened through centuries of war, tumult, and conquest.

The present House of Lords itself is the direct
result of the Saxon's unwillingness to bother
with government, and his willingness to leave
such matters to those of most leisure and most
wealth, and therefore, in all probability, to those
of most capacity and most experience in such
matters. It was, and is, the common-sense view
of government, as over against the theoretical
view. The danger in such a view of government, of course, lies in the fact that the govern-

ors, whether kings, or nobles, or statesmen, may grow to feel themselves paramount, and undertake to demand from the governed what they have no right to demand; such as taxation without representation, or a full purse for the king by unjust requirements, and without rendering an account. But these peaceable Saxons, on each and every occasion when their independence has been threatened, have risen in a mass, asserted their liberties, and then left their kings or gentry again to govern. The Magna Charta, and the revolt led by Simon de Montfort, and the head of Charles the First, are all warnings to whom it may concern that the Saxons are not to be meddled with, and are not to be anybody's subjects. Thus began the history, and the fact, of democratic government. Love of the land, industry, privacy, personal liberty; these were sought and found in this island by the Saxons, and they have been preserved there ever since.

The London policeman with his hand uplifted, who has become part and parcel of the rhetorical stock in trade of American ambassadors, is the symbol of the Saxon's willingness to abide by the law, so long as the law is of his own making, and facilitates his getting about his business quickly and with a modicum of friction. That policeman is simply the embodiment of the spirit of the race which has fought off Jutes, Angles, Danes and Normans; which has broken nobles, and beheaded kings in order to be let alone to attend to their own affairs in their own way. They are not jealous of the law as are the French, because they make the law for their own convenience, and because they know that it applies with equal force to all. They do not disregard the law as do we Americans who are overrun with amateur law-makers, because they realize that they can and do make the laws, and that to disregard rules of their own making makes either sport or government a nuisance. The coster-monger's cart and the coroneted carriage in London streets have equal privileges, no more, no less, the one than the other. You may see both dealt with, with imperturbable impartiality by the police any day in the streets. The poisonous philosophy of socialism, whether it be eleemosynary socialism, or predatory socialism, which would make the State a distributor of the surplus of the strong for the propagation of the weak, makes its way but slowly among those of Saxon blood. "If I were to be asked," says Montesquieu, "what is the predilection of the English, I should find it very hard to say: not war, nor birth, nor honors, nor success in love, nor the charms of ministerial favor. They want

men to be men. They value only two things —
wealth and worth."

No State can make men men. No State can
produce wealth and worth. These three — men,
and wealth, and worth — are produced, and
produced only, where men measure themselves
against men for the mastery over the fruits of
the earth, without adventitious aids of any kind,
and under the protection of laws that all make
and all obey.

In these modern days, when so many strive to
become members of Parliament, and when all
sorts of pressure, financial and otherwise, is
brought to bear to secure a peerage, it is interesting to remember that both the House of
Lords and the House of Commons owe their existence to the fact that the Saxons did not wish
to be bothered by attendance at their assemblies.
Somebody must go, and so one or two were
chosen by each community to represent the rest;
and the wise men of the *Witenagemot* of old, together with the heads of the great church establishments, gradually came to be looked upon as
the King's counsellors, and were called together
to confer upon such questions as concerned the
whole commonwealth.

It is by no means a good sign at the present
time that, instead of wishing to attend to their

own business, so many butchers and bakers and
candle-stick-makers are eager to enter Parliament, to attend to other people's business. It is
not the good old Saxon way.

In America, as in other democracies, our mistakes and our political troubles have mostly
arisen from a wrong interpretation of "government by the people." It has never meant, and
can never be successful when it is interpreted as
meaning, that each individual shall take an
active part in government. This is the catchpenny doctrine, preached from the platform by
the demagogue. The real spirit of "government by the people" is merely that they should
at all times have control, and keep control, of
their governors, as these Saxons have done.

No one would dream of harking back to the
primitive days when every man sewed together
his own skins for clothes and for foot-wear,
made his own hut, caught his own fish, killed
each for himself his meat, and picked each for
himself his berries, and was his own priest, his
own physician, and his own policeman. We
now know that this was waste of time and energy.
We find it more convenient, and more conducive
to a long life, and a comfortable life, to divide
ourselves up into bakers, and butchers, and tailors, and berry pickers, and priests, and police-

men, and physicians. It is only in politics that we grope blindly amongst primitive methods for a solution of the problem of government. France, with her fantastic theories, and what proved her horrible fiasco, influenced our beginnings, and followed by that have come the Irish with their hatred of England and the English; and the mating of the French philosophy, with the Irish fact, has turned us aside from, and made us hesitating in, our allegiance to the only form of free government which has ever been successful in the world, and which is ours by ancestral right. It must be a poor race which cannot throw up from the mass of men a certain number whose wealth, leisure, and ability fit them for the work of governing; just as others amongst us are best fitted to bake or brew, or teach or preach, or make clothes or hats, or to dig in the fields. To say that every man is fitted to govern is to hark back to the days when every man was his own huntsman, fisherman, cook and tailor.

We have millions in America who are just learning the alphabet of free government, and they are still flattered by political parasites with loud voices and leather larynxes. Our parliaments and assemblies have too large a proportion, not of the brawn and brains that have made America a great nation in fifty years, but the semi-successful, the slippery and resourceful who live *on* the people, and *by* the people, and *for* themselves.

He is but a mean American who believes that this will last. The time approaches when Americans will slough off this hampering political clothing, put upon them by Latin and Celtic parasites, and insist upon being governed by the best amongst them, by the wisest amongst them, by the successful amongst them, and not by those whose living is derived by governing others, because they cannot govern themselves. It is not because we are fools that the present condition continues, it is because we are weighed down with the responsibilities of nation making. We have succeeded commercially and in all material ways marvellously. In fifty years we have become the rival of the strongest, and the commercial portent to which every finger in Europe points. Let this same energy be turned upon setting our domestic political affairs in order and the change in government will be as complete, and come as quickly, as in other matters. We have allowed our idlers to govern, with a splendid honor-roll of exceptions; we shall ere long insist that our ablest shall take their places in the good old Saxon way.

Strangely enough, however, the House of

Lords still remains the most democratic institution in England. It may still claim for itself to be the *Witenagemot*, or gathering of wise men, and one wonders why it does not defend itself along those lines.

It is not a house of birth or ancestry, for it is composed to-day to an overwhelming extent of successful men from almost every walk in life. No one cares a fig what a man's ancestry was in this matter-of-fact land if he succeeds, if he becomes rich and powerful.

William the Conqueror himself was a bastard, and his mother was the daughter of an humble tanner of Falaise.

The mother of the great Queen Elizabeth was the daughter of a plain English gentleman.

A pot-girl of Westminster married the master of the pot-house. After his death she consulted a lawyer named Hyde. Mr. Hyde married her. Mr. Hyde afterward became Lord Chancellor, with the title of Lord Clarendon, and his wife, the former pot-girl, bore him a daughter. This daughter married the Duke of York, and became the mother of Mary and Anne Stewart, both afterward queens of England.

It is evident that if queens of England may have a barmaid for grandmother, lesser mortals need not fret on the subject of ancestry.

The Englishman would not be what he is, nor would he in the least be transmitting his very valuable Saxon heritage, if he gave up his democratic custom of an aristocracy of power for the feeble continental custom of an aristocracy of birth. What the one and the other is to-day answers the question as to the relative merits of the two systems without need of discussion. The English, though nowadays many of them do not know it themselves, are the most democratic of all nations.

William the Conqueror divided England among the commanders of his army, and conferred about twenty earldoms; not one of these exists to-day. Nor do any of the honors conferred by William Rufus, 1087–1100; Henry the First, 1100–1135; Stephen, 1135–1154; Henry the Second, 1154–1189; Richard the First, 1189–1199; or John, 1199–1216.

All the dukedoms created from the institution of Edward the Third, 1327–1377, down to the commencement of the reign of Charles the Second, 1649, except Norfolk, and Somerset, and Cornwall — the title held by the Prince of Wales — have perished.

Winchester and Worcester, the latter merged in the dukedom of Beaufort, are the only marquisates older than George the Third, 1760–1820.

Of all earldoms conferred by the Normans, Plantagenets and Tudors, only eleven remain, and six of these are merged in higher honors.

The House of Lords to-day does not number among its members a single male descendant of any of the barons who were chosen to enforce Magna Charta. The House of Lords does not contain a single male descendant of the peers who fought at Agincourt. There is only a single family in all the realm, Wrottesleys, which can boast of a male descent from the date of the institution of the Garter, 1349.

In a word, the present House of Lords is conspicuously and predominantly a democratic body, chosen from the successful of the land.

Seventy of the peers were ennobled on account of distinction in the practice of the law alone.

The Dukes of Leeds trace back to a clothworker; the Earls of Radnor to a Turkey merchant; the Earls of Craven to a tailor; the families of Dartmouth, Ducie, Pomfret, Tankerville, Dormer, Romney, Dudley, Fitzwilliam, Cowper, Leigh, Darnley, Hill, Normanby, all sprang from London shops and counting-houses, and that not so very long ago.

Ashburton, Carrington, Belper, Overstone, Mount Stephen, Hindlip, Burton, Battersea, Glenesk, Aldenham, Lister, Avebury, Burnham, Biddulph, Northcliffe, Nunburnholme, Winterstoke, Rothschild, Brassey, Revelstoke, Strathcona and Mount Royal, Michelham, and others, too many to mention, have taken their places among the peers by force of long purses gained in trade.

Lord Belper, for example, created in 1856, is the grandson of Jedediah Strutt, who was the son of a small farmer, and made wonderful ribbed stockings.

> "Wealth however got, in England makes
> Lords of mechanics, gentlemen of rakes.
> Antiquity and birth are needless here:
> 'Tis impudence and money makes the peer.
> .   .   .   .
> Great families of yesterday we show;
> And lords whose parents were the Lord knows who."

The Saxon system still prevails. Those who push themselves to the front, those who accumulate a residue of power in the shape of leisure, are called upon to govern so that the others need not be bothered by such matters. It has been harder in some ages than in others for the man, unassisted by birth, to rise. But there has been no time in England when it has been wholly impossible. As a consequence of this, there is probably no body of men in the world who combine such a variety of experience and knowledge amongst them as the House of Lords. There are one or more representatives of every branch of human industry and professional skill.

Strange as it may seem, there is no assembly where a man could go — granted that all the peers were present — where he would be more certain of getting sound advice upon every subject, from higher mathematics and abstruse law down to the shoeing of a horse or the splicing of a cable.

Why the English themselves, or, at any rate, certain of their number, wish to abolish this assembly of the picked brains and ability in every walk in life, from literature and chemistry to beer-brewing and railroad building, I, as an American, cannot understand. It is the culmination of the essential philosophy of Saxondom. This is what the race has been at for two thousand years, not to be too much governed by, but to permit to govern, those who have proved themselves most capable of doing so.

The average number of barons summoned to Parliament by Edward the Second was 74; the average of the reign of Edward the Third was 43. At the beginning of the reign of Henry IV the lay members of the House of Lords consisted of 4 dukes, 1 marquis, 10 earls, and 34 barons. Henry VIII only assembled 51 peers in his Par-

liament; while only 82 sat in the first Parliament
of James the First; and 117 in the first Parliament of Charles the First. At the end of the
reign of Charles the Second there were but 176
names on the roll of the Lords. The roll was increased to 192 peerages before the death of
William the Third; to 209 before the death of
Anne; to 216 before the death of George the
First; to 229 before the death of George the
Second; to 339 at the death of George the Third;
to 396 before the death of George the Fourth;
to 456 at the death of William the Fourth;
to 512 in 1881; to 541 in 1892; and the total
number at the present time (1908), including
Spiritual and Law Lords, is 853, 200 of whom
have been created since 1882, and nearly half of
them since 1830.

Ah, but some one answers, suppose these men
govern badly, or suppose they cease to represent
the nation, or suppose the sons of these men are
not of the calibre of their fathers. The last supposition is easily answered. We have seen already what a mushroom assembly it is from the
point of view of ancient lineage. They are by
no means all gentlemen, in the technical sense
of that word; and by no means without exception worthy. But that only adds the necessary
human factor of fallibility.

The adult males in a town meeting in Hingham, Massachusetts, for example, could trace back to male ancestors, who attended that same town meeting an hundred years before, in greater numbers, in proportion to their total number, than could the members of the House of Lords to ancestors who had sat in that same chamber. Nor is it easy to see wherein they fail to represent the nation, since they come from every and all classes; nor why they should govern badly, since they are chosen only after proving themselves to be of superior ability and sound judgment. It is true that a son may not turn out to have the same ability as his father, but if the son of a Rothschild has ability enough to keep the money his father made, he must, in these days of liquid securities, be a man of no small ability. Those who are weaklings do not last long in the hurly-burly of the modern world. We have seen how very few peers are the male descendants of houses dating back any distance. God and nature turn out the incompetents almost as quickly as would the electorate. The chances of any living man having a male descendant able to keep what was left him, and also able to get more, and beget more, an hundred years after his time, is very small indeed.

Indeed, this system evolved from sound Saxon sense has done more than anything else to produce that wholeness in the English social body which is a salient feature of English life. There are, or at any rate have been until very lately, fewer disquieting social and political segregations due to class distinctions in England than in any other nation in the world.

Grandsons, and younger sons, of peers drift back into the upper middle class and remain there unless they rise by their own exertions; while there is a continual absorption of the strong, the competent, and the successful into the peerage. This mixes up and leavens all classes. Noble sons become commoners, noble commoners become peers.

This is what explains the existence of the House of Lords in so democratic a country as England. It exists because it is the most democratic institution in England, and because in the long run it has been recognized as an assembly whose opinion is as nearly as possible the opinion of a consensus of the competent.

But here again we must bear in mind that we are neither defending nor attacking. This upper chamber so nearly represents what these early Saxons were, perhaps not in its details aware of, striving to produce, *viz.*: government

with as little government as possible, and that,
by those with the leisure and capacity to do it,
that it deserves attentive study.

These people who have governed more of the
world, and a far larger population, than any
other people since time began, deserve respectful
consideration for their methods in, and their
philosophy of, government. Any socialistic
sneering, or republican ribaldry, on the subject
of the British system of government, must necessarily react upon the foolish one who indulges
in them. The ready answer is: We are taking
charge of one in every five square miles, and
one in every five inhabitants of the globe; if you
can do it better, why do you not do it?

It is a notable feature of the history of this
great governing people that they have had little
desire to take part in the governing themselves.
The gathering of the wise men, the assembly, in
short, at which the nation sat in council, was
open to all, but by a natural process was reduced
to the attendance of those who could afford the
time and the money to go. By an easy step those
who had the time and the money gradually became the great ones of the land.

William the Conqueror only imitated the example of his predecessors in calling together the
wise and the great of the nation to consider the

customs, and thence to determine the laws, of the kingdom.

It was Simon de Montfort who led the freemen against the barons grown too proud, conquered them, and summoned a parliament by directing the sheriffs to return two knights for each county, and two burgesses for each borough in the kingdom; and there you have the beginning of Parliament. They were not clamoring to govern, but they found themselves forced to take a hand lest the barons should grow to think governing their right.

The statute of a generation later than this time, which still remains on the statute book, begins by declaring that no tax or aid shall be taken without the good-will and assent of archbishops, bishops, earls, barons, knights, burgesses, and *other freemen* of the land.

The profound and real difference between the philosophy of democracy and the philosophy of aristocracy is that the former emphasizes the identity of men, and the latter the diversity of men. The one makes democracies, the other makes monarchies. But men are all alike, and they are all unlike, and either proposition, carried to its extreme, defeats itself; in the former liberty becomes licence, and in the latter order becomes despotism. The pendulum swings ack and forth between the two extremes, and down to this day the English have succeeded in reconciling the claims of both philosophies, and of keeping the peace between them. Their gift of the solution of the problem of government to mankind rivals the great gift of Art by the Greeks, and of Law by the Romans.

But even to this day these common-sense people care nothing for the fiction, for the trappings, of government. Even now acts of Parliament begin: "Be it enacted by the King's most excellent Majesty, by and with advice and consent of the Lords spiritual and temporal, and Commons in this present Parliament assembled." The King knows, and the Lords spiritual and temporal know, and the Commons know, that the King does not make the laws, or enforce the laws, but they are all equally willing to have him appear to do so. They have no taste for ostentatious participation in governing even now. They would still rather mind their own business, though there are, alas, signs nowadays that they are losing somewhat their Saxon heritage in this respect.

In the past they have taken a hand in governing only when their governors overstepped the bounds, and attempted to govern with the physical and financial aid, but without the consent of the governed. Then, over and over again, against barons or king, or whomsoever it might be, they have risen and demanded to be governed as little as need be, but according to their ancient custom of personal liberty for each one.

One hears occasionally in the inebriation of exuberance which vents itself in song, that: Britons never shall be slaves. It is well known, of course, that Britons have been slaves, and worn the collar of a Roman master, but the Saxons, their successors, never have been slaves. This is interesting because practically down to 1867, or forty years ago, the English government has been in a very few hands indeed.

The temptation must have been constant ever since the Romans left and the Saxons came, for the small governing class to usurp all power. And yet with practically no voice in the government, this has never been accomplished, for it has always been prevented by the people themselves.

It should be remembered that long after the development of government into a House of Lords and a House of Commons, these two bodies were controlled by a very few men. It is said that as late as 1793, out of 513 members of Parliament, 309 of them owed their election to the nomination either of the Treasury, or of some 162 individuals who controlled the voters.

The House of Commons of 1801, including the Irish and Scotch members, consisted of 658 members, and of these 425 were returned either on the nomination, or on the recommendation of 252 patrons.

Thus has England been governed persistently by the few. Nor has this been against the wishes of the many. We have seen how, time after time, the many have demanded, and conquered for themselves, what they considered to be for their welfare and their happiness; but constant personal participation in government has not been deemed a necessity of personal freedom, but rather, indeed, a drag upon it. I am inclined to look upon this as the most important factor in their wonderful growth as a nation.

In 1832 the borough franchise was confined to householders whose houses were worth not less than ten pounds a year, and the county franchise was enlarged by the admission of copyholders, leaseholders, and of tenants whose holding was of the clear annual value of fifty pounds. Then and there, and for the first time in the history of the nation, England was practically governed by the middle class.

In 1867 this was followed by a still more sweeping reform, and, by the act of that year, every freeholder whose freehold was of the value of forty shillings a year; every copyholder and leaseholder, of the annual value of five pounds; and every householder whose rent was not less than twelve pounds a year, was entitled to vote for the county. Every householder in a borough, and every lodger who paid ten pounds a year for his lodging and had been resident for more than twelve months, was entitled to vote for the borough member. This is to all intents and purposes male adult suffrage.

Nevertheless, up to the election of members to this present Parliament, when an unusual number of labor members were elected, Parliament has been composed of an overwhelming majority chosen from the leisure classes.

Pitt once said that an Englishman with an income of ten thousand pounds a year had a right to be a peer. The English voter still, to a large extent, takes the same view. He seems to hold that those have the best claim to go to Parliament who have the leisure and wealth to enable them to go conveniently. Even now when a dangerously large number of people — some say thirty millions — are always on the verge of starvation, the voter is but little touched by that despair of the individual in his own manhood, reduced to a system, known as socialism. He still believes in his gentry as most to be trusted, and best qualified to govern.   He has a rooted distrust of those who wish to be paid to govern.   He has not ceased to look upon the business of governing as a duty, not a trade.

Some instinct tells him, for no one would accuse the British voter of being either a philosopher, or of being unusually intelligent even, that the solution of the problem of his lack of wealth does not lie in the fact that his gentry have too much.   To take another man's coat does not take with it the ability to keep that coat against all comers, any more than to exchange gloves with the man who has just knocked you out in a sparring bout would enable you in turn to knock him out.   That easy solution of inequality, that because somebody else has more, therefore it is that I have less, has not fooled the Englishman as yet.   He has only to look across the Channel to see the results of that philosophy.   When he looks he sees a nation that has so belittled its men that they can only prevent themselves from being swallowed up by their enemies by lending their hard-earned gold to Russia, an autocracy with which, of course, an honest republic could have nothing in common, and by accepting the friendship of England, a monarchy, because England wishes a buffer-state between herself and Germany.

In an hundred years England has grown great, while, since the Revolution, France has diminished to the stature of an epicene amongst nations, trafficking in her ideals and in her honor, and advertising the virtue of her capital for sale to all comers as her principal stock in trade. She is like a pretty woman who will sell anything for security and comfort. This lesson has not been lost upon the Englishman, dull as he is.

Fox, Liverpool, and Lord John Russell, all entered Parliament before they were of age, though this was technically a breach of the law, which required that a member should be of age, a male, and of some wealth. So closely indeed have these people clung to their tradition about the land, that many, no doubt, will be surprised to learn that it was only at the beginning of the reign of the late Queen Victoria that one could become a member of Parliament without being the possessor of a certain amount of landed property. He must be a landlord, in short.

He might have thousands invested in securities of all kinds, that mattered not; he must be a landholder. They came to England to be free landholders, and when Queen Victoria came to the throne that was still their ideal of what a man fit to assist in governing should be.

As late as the middle of the eighteenth cen-

tury England was almost entirely rural. The
greater number of the towns were merely country
towns. Perhaps the secret of the independence
and the homogeneity of the population is to be
found in this multitude of men who firmly believed in the land, were permanently settled upon
the land, and whose claim to personal dignity and
political and social distinction rested upon the
possession of the land.

We have heard in our own day, in America,
often repeated, the cry: Back to the land!
Nowhere will one find stronger arguments to
support such advice than in the history of the
Saxons in England. One might choose as the
three requisites of a people that should prosper
and conquer, that they should believe in God,
live on the land, and let their leaders govern.

It is only in comparatively recent times that
England has ceased to be a nation of farmers.
In the middle of the fourteenth century the population of England and Wales was probably about
2,300,000; at the end of the seventeenth century
something over 5,000,000; and in 1831, 14,000,000.

The expansion of England into an empire
grows as naturally and as surely out of this love
of theirs for the land and liberty as the first
settlements of England by the Saxons grew out
of this same desire.

Their Saxon plain was crowded. The Jutes led by descendants of the warlike and roving Odin, needed companions in arms, and these Saxons followed them on one of their excursions to England.

Finding that the Saxons settled peaceably and industriously on the land, and acted as a buffer-state between their own settlement and the roving Britons, they induced still more Saxons to come over, and more came, and then more and more, until they became the predominant factor in the settlement of the country.

They were not, as is generally supposed, and as is often erroneously stated, of the fighting, marauding, restless breed of the piratical races, which from time to time ravaged the coasts of both what is now England and what is now France.

In spite of their many wars, the English, as were their peasant ancestors the Saxons, are not a warlike people. *Si res poscat*, writes Tacitus. If it is *worth while* they fight. But they fought not as did the fiercer tribes, merely for the love of fighting. Read their history and you find — and it greatly alters certain preconceived opinions — that they were not, and are not, a war-loving, or a quarrelsome race.

It is often said that England is always fighting

somewhere. When one considers the enormous area of land, and the varied populations she controls, it is not surprising that she should have constant trouble on her hands. On the other hand, if one investigates these wars, big and little, they all fall under one general head: the protection of her subjects in the possession of the land.

The two wars with China were to protect her landowners in India who trafficked in opium with the Chinese. The war in the Crimea was against Russia, looming up as her rival in India. The support of the Allies against Napoleon was a necessary commercial expedient to save her shipping and her commerce. The war with America was again, at first, a question of commercial significance alone. The war in Africa was plainly enough for the upholding of the status of her citizens against the Dutch. There is a superb selfishness involved in each and every one of these conflicts. No one can defend for a moment the terrible hypocrisy of the race, in their insistence upon the right of their traders to debauch the Chinese by the sale of opium against the wishes of the Chinese authorities. Imagine the horror of the Englishman should a neighbor nation insist upon the right to sell cocaine in England whether he liked it or not, and give as a reason that a certain colony derived a large revenue from the sale of cocaine, which would be cut off if England refused to allow its sale in her territories. This is exactly what happened in China. The British colony of Hong Kong is a monument to England's infamous selfishness where her trade is concerned. Hong Kong was taken from the Chinese as an indemnity for daring to make war upon England's opium trade.

The war with America was due to selfishness, coupled with forgetfulness. The Englishman went to America, almost exactly as the Saxon went to England. He went for land and liberty. The settlers were agriculturists, who founded free estates and drove off the warring, nomadic tribes, just as the Saxons drove off the Britons. These American settlers were of the same class as those they left behind them. Let us get it out of our heads and keep it out, that England is an aristocracy. It is not and never has been. It has not and never has had a *noblesse*. At once, indeed, almost before they set foot on land, the wiser and wealthier among them, are set up in authority over them, not to *rule* them, but to *govern for* them. Here we have the same institutions again, and the same dogged insistence upon liberty to till the soil in peace. But when England, forgetting her own history, and her own blood, set out to rule and to tax without representation these people, she was precipitating exactly the same kinds of conflict as had taken place between John and the barons; between Simon de Montfort and the barons; and between Charles and the Parliament. The result was foredoomed. The Saxons can only live in one way, and that is by ruling themselves. As the greatest representative of the Saxon race of the last two hundred years put it: A government of the people, for the people, by the people. Their confidence in this form of government has resulted in forcing its adoption upon all peoples, and all countries, that they control. That any family, clan, tribe, or nation should wish to live under other than this Saxon arrangement, is to them unthinkable.

Lord Curzon, late viceroy of India, in a volume entitled, "Problems of the Far East," writes as follows in his dedication: "To those who believe that the British Empire is, under Providence, the greatest instrument for good that the world has ever seen and who hold with the writer, that its work in the Far East is not yet accomplished, this book is dedicated." Where, in the history of mankind, may one look to find such a magnificent assumption of virtue and omniscience, coupled with incomprehensible self-satisfaction? It makes one fearful for the destinies of the race when one sees it proclaim itself thus arrogant. Here is a haughty egotism that would make Alexander, Cæsar, or Napoleon turn pale. Who believes that the world is better where England dominates? The English. Who believes that India is happier? The English. Who believes that Ireland is happier? The English. Who believes that the East under English protection is happier? The English. Who believes that North America is happier? The English. But what do the four hundred millions of people, controlled by these million English gentlemen, whose omniscient prophet Lord Curzon is, — what do they think? What do they say? Personally I am not questioning or criticising. I am merely a child making notes. This amazing assumption that England has done more for the world than any other agency, is a characteristic of these people that cannot be too often insisted upon. As I have said before, it is not a pose with them. It is not impudence, it is their rooted belief in their own superiority. Anybody who starts out to have dealings with them, either personally or along international lines, must take that into consideration. They know only one way. That is their way, and their way is the best way and is sanctioned by God, who, by the way, is the God of the English national church.

It is magnificent, is it not? but it makes one stop just for a moment to get one's breath.

Let some one tell us what fantastic arrangement of molecules turned the youthful rake into a St. Augustine, the unknown country lad into a Shakespeare, the Corsican peasant into a Napoleon, or the Western rail-splitter and country lawyer into a Lincoln, and when these are all explained, there will remain an even greater mystery: how these Saxon peasants became the English Empire of to-day.

It is said often enough that a man who restricts his energies to the pursuit of one end, who thinks of nothing else, saves himself for that alone, keeps his eyes fixed on that alone, is likely to succeed even though he be of mediocre powers. The fable of the hare and the tortoise was written as a brief commentary on this fact, that it's dogged that does it! These Saxons, since the historian's first introduction to them, inhabiting that Saxon plain, have had apparently but one aim: possession of the land in peace. Little by little they have become the inheritors of one-fifth of all the land there is. We have traced here, by a mere thread of narrative, their history, and we have noted their present status among the nations of the world. We have seen nothing brilliant or heroic, nothing Napoleonic in this story; but merely steady growth along ever the same lines, aided by a genius for compromise. They stop and wait when they must, they fight when they must, they even pay to be let alone when they must, they spill over into other countries when they must, but land and liberty they keep ever before them as their goal. Who are the English, what are the English? They are Saxons, who love the land, who love their liberty, and whose sole claim to genius is their common-sense.

III

THE LAND OF COMPROMISE

THERE are people, both English and foreign, who instead of Compromise, write Hypocrisy; others still who write Conciliation; while the more vehement write Pharisaism.

What has been written in other chapters of the origins, development, and the manners and customs of the English, calls now for something in the way of an explanation. The statements therein contained must seem to the careful reader, like a mere tumbling together of haphazard and often violently contradictory facts. There must be some string of philosophy of life upon which to place such an odd lot of jewels, some precious, some false, and many that are ill-assorted, and which apparently do not in the least belong side by side. Here we have a king who is not a king in any autocratic sense; a free people who are not a free people; a constitution which is not a constitution; an aristo-

cratic House of Lords composed of successful
merchants, manufacturers, journalists, lawyers
and money-lenders, leavened by a minority of
men of ancient lineage; a State Church which
is not a State Church; a nation professing
Christianity, but nevertheless continually at war,
sodden with drink, and offering all its prizes of
wealth and station, to the selfish, the successful
and the strong, who have possessed themselves,
— some thirty-eight thousand of them, — of
three-fourths of the total land area of England
and Wales, and who, with their State priests in
Parliament, to voice the fact that they are a
Christian nation, spend the bulk of their income for war, drink and sport.

All this is not my business, or yours, gentle
reader. We can neither mend nor mar. If
these forty millions choose so to live in their
island home, it is no affair of the outsider; unless it is attempted by these same islanders to
pose as the missionaries of light to the rest of the
world. This is exactly what they do. They not
only pose to all the world, but they have imposed
themselves upon one-fifth of the world, with this
rather shabby article of civilization, as their
sample of salvation. One need not, however,
refrain from criticism on the score of the sensi-
tiveness of the patient. The British public is as

impervious to criticism as an elephant's hide to stabbing by sticks of boiled macaroni.

Yesterday was Sunday. London was silent and solemn, in the gloom of a depressing orthodoxy, which denies drink, food and amusement to all except the rich. I was present at the Christian Science church in the morning, and listened to two young people, standing side by side at separate reading-desks which were enshrined in a profusion of lilies. Their appearance was that of rather self-conscious drapers' assistants, their voices were mechanical and their pronunciation provincial. The young woman read passages, which she prefaced as from "Mark," "Luke," "Matthew." Why they were deprived of their usual titles of courtesy, I am at a loss to know; just as I have always been at a loss to understand why such titles as: "Jesus Christ and the Social Question," and the like, are paraded in print, titles that even a heretic, if he be a gentleman, must regard as unscholarly, or offensive, or callously vulgar; or to put the best face upon it, an effeminate display of that carefully shielded hot-house courage, known as opportunism. The young man responded with commentaries from a volume which he told us was written by "Mrs." — why "Mrs.", if the other authors were titleless? — "Mary Baker

G. Eddy." These commentaries were a meta-
physical jargon which left me mentally bewildered. I am more or less familiar with the
common terms of psychology, but I heard them
now flung together, as a child might toss its
alphabet blocks together on the floor, spelling
no words to be found in any known dictionary.
The audience must, I thought, be of a superior
order of intellectual development, and I looked
curiously at the faces around me. I have sat
often in the House of Commons, and in the House
of Lords, and if I am any judge of physiognomy,
these listeners to what was Greek to me were
certainly inferior in intelligence to the average
of those in either of the two chambers. It was
with a start of surprise, too, that I heard amongst
these sickless ones, coughing and hawking, indi-
cating that they had failed to Bakerize the then
prevalent epidemic of influenza.

In the afternoon I attended the church of the
Jesuit Fathers, where I heard Father Bernard
Vaughan, who is, I believe, castigator-in-chief to
the sins of London society, preach upon the subject of the Devil. He told us that science and
philosophy had nothing to do with this question,
and that there was of course a personal Devil now
just as much as there was a personal Devil at
the time when our first ancestors, Adam and

Eve, committed that fatal pomological mistake in the Garden of Eden.   This I believe is true!   It may be a somewhat Jesuitical way of putting it, but taken one way or the other it may be believed by all, believers and doubters alike.

In the evening I was present at the cathedral church, St. Paul's, where I heard a distinguished cleric of the State Church, in a foggy, but far-reaching, voice, calling upon "this Christian Empire of Great Britain" to interfere to prevent the horrible atrocities now practised upon the natives of the Congo Free State.   He pictured the cannibals of that region as having been "free" and "happy,"— what glaring and ridiculous hypocrisy! — until King Leopold, through his agents, had enslaved them into the search for the rubber, which alone of commercial articles, is as elastic as that monarch's morals.   As I sat and listened in these very different places of worship, and in no scoffing mood, — for he is a braver man than I who is not drawn to think of his latter end during a Sunday spent in London, — I was impressed by the aloofness of each and all of these services, from any connection with the sad problems that confront England on every hand.

Here was a handful of Englishmen and Englishwomen in a costly tabernacle, attempting to mezmerize the world with the cabalistic messages

of a rich and uncultivated old woman hailing
from Massachusetts.   There was a church full
listening attentively to a mediæval portrayal of
the Devil as a terrorizer of sinners; and, last of
all, a high officer of the State Church, lashing a
foreign potentate, who is best known on the Continent by the name of a popular harlot.   Mrs.
Eddy, The Devil, and King Leopold! Strange
texts, for a people at close grips with poverty,
high taxes, drunkenness, gambling, and lack
of schooling at home; people peddling opium to
the Chinese, pandering to priestcraft in Ireland,
with twenty-five thousand Chinamen slaving in
their gold-mines in South Africa, and with hundreds of thousands dying of starvation in India
on their hands abroad.

Some people call this hypocrisy, some pharisaism.   But there is no need of harsh names.   He
can have had but little practise with the pen who
does not find it easy enough to call names, to
fling epithets; but he who does it is quite unworthy to be trusted with so dangerous a weapon,
and so useful a surgeon's knife.   I write these
things to explain, not to revile.   This is a great
country, — we have said it scores of times already in these pages, and therefore it is worth
while getting at the meaning of these things.
They are not pharisees, they are compromisers.

They have drilled themselves through centuries, till this mental haziness, which permits them to hold two contradictory propositions at one and the same time, has become a part of their being.

Their King, though King by right of birth, has been set aside, has been beheaded, and is now in the hands of a cabinet, chosen, not as it used to be, by him, but by his people.   George the First, who could not speak English or understand it, when he came to the throne, and who was wont to communicate with his ministers in bad Latin, gave up attending the meetings of the cabinet because he could not understand its discussions; thus was the last link snapped in the chain which held the cabinet in the grasp of the King.   As late as the time of Queen Victoria, she besought her friends in the Parliament not to impose Gladstone upon her as Prime Minister again, a man whom she disliked, but they were helpless. Gladstone was the man appointed by the suffrage of the people, and Queen Victoria must accept him.   So little is the King, King.   On the other hand, in the case of this present King, the King is the people plus the experience, the knowledge, the impartial situation, and unprejudiced mind, which the people ought to have before making a decision, or passing judgment.   That is the ideal constitutional ruler, and the present King comes very close to the ideal.   At any rate, King Edward the Seventh, is, through his popularity with all classes, more powerful than any man, any class, any sect, any minister, or either of the houses of Parliament.   His wisdom is not the wisdom of the people, with the knowledge they have; but the wisdom of the people, with the knowledge and experience he has.   It is the knowledge of many, filtered through an unique experience, and this comes close to being the acme of common-sense.   He is the most astute diplomatist, and the most useful and charming gentleman in Europe.   So much is the King, King!

The people is a free people, in the sense that nowhere else in the world is the individual so little ruled, hampered or oppressed; but politically they are bound fast by the chains of a House of Lords, which, entirely independent of them, rejects their measures when it so pleases.   And here again is still another anomaly, for I believe that the House of Lords, is, as a rule, a surer interpreter of the sober wishes of the English people as a whole, than the House of Commons.

The constitution is so loosely mortared together that you can take a brick out, or put a brick in, without greatly disturbing the house of the State, which has been put together slowly, from old customs grown to be laws.

The State Church may have its chief priests appointed by a Prime Minister like Walpole, who was a loose liver and a hard drinker; or by a Chamberlain, who is a Unitarian; or by a Morley, who is an agnostic; or even by a Jew like Disraeli, whichever one may, or might happen to be, Prime Minister. The high priest of this church, the Archbishop of Canterbury, is paid a salary of $75,000 a year, and the Bishop of London a salary of $50,000 a year, while the bulk of the clergy live on pittances, and thirty millions of its flock are, it is said, continually on the verge of starvation. What could be more grotesque? On the other hand, the Bishop of London, unless I am woefully mistaken in my man, is one whose fine spiritual sincerity shines in his face, and whatever his intellectual calibre, his influence must be worth many times ten thousand pounds a year to London. Though I know nothing of him personally, I feel very sure that very few hundreds of those thousands of salary go for his personal comfort. Here again the theory of such payments to any priest is wrong, exasperatingly wrong, but in this particular case, it no doubt works well, not to say nobly.

The King, the people, the constitution, the

church, we have glanced at their contradictions.
Each and all unexplained are indefensible, but
by compromise they are made to work. It is
this constant search for the feasible, for the convenient, for the conciliatory, for the instantly
practicable, and the total ignoring of the logical,
and sometimes even of the true and the right,
which has given the name *Perfide Albion* to England and made her so vulnerable to the accusation of hypocrisy. We all know how in this
complicated society of ours, in order to be free to
do even a little, one must escape from the tyranny
of trying to do too much. All the pictures may
not be painted on one canvas, all the books
may not be written in one chapter, all the
legislation may not be accomplished in one
session.

This philosophy of subordinating high principles to practical exigencies has reached its
climax in the House of Commons. In the first
place, the chamber where the commons meets has
not seats enough for its members. If all attended at any one session, many would be forced
to stand. Every conceivable question comes up
for discussion in this assembly, which deals with
the whole Empire. This, by-the-way, makes it
the most cosmopolitan, the most influential, and
the most interesting legislative assembly in the

world. A member asks that a clock on a certain public building in London be regulated; another member calls attention to the condition of the Zoological Garden; still another to the proposed improvements of the Marble Arch; another member asks about the housing of the Chinese laborers in Africa; another asks whether the furniture in Irish school-houses is to be paid for by the State or by the local rate-payers; another asks a question about the theft of the Crown jewels at Dublin; another asks about the plan for a governor of Macedonia; another brings up the question of the playing of hand-organs in the public streets of London; another asks if a sample gun of those to be provided for the new territorial army may be brought up to the House, for the inspection of the members; a Welshman rises to complain that the new army scheme does not consider sufficiently the feelings of the Welsh; an officer of the Yeomanry asks who is to pay for his horse if the horse dies while on duty; Irishmen are continually to the fore with questions concerning the Emerald Isle.

One wonders, as one sits and listens to this hodge-podge of questions and answers about everything under this British sun that never sets, how anything is ever done. The present Parliament (1908) contains six hundred and seventy members.   More than one-eighth of the total are irreconcilable Irishmen, who are there to bribe, bully or balk the House, if thereby Ireland may have a parliament of its own. Fifty-four are labor members.   Think for a moment of the problem of dealing with the affairs of the greatest Empire we know in such an assembly, with its multitude of interests and its variety of personalities.   No wonder there is conciliation, even to the point of flabbiness, otherwise nothing could be done. The Minister of War, with a rotund person and the face of a cherub, answers attacks, not in the voice of Mars, but in the falsetto and piping tones of peace.   So with the other ministers.   All are tainted with this love of compromise.   Even the upright John Morley, independent politically, easily first among writers of lucid English prose, bends to defend India's exchequer in the sale of opium to protesting China.

His Majesty's government licenses opium dens in Hong Kong, the Straits Settlements, and Ceylon, and in certain other Crown Colonies, deriving a considerable income therefrom.   In the year 1907 there were in Singapore alone 97 licensed shops for the retail of chandu, which is opium prepared for smoking; and 449 rooms licensed for smoking it.   It may be said that this is not a direct revenue to the government of His Majesty, but as the Straits Settlements at any rate have for many years contributed one-fifth of their annual revenues to Imperial defence purposes, it is a mere evasion not to recognize it as such. This form of compromise is merely a mush of concession. It is not the philosophy of getting things done by giving way a little here and a little there which is the pith of English administrative success all over the world, rather it is cold-blooded drowning of honor in selfishness. If there is advantage for England, other things, be they even truth and right, must retire into the background.

> "Ill fares the land, to hastening ills a prey,
>   Where wealth accumulates and men decay."

As Mr. Bryce wrote in the "American Commonwealth," in spite of much political machinery which works badly, and many social characteristics which seem to point to disaster, there is a certain something of buoyancy, of vigor, of hope, in the Americans that convinced him of their future triumph over all difficulties. Something of the same thing is true of Mr. Bryce's own country. The people of one locality can never be made completely familiar with the temper, tone and atmosphere of the people of another locality from a distance. Englishmen may read of

America, and Americans may read of England, and yet both Englishmen and Americans find, upon personal acquaintance with one country or the other, that there is a certain vaporish something that has not been communicated, or even brought much nearer, by steam, or photography, or electricity, but which makes all the difference. One may know all about the situation, the geology, the history, the fauna, the flora, the climate, the population, the industries, even the laws and customs of a place, and still miss entirely its personality — just as photographs, and letters, and the descriptions of a third person, cannot transfer the real presence of an individual. This something, which explains how this vast Empire of jarring interests works at all, is this people's genius for politics and for governing, for conciliation and compromise. They do get on somehow, there is no denying that, and thus far they have got on remarkably well. I think their passion for personal freedom has made them chary of treading on one another's toes, has made the give and take of living together a science, an intuitive possesion of all of them, from the highest to the lowest. Each one realizes that he cannot have his place without leaving the other fellow in peace in his place. The philosophy of social convenience, though perhaps not a high phase of social economics, is, they feel, a comfortable working hypothesis.

It is difficult with such a people to discover what are their ideals, what are their real likes and dislikes, what they spend themselves for most willingly. The word "spend" may help us. Some of our expenditures may be simply silly, may have no significance. Benjamin Franklin tells us that he first learned economy when he discovered that he had paid too much for a whistle. Robert Louis Stevenson comments upon this by saying that what annoyed him in life was not that he sometimes paid too much for a whistle, but that he often found himself the purchaser of a whistle that he did not want at all. But when we find an individual, or a nation, spending large sums persistently for this or that we cannot be wrong in supposing that here at last is a key to character. A man who year after year spends largely for vintage wines and delicate edibles can hardly make us believe that he is an ascetic. Money is the blood of the body domestic and the body politic. The individual may claim for himself what virtues he will, the nation may assume to possess such high qualities as it will, but when one discovers how a household, or a nation, spends its money, one has something tangible to hang guesses at character upon.

Even at the risk of wearying the reader, let us repeat some facts and figures as to the make-up of the population of England and Wales. It is composed of 15,728,613 males and 16,799,230 females, or a total population of 32,527,843. Unlike our population, it is to an extraordinary extent homogeneous. There are only 247,758 foreigners in all amongst them. Of these foreigners some 82,000 come from Russia and Russian Poland, 49,000 come from Germany, 20,000 from France, 20,000 from Italy, and something over 16,000 from the United States of America. London alone has a population of 7,113,561 (1906). Roughly divided into classes, the bulk of this population is made up as follows:

	MALE	FEMALE	TOTAL
Professional Classes	651,543	321,142	972,685
Domestic Servants	304,195	1,690,722	1,994,917
Commercial	1,779,685	78,769	1,858,454
Agricultural and Fishing	1,094,765	57,730	1,152,495
Industrial	6,326,788	2,023,388	8,350,176
Unoccupied	1,977,283	9,017,884	10,995,167

In 1901, seventy-seven per cent. of the population was urban, and twenty-three per cent. rural.

They are a pious people, or lay claim to be. There are some 28,000 clergymen of the Church of England, and about the same number of priests, nuns, preachers, ministers, and lay-readers, or about one for every five hundred and eighty men, women and children in the island. All along their coast men and women are forbidden to go in bathing together, and a man may not accompany his own wife into the water. In the great city of London everything closes at a half hour after midnight, and you are driven from the restaurants and cafés into the street. On the other hand, England in a fit of mawkish prudery rescinded the Contagious Diseases Act, and hundreds of her soldiers and sailors are always in hospital as a consequence; and London streets are free day and night to perambulating disease, which bedizens itself with baits for the unwary. The other day a workman's widow and children were virtually deprived of any real compensation, under the Workmen's Compensation Act of 1906, by being obliged to share it with a number of his real, or supposed, illegitimate children.

There is now under discussion (1908) in Parliament a new Licensing Act. On the first of January, 1908, there were in England and Wales 95,700 licenses, or 27.62 per 10,000 of the total population. It would seem fair enough, in all conscience, to decrease this number, even though certain vested interests in the beer and liquor trade lost some revenue by the operation. One would think that at least the bishops and clergy would be unanimous in favor of such a bill. Not at all. They are divided and one bishop at least, there may be others, has already written a letter denouncing the bill on the ground that investors in brewery shares would lose by the passage of the bill. Apparently even the spiritual lords of the church cannot overcome the national obsession of keeping the main chance ever in view. This bishop holds with Frederick the Great that: "Hier muss ein jeder nach seiner Façon selig werden."

If a brewer, when he sells enough beer, is made a peer, no wonder the average bishop is confused, and concludes, as do all Englishmen, that Doctor Johnson was right when he said that "there are few ways in which a man can be more innocently employed than in getting money." They spend four pounds sterling per head for drink, or some $750,000,000 a year, and in the year 1906–7 the navy cost $157,170,000. The revenue derived from excise taxes, exclusive of additional beer and spirit duties, collected for local authorities is $151,750,000 (1906–7). In 1906 these people drank 1,223,187,000 imperial gallons of beer, or 28 gallons each, for every man, woman and child, including the teetotalers. In addition they drank 39,264,000 gallons of spirits, and 13,278,000 gallons of wine; not to mention that they used 269,503,000 pounds of tea, or a little over six pounds per head.

The statement made in a previous page, that this Christian country spends its money for drink, sport and war, now proves to be not malicious, or even harsh, it is merely true; for during the last year (1906–7) they spent the colossal sum of considerably over a thousand million dollars for drink, sport, and the navy, while the total national expenditure for the same year was $697,-076,250, which is much less than was spent for drink alone! As an offset to this, there is a State Church, worth in its own right over $500,000,000, and toward the support of which Mr. John Bull contributes some $36,000,000 a year.   This little kingdom of 121,115 square miles, with a population of only forty-odd millions, controlling possessions aggregating over 9,000,000 square miles, and a population of over 400,000,000, carries in addition, the burden of over 1,000,000 persons enrolled as paupers; is taxed to the amount of $75,000,000 a year for their support, and spends nearly $20,000,000 a year under the general head of Law and Justice to keep her population in order.   When, in addition to these expenditures, it is recalled that John Bull has a national debt now standing at $3,870,823,520 gross, $3,655,817,090 net; on which he pays interest annually to the amount of $142,500,000, the wonder of the student of his affairs grows apace. For these are nice round sums for any nation to spend, no matter how rich, when it is remembered that they are expenditures which are in no sense productive.

Drink	$750,000,000
Sport	220,000,000
Navy	157,000,000
Paupers	75,000,000
Interest National Debt	142,000,000
	$1,344,000,000

Estimating the population at 40,000,000, these figures mean an annual expenditure of $366 per head for every man, woman and child on whistles that they ought not to want, at any rate in such profusion as this. Indeed this is proved beyond cavil by the fact that 361 out of every 400 of the population die leaving less than $1,500. Much as we may believe in the wholesomeness of a sound glass of wine, firmly, as I personally, at least, believe in the value of sport, one cannot bring oneself to accept such prodigal expenditures as these as necessary. It is a question indeed if they be not actually criminal, and bound ere long to bring disaster.

Besides these expenditures there have arisen in the last few years a number of local bodies which are empowered to borrow and spend. The local debt in England and Wales in the last thirty years has risen from $460,000,000 to over $2,250,-000,000. The expenditures of local bodies in the last twenty years have risen from $275,000,000 to $700,000,000, indeed the local bodies in England and Wales are spending more each year than the Imperial Government of the United Kingdom. The national net expenditure in 1870 was $308,373,880; in 1890 it was $396,662,605; in 1900 it was $643,170,720; and in 1907, $657,-731,250. The national expenditure has more than doubled since 1870, and has risen 50 per cent. in a dozen years. The principal items of increase are:

	NATIONAL DEBT SERVICE	ARMY AND NAVY
1870	$134,922,655	$113,742,275
1907	158,090,460	285,772,880

	ELEMENTARY EDUCATION	CIVIL SERVICE
1870	$ 6,029,540	$29,724,585
1907	77,137,230	46,996,895

These vast increases matter not at all if the national wealth and prosperity increase at the same ratio, but what is the answer to that question? It is an answer full of peril for England. Income, subject to income tax, in Great Britain in 1892, amounted to $2,685,756,000; in 1905 it amounted to $3,096,640,485; an increase of only $410,884,485. The income subject to income tax in Prussia increased in those same years from $1,490,349,405 to $2,505,205,115. There is no German income tax, and these are merely the figures for Prussia. There should be added, therefore, about 50 per cent. for the whole of Germany. British income subject to tax has increased 15 per cent., while in Germany it has increased 60 per cent. British savings banks deposits from 1901 to 1907 increased $85,000 000; while German savings banks deposits increased $860,000,000 during the same period.

Figures are of small value as dry bones, but clothed in flesh and blood they become personalities. These few figures mean that England's wealth has increased by no more than the population, it has remained stationary in short; while in the rival country, Germany, it has increased by 60 per cent. British expenditure must go on increasing for army, navy, and education, if for no other reason than as a defence against war and commercial invasion. These figures therefore present a problem that cannot be laughed away. If the income tax and death duties are to be increased, then capital, which is the very blood of increased commercial and industrial prosperity, is gradually thinned and weakened. I have the good authority of an eminent English financier for stating that the English income from foreign investments is calculated to be $450,000,000 a year; and that foreigners pay the English for carriage of freight about the same amount annually, but even this fine total of $900,000,000 income is not compensating England for the surpassing onrush of prosperity in America and Germany. As we have said before, not to go ahead is to fall behind, and England for the first time in her history is falling behind.

This enormous income from foreign investments too is a bad rather than a good sign, since it means that English capital is drifting away from use in England, and for the employment of English labor, to assist in the development of rival industries in foreign lands.

There must needs be colossal strength and pluck, marvellous financial elasticity, unbounded confidence, tremendous earning power, and a vast reservoir of national virtue somewhere, to explain these huge incongruities. One begins to understand the reasons for the nonchalant self-satisfaction of the English, which Germans, Frenchmen, Americans, and others, are fain to call conceit, or obstinacy, or stupidity, as the occasion demands.

One may note just here the curious fiction that England is the land of free food, a fiction, but firmly believed both at home and abroad by the uninformed. As a matter of fact the receipts from customs duties upon the things that the English eat, drink, and smoke, plus the excise taxation of them, make together much the largest item of the Imperial revenue of the United Kingdom. Let us look at the figures. For the ten years ending March 31, 1898–1907:

NET RECEIPTS FROM CUSTOMS

Tobacco and Snuff	$608,500,000
Tea	289,000,000
Spirits	218,000,000
Sugar (last six years only)	175,500,000
Wine	69,500,000
Currants, etc.,	21,000,000
Corn and Grain (two years only)	12,000,000
Coffee	9,000,000
Total	$1,402,500,000

NET RECEIPTS FROM EXCISE

Spirits	$884,500,000
Beer	629,500,000
Total Net Receipts from Customs and Excise	$2,916,500,000

This works out at an average of $291,650,000 yearly, or at $5,605,000 weekly, or at the rate of $690 yearly per 100 of the population during the last ten years. When it becomes thus apparent that the English are taxed for what they eat, drink, and smoke at the rate of over $5,000,000 a week, the fiction of free food is blown to the winds, and the Land of Compromises rejoices in the possession of yet another strange contradiction which troubles nobody, and which is still used by politician and layman alike as though this at least were one of the fundamental truths of their insular social economy.

These brief glimpses of the expenditures, burdens and responsibilities of Mr. Bull explain why that gentleman's portrait shows a broad, red-faced, big-waisted, heavy-shouldered, piano-legged countryman, with a bulldog at his heels. Note the bulldog! The characteristics of the bulldog are that he is slow to anger, but once he takes hold he never lets go till you break his jaws or scald him nearly to death with boiling water.

Only a slow man, a safe man, a man without nerves, who can eat and drink copiously, and sleep dreamlessly, and shake off annoyances easily, can keep his place in the world with such burdens upon his shoulders. And when we look a bit further into his house-keeping accounts we find this to be the case. He spends some $380,000,000 a year for bread. In 1906 he used

267,022,000 bushels of wheat, and wheat products, or 6.12 bushels per head; $190,000,000 for butter and cheese; $405,000,000 for milk, sugar, tea, coffee and cocoa, and he washes these down, and some millions of tons of beef, mutton, pork rice, potatoes besides, with heavy malt liquors, brandy, gin, whiskey, and wine, which cost him $750,000,000 a year. And everywhere, from highest to lowest, the wastefulness and the bad cooking, and the spoiling of good materials, go on apace, to the astonishment and horror of every Continental who visits England.

Mr. Bull is apparently not greatly disturbed by these significant figures. Here and there a voice is raised to protest or to warn, but the voice of the professionally patriotic politician is always louder in denial. The political Cleopatra is always ready to put a broiled fish on the populace Antony's hook. Who could have made a French statesman at the end of the reign of Louis the Fourteenth believe that within an hundred years France would be in the financial gutter, begging for a loan from Messrs. Baring, and Labouchère in London! Who would dare whisper such a thing in regard to England to-day, lest he be laughed out of court!

On the contrary, England is the most hopeful of all the nations. There is less political pessimism than in France, Germany, Russia, Italy, or even in America. There is less of that fatigued way of looking at things here than in the rest of Europe. Compare the speeches delivered in and out of Parliament by politicians big and little, with the speeches of politicians delivered elsewhere at this moment in the world and one is impressed first of all by their healthier tone. Every now and again in Germany, in France, and in America, there is an undertone of discouragement, of despair, as of men whose nerves had collapsed and left them peevish. Though the problems here are faced as courageously and discussed as frankly as elsewhere, there is no throwing up of hands in despair, no dyspeptic politics to put it briefly. The men in control, I judge from the look of them, are men who eat, and drink, and sleep, and play more than the men of other nations, and their nerves are not so close to the surface. They remain youthful longer than we do.

A quicker, more sensitive, less easy-going, less good-natured individual than John Bull would be goaded into extreme measures by some of the precedent-supported blundering in his political and economic household. The moment one investigates the poor-laws, the ecclesiastical system, the school arrangements, — now in a worse tangle than ever—the method of administering justice, one is forced to admire the rough optimism which can submit good-humoredly to the awkwardness of methods which are retained merely because they are the methods of the forefathers. Factory hands, small farmers, clerks, shop-keepers, laborers, farm hands, employés in factories, mines, and other industries, even in the country towns where there is no excuse for crowding live in small, badly arranged, and badly ventilated houses, with no conveniences; such as hardly exist in either the city or the country districts of America.

In the time of Henry the Eighth, one-fifth of all the land in England was in the possession of the church. Much of it was then, and has been since then, distributed by royal favor and royal grants. Go where one will in England, even to-day, and upon questioning the inhabitants of this town or that as regards the ownership of the land, one finds that a very few people are in possession of all the land, and not only the farmers but the townspeople themselves are their tenants. These landlords have inherited, or purchased, these large holdings, first, because in years gone by land rents paid well, and, secondly, because peculiar social advantages and certain definite political preferences, as well as direct political influence over the tenants, went with, and still go with, the land. Men who make a fortune almost without exception invest a part of it in country estates, and lay the foundations for social and political power in this or that county. Many of England's large landowners to-day are comparatively new people of this type. So far as this matter of land is concerned, it is a burning question in Ireland, in Scotland, and in England at this very day. The great, very great, majority of Englishmen have not a square foot of land they may call their own, they are tenants, and they pay $500,000,000 a year rent divided as follows:

From	Farm Lands	$175,000,000
"	Lands Bearing Dwelling-Houses, Factories,	
	Business Premises, etc., ...	255,000,000
"	Sporting Rents, etc., ...	5,000,000
"	Mines, Quarries, etc., ...	35,000,000
"	Other Property	30,000,000

This fact becomes the more clear, and one may add the more lugubrious, when we know that the whole area of the United Kingdom measures 77,000,000 acres, and nearly 77,000,000 are in the hands of a comparatively small number of owners.

For England and Wales alone the figures are as follows:

NUMBER OF OWNERS		CLASS OF OWNERS		ACRES
400	. . . .	Peers and Peeresses	. . . . .	5,729,979
1,288	. . . .	Great Landowners	. . . . .	8,497,699
2,529	. . .	Squires	. . . . . .	4,319,271
9,585	. . . .	Greater Yeomen	. . . . .	4,782,627
24,412	. . .	Lesser Yeomen	. . . . .	4,144,272
217,049	. . . .	Small Proprietors	. . . .	3,931,806
703,289	. . . .	Cottagers	. . . . . .	151,148
14,459	. . . .	Public Bodies	. . . . . .	1,443,548
		Waste Land	. . . . . .	1,524,624

In short, more than half the area of England and Wales is owned by a few thousand people. Of the 77,000,000 acres, 40,426,900, or more than one-half, are owned by 2,500 persons, and 38,200 persons own three-fourths of the total land area of England and Wales.

That this arrangement is not satisfactory goes without saying, and various legislative measures are proposed, some of which are now under discussion in Parliament, to remedy this injustice. In France the rural population is 65 per cent. and the urban population 35 per cent. In Great Britain the census returns for 1891 showed that 71.7 per cent. of the population was urban and 28.3 per cent. rural, while in 1901 the drift from the land had still further increased, 77 per cent. of the population being classed as urban and only 23 per cent. rural.

After Henry the Eighth had deprived the monasteries and the high church dignitaries of their land, land became plentiful. Vast tracts of ground were thrown open to the acquisition of lay proprietors. Indeed these released estates in the days of Queen Elizabeth were so plentiful that an act was passed obliging every man who built a cottage to "lay four acres of land thereto." The cottager thus was forced by law to become a small farmer, and as we have seen in other chapters these small farmers were the defence of England. It is hard to believe that such a state of things, as regards the land, ever existed, when we see how to-day the land is back again in the hands of a very few owners.

Thus it is seen that the first, fundamental, and unavoidable payment by an Englishman is always for rent. In addition to this, with great good nature, he submits to the most ridiculous poor law in the world, a compound of socialism, sentimental philanthropy, and outgrown custom, by which he is taxed enormously for the support of the poor.

Up to 1834 the matter of poor law relief had been going from bad to worse, until at last the land was taxed so heavily for the support of the poor, who of course increase exactly in proportion to the relief offered, not only in England but everywhere else as well, that the farmers could not afford to cultivate it. Then came a change and a gradual remodelling of legislation.

	POPULATION	PAUPERS	EXPENDITURES
In 1841 . . .	15,914,148	1,299,048	$23,804,645
" 1851 . . .	17,927,609	941,315	24,813,520
" 1861 . . .	20,066,224	883,921	28,894,715
" 1871 . . .	22,712,266	1,037,360	39,433,620
" 1881 . . .	25,974,439	773,198	40,075,050
" 1891 . . .	29,002,525	728,042	43,216,590
" 1901 . . .	32,527,843	778,084	57,744,425

The total number of paupers receiving relief on January the first, 1907, was 920,838, while the total cost of relief of the poor for the fiscal year 1906 was $70,251,310.

These sums of money are, it must not be forgotten, quite outside the enormous sums expended in private charities. The city of London alone, it is calculated, contributes more than $25,000,000 a year in private charity, and the various temperance societies also, and they are a drop in the bucket among charities, spend every year an amount represented by a capital of $12,000,000, in a rather Liliputian attempt to prevent the Brobdignagian British giant from lifting his costly $750,000,000 drinking cup to his lips. Only the rich man can own land in a country where thirty-two million people spend such sums for drink and over seventy million dollars a year for the official relief, and almost as much more for the private care, of their shirkers, incompetents, and helpless; and where land itself cannot be bought at its agricultural or productive value, but must be paid for at the artificial valuation that it has acquired through this feudalistic desire on the part of rich men to become great landowners.

When one hears, and one does hear it on every hand just now, how poor are Englishmen, one has in this land question some explanation of the secret. It is not only a material and mechanical change that has taken place but a spiritual change. Democracy under one name or another is in the air just now. Men can have land, and liberty; that has been proved. And many more men want it. The tenants on large estates fifty years ago were, to all practical intents and purposes, political and economic slaves, and to some extent they are slaves still. They find more rights and more freedom in the cities, and they flock thither; and it is this combination of democracy and landholding by a few that has so radically changed the grouping of the population of Great Britain, till now 77 per cent.

live in cities, and only 23 per cent. in the
country.

Whether as a result of this or no the birth
rate has been steadily decreasing, until 1907
showed the lowest birth rate on record. Pauperism increases, the deportation of men increases,
expenditure for drink increases, expenditures
national and local increase, while the national
wealth remains at a standstill, and the birth rate
decreases.

One is led naturally enough to inquire what
the church, with its bishops in the House of
Lords, and its twenty-eight thousand clergy, is
doing to modify, or even to influence, this condition of affairs. Here again, one is surprised to
find only conciliation, compromise, and optimism
at work. Even in the realm of spiritual and
ethical things, the immediately feasible is the
watchword. The land question is an important
factor in all ecclesiastical problems to begin with,
since the church is a landowner, and because the
ecclesiastical system includes as many incongruities and contradictions as can well be imagined.
It has been said of it that it has a Catholic ritual,
a Calvinistic creed, and an Arminian clergy,
which is true enough for a witticism. A more
savage criticism is that of Jowett, who, writing to
Caird, said: "In another ten years half the

English clergy will be given up to a fetish priest-worship of the Sacrament." This prophecy has come true to a sufficient extent at least to cause grave trouble. The Church of England holds fast to the three orders of the clergy, to tactual succession, and, until recently when an act of Parliament made it possible for a clergyman to become again a layman, to the indelibility of its ordinations. And yet the two archbishops, and all the bishops, are practically appointed by the Prime Minister, who may be, as we have seen, a Jew, a Unitarian, or an Agnostic.

In the United States of America one church differs from another only in being a little better than any other. The men and women of each congregation control the church property, the minister, alas, being all too often considered as church property as well, and choose their own minister. Even in the American Episcopal Church, any particular bishop would find it difficult to interfere successfully with any particular congregation's choice of a rector. There is, too, in too many of these congregations, a noticeable, not to say very remarkable alliance between wealth and goodness, since the church officers are almost invariably the wealthier men in the congregation.

The American notion of a church as a club, or

as a social ladder, does not obtain in England, except that there is perhaps a tendency on the part of men grown rich to leave the dissenters' chapel for the more aristocratic ministrations of the church.   Why a man or woman who enters a church to worship God should be warmly greeted and, later on, gradually entertained socially, as though this were a usual quality and manifestation of the Kingdom of Heaven, a prevalent notion in America, has not as yet dawned upon these dull English people.   That a woman should seek social recognition through membership in the altar-guild; or worship in and serve the parish, with an eye to dinners and dances; or that a man should be ostentatiously deeply, darkly blue in his orthodoxy, and at the same time peddle bonds that he knows to be of easy financial virtue amongst his friends, is a refinement of ecclesiastical-social diplomacy to which they have not attained.

Mr. John Bull says his prayers under totally different auspices.   The majority of the churches of England are private property.   When a large estate is purchased, the parish church or churches go with the other property.   The landlord, or the patron of the livings, as he is called with reference to his relations to his church property, chooses the clergyman for every parish on his property, and sees to it that the revenue attaching thereto goes to him. He can sell this church living or let it to whom he will, and although each incumbent is put over the parish for life, at his death the patron may again bestow it upon some one else. So secure was this tenure of the parson in his parish that it is only recently that an act of Parliament permitted his dismissal, even for drunkenness or debt.

The people of a parish have well-defined rights to the services of the parson, to sittings in the church, to burial in the churchyard, and to the sacraments, but to little more. George William Thomas Brudenell Bruce, fourth Marquis of Ailesbury, who died some years ago, was the patron of nine such livings. He married a girl of unexceptionable immorality from the variety stage, was part owner of several music halls, and added to his notoriety by being ruled off every race-track in England, as a cheat and a blackguard. There is always a large number of these livings for sale, which are advertised just as are other investments. A wealthy man's daughter marries a clergyman, and the father, if he be of the right sort, purchases one of these livings and presents it as a wedding gift. In families where there are one or more of these livings, one of the sons becomes a clergyman, just to keep that much income in the family. A clergyman with capital at his disposal, invests some of it in such a purchase, and enjoys the income thereof, and an agreeable way of exercising his professional energies, at the same time. Younger sons were wont to take to this profession, and with reason, since it is the only one in which a man may retain all the prerogatives and privileges of a gentleman, and have all the amenities of social courtesy shown him, without the possession or expenditure of money.

On finding out this much about the State Church of England, one expects to find one thing, and finds quite another. Again, somehow, the machinery works. In the city, and in the country districts as well, these men are the dullest men in the pulpit, and the most companionable men out of it, to be found anywhere. They work hard and conscientiously, most of them, and are, as a rule, popular, very often indeed the most popular, and with the greatest influence for good in their several communities. The demand for the disestablishment of the church is seldom bolstered by any argument now-a-days from the laxness or incompetence of the clergy. The demand is based rather upon such arguments as these: that the State should represent the whole people in religious as in other matters; that

Parliament is not a fit body to deal with church matters; that establishments obstruct political and social reforms; and that established churches being subject to State control cannot possess a certain necessary liberty of adaptation.

In the last quarter of a century the Established Church has collected and spent an enormous sum, estimated at some $450,000,000, in domestic and foreign missions, in renovating old churches, in establishing new ones, and in founding and supporting institutions for carrying on the different branches of its work. The church population of England is estimated to be about half the total population; and whatever be the comparative strength in numbers of the Established and Dissenting Churches, there can be no question of the superior influence of the 28,000 clergy of the State Church. Whether the system be right or wrong, these clergymen are, man for man, stronger men than the dissenting ministers, and not only in the palaces but in the slums also, they wield a more constant control. In spite of Ruskin's bitter comment: "Our national religion is the performance of church ceremonies and preaching of soporific truths (or untruths) to keep the mob quietly at work while we amuse ourselves," it must be admitted that to-day, either because the fear of disestablishment stares them in the face, or because attendance at church has woefully decreased, while indifference and unbelief have increased, the clergy are an energetic, hard-working, and sincere body of men.

But what if they were a far greater power for good than they are! What if they were not divided among themselves as to ritual, exegesis, and theology, as well as upon outside questions of education, the licensing bill and other matters! They would even then be overwhelmed and lost in the sea of troubles that confront them. They are as a pitchfork against the sea.

Of what education is doing to palliate these evils we have seen in another chapter, and it is little enough.

Mr. Balfour, the late Prime Minister, says: "The existing educational system of this country is chaotic, is ineffectual, is utterly behind the age, makes us the laughing-stock of every advanced nation in Europe and America, puts us behind, not only our American cousins, but the German, and the Frenchman and the Italian."

The truth of the matter is that the whole Imperial situation has so changed in the last fifty years that the old makeshifts and compromises no longer suffice to meet the situation.

In 1860 the United States was on the verge of a four years' struggle for national unity, and

England was looking on, the majority of her citizens believing that the end of the Republic was in sight. Even Gladstone was an investor in Confederate bonds. Germany was not even a nation. Japan was known to the outside world as a gentle, courteous people, still steeped in feudalism and proficient in delicate iron and enamel work.

What Englishman thought then that America would produce so much steel and iron that she could afford to undersell the Englishman at his own door? In those dark days what Englishman dreamed that the Republic across the water would produce 2,592,320,000 bushels of corn, or 78.8 of the world's total production; 634,087,000 bushels of wheat, or 20.7 of the world's entire crop; 13,346,000 bales of cotton, or 71.3 of the world's total; 25,780,000 tons of pig iron or 42.2 of the world's total; 162,600,000 barrels of petroleum, or 62.5 of the total supply; 918,000,-000 pounds of copper, or 57.5 of the total supply; $89,620,000 of gold, or 22.1 of the world's total output; and $37,914,000 of silver, or 35.5 of the total; 298,859 tons of sulphur, or 35.8 of the total; 455,000,000 tons of coal, or 37.3 of the world's supply? Since those days the United States has grown portentously. With an area of 5.9 of the world's, and a population of 5.2, we supply 43 per cent. of the world's total production of wheat, corn, and oats. We mine 35.5 per cent. of the world's silver, 22.1 of the gold, and have 21 per cent. of the cotton spindles. What Englishman, with the Armada and Trafalgar in mind, believed that Germany would build ship for ship with him, and give him anxiety as to his island's safety from her attack? What Englishman dreamed that he would rejoice to see his country the ally of pagan Japan, become a naval power to be reckoned with?

The world has changed, but he has changed least of all. He has as little sympathy as ever with the foreigner. He cannot see what these changes mean. Even the one solution of the problem right at hand, namely an Imperial Federation, with a wise scheme of tariff regulations binding together his vast interests all over the world, is made almost hopeless by his complacent condescension toward the colonials. Ask the Canadian how he likes the Englishman, not the politician, not the panderer who speaks for publication, but the man in the street. I have heard the answer an hundred times. I have heard it in Cape Breton, and from there all the way to Vancouver, and it is not reassuring. Ask the Australian how he enjoys a visit to England, and what hospitality he receives there. Ask the

South African how he looks upon the Home Government, which has handed him over to his enemies again. He will probably tell you the story of a certain husband's view of compromise. He was complaining to a friend that he liked to sleep between cotton sheets, but that his wife preferred linen sheets. He found linen sheets cold and disagreeable and they could not agree. "What do you do about it, how do you arrange matters," asked his friend. "Oh, we compromise!" replied the husband; "we use linen sheets!"

Oh, we'll compromise, says England to her South African colonist, and hands him over to the Boers. One hears vague tales, too, of Indian princes, not talking for publication, who are restless and dissatisfied, and of a semi-educated Indian populace demanding some share in government. Of all follies, the worst is a system of bringing these Indians to England, educating them, entertaining them, letting them dance and flirt with their women, permitting at least one of them to marry an English lady, and then sending them back to India to live in dependence, and as the inferior of the least important British official. Is it any wonder that this compromise brings anger and dissatisfaction?

Close at home, it is the same easy compromise.

A palpable disproportion of Irish members in the House of Commons, but servitude for Ireland. (The Irish point of view.)

A State Church, some of whose members and leaders take sides with the brewers against temperance reform. Years of wrangling between Churchmen, Catholics, and Nonconformists over the school question.

National unanimity in playing ostrich, and burying their heads in the sand on the question of England's continued commercial supremacy.

Always wide advertising of the fact that England still leads in the volume and value of her export and import trade over Germany, or the United States, or other rivals, but no honest analysis of the facts.

What boots it how fast England goes ahead, if her rivals go ahead faster than she does? What a silly fellow we should dub the youth who congratulates himself upon having grown so much stronger, so much heavier, so much taller in ten years, if all his rivals had during that time grown even stronger, heavier and taller than he. Between 1886 and 1906 Germany increased her exports of manufactured goods $415,000,000. During the same period England increased hers $300,000,000. Far more important even than that, Germany is keeping her men at work in her industries and on her soil. In 1894 Germany exported 26 out of every 10,000, in 1907 she exported 4 out of every 10,000 men. In 1894 England exported 9 out of every 10,000 men, in 1907 she exported 40 out of every 10,000 men. Between 1903 and 1907 the increase of men leaving England for other countries was 61 per cent. and unemployment was greater in 1907 than for ten years previously.

It must be exasperating to the Germans to read the English papers, which comment in sorrowful tones upon Germany's debt, Germany's deficit, and Germany's financial difficulties generally, in a tone of aloofness and self-satisfaction. One would suppose England had no debt, that England's total export and import trade had not decreased during the one year 1908 by $570,000,000, that England was not taxed to death, that England was not drink mad. It is no concern of ours. England is our play-ground, and the English our inexhaustible source of amusement, but it is not to be wondered at that the Continent wearies sometimes of England's constant suggestions that she is not as others are. The temple of the world has echoed and re-echoed for many years now with the Pharisee's prayer, and the accent is unmistakably cockney.

Germany in the twenty years of the present

Emperor's reign has increased her population from forty-eight millions to sixty-three millions. A comparison between the three countries, Great Britain, Germany, and the United States shows the long strides the rivals of Great Britain are making.

EXPORTS

	GT. B.	GER.	U. S.
1890. In millions of £	263	158	176
1907. " "	426	342	370
Percentage of gain during period	62	116	110

IMPORTS

	GT. B.	GER.	U. S.
1890. In millions of £	420	224	164
1907. " "	645	477	286
Percentage of gain during period	53	113	74

MANUFACTURED EXPORTS

	GT. B.	GER.	U. S
1890. In millions of £	228	107	35
1907. " "	342	240	147
Percentage of gain during period	50	124	320

POPULATION

	GREAT BRITAIN	GERMANY	UNITED STATES
1890	37,400,000	49,400,000	62,600,000
1907	44,000,000	62,300,000	88,000,000
Gain	6,600,000	12,000,000	26,000,000

EMIGRATION

	BRITISH	GERMANY
1890	109,000	97,000
1907	235,000	31,600

GROSS RAILWAY RECEIPTS

	GT. B.	GER.	U. S.
1890. In millions of £ . . .	79.9	65.0	217
1907. " " . . .	121.5	131.6	494
Percentage of increase . . .	52	102	126

CONSUMPTION OF COAL

	GT. B.	GER.	U. S.
1890. In millions of tons . .	151	104	135
1907. " " . .	202	199	370
Percentage of increase . . .	33	91	174

PRODUCTION OF PIG IRON

	GT. B.	GER.	U. S.
1890. In millions of tons . .	7.9	4.6	9.2
1907. " " . .	10.1	12.6	25.7
Percentage of increase . . .	27	174	179

SAVINGS BANK DEPOSITS

	GT. B.	GER.	U. S.
1890. In millions of £ . . .	115	185	310
1907. " " . .	230	466	699
Percentage of increase . . .	100	151	125

With this condition of affairs in plain view, one party at least in the State is coquetting openly with socialism. Old age pensions are now a fact and free food for school children is under discussion. Five shillings a week for those seventy years of age or over! Why not sixty-three years of age, why not fifty-five, why not Professor Osler's limit of forty years of age? Does anyone suppose for a moment that the old fellows of sixty-five will not be jealous of the old fellows of seventy; and the old fellows of fifty-five of the old fellows of sixty! Up to December 31, 1908, the number of pensions actually granted was 596,038. Roughly speaking one person out of every seventy is now in receipt of an old age pension. Is human nature a different thing in this island? Will men save here who are being saved for? Will men work here when others must work for them? On the contrary, less here than in almost any other country. They are slow, stolid, cold-blooded, and selfish. A fight, or drink, or sport, these rouse them, but little else does. For the last twenty years the only compromise with the British workmen has been that of the rest of the country sleeping between his sheets! His savings bank deposits are only some $265,000,000, and here it must be remembered that thousands of people who do not belong in any sense to the working classes use the savings banks for their savings. It would take three times this amount to pay his drink bill for one year. But nobody dares take his cup away from him. Instead of that it is proposed to promise him support in his old age, so that he need not save at the public house in the meanwhile.

This matter of old-age pensions is an insidiously elastic form of outdoor relief, which will be stretched to suit the political exigencies of the hour, and a very enticing invitation to shiftlessness, to trust in God and let the powder get damp. It is the beginning of the change of English attitude from frank and free individualism to the fashionable present-day effeminacy of State support.

The important and the forbidding feature of this new departure of State aid is not the fact itself, or the method of working it out, or even the consequences, but the cause. Why is such legislation deemed necessary? In a nutshell the reason is this: The birth-rate is dropping as we have noted elsewhere. The birth-rate which twenty-five years ago was 36 is now 28 to 26 per 1,000. The effect of this is that the number of the young has decreased in proportion to the whole population; while the modern lengthening of life has increased the proportion of the old. The number of children under fifteen has decreased so rapidly in the last twenty-five years that there are to-day 1,200,000 fewer in proportion to the whole population, while the proportion of the old to the total population, people over sixty years, has increased in the same time by 500,000. In short the proportion of old people has increased by half a million, while the proportion of young people has decreased by nearly a

million and a quarter.   This is a serious matter
anywhere, but to this manly and vigorous and
self-reliant race it is, unless remedied, the beginning of the end.   It is this aspect of the situation
which to the onlooker is much the most serious
feature of this new legislation of support by the
State.   If the children are to be State educated,
and the aged to be State supported, and tariff
reform is to follow to enable those between
fifteen and sixty to make enough in forty-five
years to be able to take care of the unfortunate
young and the shiftless old as well as themselves,
the whole complexion of British life is bound to
change.   Sturdy self-reliance, and common-sense,
and manly dealing with their own affairs and
the Imperial affairs so largely intrusted to
them, will, if they do not disappear, droop into
a tendency to lean upon the State — the State
which is after all here and everywhere the
phantom self of every man in it.   Is the individual less a man?   Then just so surely is the
State less to be respected.

What did all these things matter to England
fifty years ago, or even twenty-five years ago.
She had been unbeaten on land, or at sea, for as
long as a man's memory could go.   She was so
easily first in shipping and commerce that there
was not only no rival, but no second, the rest of

the world was nowhere. Why not be generous and conciliatory, why fash one's self about education, the quarrels among the sects, the demands of labor, the partition of the land, the drink question, when there was so much and to spare! Compromise, smiling compromise if possible, was easier, was more soothing to the nerves, and was found to be the cheapest oil for the machinery of State. But when everybody compromises, from bishops to barmaids, somebody must be paid some time, — yes, there is always the Devil to pay! And now he is presenting his accounts all round. "Disestablishment" is handed to the bishops; "no more barmaids" is handed to the barmaids; "reduction of the forces, and of pay" is handed to the army; "unemployment" is handed to the workman; and "increased taxes" distributed liberally to everybody; and ministers of State themselves throw up their hands and complain of the difficulty of riding the two horses at once, "of economy and efficiency." If economy had been ridden with firmer hands and a more confident seat in the saddle, there would have been no need of such a simian straddle as that. Compromise loses any intellectual defensibility, and becomes a term of the circus, when it is thus used. Compromise which gives as much liberty as safety permits to two opposing

factions, may have its political u[...]
mise, powdered and painted, [...]
spangles, kissing its hands to [...]
contemptible thing.

We have seen how in church, in [...]
expenditure and in governing, compromise has
been the offered solution. In the days of prosperity it may serve the purpose well enough, but
must there not be an end to its efficacy some
time?

If we have learnt anything from this admirable
people, and this wonderful Empire, it has been
how much may be done by liberty loving men,
with the wealth and leisure to ensure courage,
patience and loyalty. We have watched their
history for a thousand years and more, in which
men have accepted their responsibilities, and
used their opportunities. We have seen how
neither opportunity nor responsibility has been
denied to any man. Any man may rise in church,
in State, or society. So much has ample freedom
done. Men made England, and kept her in-
violate. But now what a change! At the
hour of this writing practically every important
legislative movement is in some sort a plea and
a plan to soften men, to lesson their responsibilities, and to make them feel that they need
not earn their opportunities. This may do in

me Utopian kingdom of which I know nothing, but it is death to the Saxon. Compromise was well enough as long as it made it easier to give freedom to a larger number; but compromise is disaster, where it locks up high principle in a dark closet, and then goes fumbling and grovelling for votes. At a time when over 32,000,000 of the population of the United Kingdom are dwellers in cities and towns; this people, who, more than all others, have won their victories and achieved their development on the land and out of doors, it seems hardly the proper work of far-seeing statesmanship to weaken them still further by pandering to their own ignorant shortcuts to salvation.

These reflections must not for a moment be taken as malicious, or as seeking to give pain. We are not dealing with a pat of butter, or a bit of wood, or a handful of clay. There is good metal here, and when one draws his picture on copper, one must use steel and an acid. It would be no compliment to the English people to use the epicene style of ambassadorial compliment. A clawless kitten is not more harmless or more uninforming than a foreign ambassador at a banquet. That is his business! But as between men, we all know that America does not like England, and that Americans do not like the

English, but no intelligent American, no American indeed whose opinion is worth a fig, would rejoice to see this nation, which has taught the nations of the world the greatest lesson since Christianity, and that is the lesson of law, and order, and liberty, lose her grip. We, too, are of the Saxon breed, diluted though the blood may be, and we have our problems and our tasks, and both would be made the harder should English civilization prove a failure. Here, not long ago, was the hardiest, the best trained, the most law-abiding, and the freest people in the world, and no American who loves his own country can look on and see them emasculated with equanimity or without trying to analyze the reasons for such a change of attitude.

We have no faith in the philosophic socialism, touched up with self-conscious oratory, which governs France; none in the bureaucracy, guided by Divine Right, which governs Germany; certainly none in the autocracy, perched upon dynamite, which governs Russia. We believe that a people can be taught self-government, though the weak point in all democracies is that there is nothing the people distrust so much as the people. In England that weakness has been partially eliminated by their method of choosing as a rule their leaders and their legislators from a class whose independence has been a safeguard against corruption, or intimidation. Their governing has been a success, because it has been a friendly deference to a consensus of the competent created by themselves. No American wishes to see that solution of government, of all by the best, chosen in free and open competition, fail.

IV

ENGLISH HOME LIFE

ON entering an Englishman's house the first thing one notices is how well his house is adapted to him. It seems to have grown up around him, as in so many cases it has, and to have taken on the folds of his character, as a coat often worn moulds itself to the figure of its owner. On entering an American's house, the first thing one notices is how well he adapts himself to his house.

In England, the establishment is carried on with a prime view to the comfort of the man, and this applies to rich and poor alike and to all conditions of society. In America the establishment is carried on with a prime view to the comfort and the exigencies of the woman. Men are more selfish than women, consequently the English home is, as a rule, at any rate from a man's point of view, more comfortable than the American home; barring of course our innumerable mechanical contrivances for heating, bathing, ventilation, cooking and so on, of which even now, not only the average English house is quite barren, but also the houses of the wealthy, both in town and country. But here again it is the woman and the servants who keep house who suffer, not the man.

Men demand more, and receive more for their money than do women, hence it is likely to follow that a man's house, while it will be less attractive æsthetically, will be more carefully furnished with an eye to creature comforts than that of a woman.

An Englishman is more at home in his own house than an American, first because he is by all the inmates recognized as the absolute master there, and because he spends more of his time there. He leaves it later in the morning, returns to it earlier in the day, and gives more of himself to it than does an American. An Englishman is continually going home, an American is continually going to business. Ages of social laws, and vast accretions of social distinctions have made the Englishman who can stay at home more important than the Englishman who must go to business; consequently, all Englishmen assume that they are much at home, and little at business, whether they are or not, for by so doing they loom larger on the social horizon.

The Englishman is forever planning and scheming to get home, and to stay at home, and to enjoy the privileges of his home; while the American is more apt to devote his energies to make his business a place to go to, and in which to spend himself. Here again the social lever plays its part, for in America a man is the more distinguished from his fellows the more business he has on his hands, and he, too, assumes a busyness sometimes out of proportion to the reality.

These minor details of domestic life put their impress upon larger matters of business and politics. It would be worthy of remark should a party leader in Congress attack his opponents on the ground that a Saturday session prevented him and his followers from spending two days a week at home. But it is a matter of course in the English Parliament that Mr. Balfour should object strenuously to a plan for a Saturday's sitting which debars Englishmen from Saturday and Sunday at their own firesides; or from the pursuit of their favorite outdoor pleasures. Whether time shall be given members of Parliament to go out to dine at leisure, no matter what bill is before the house, assumes dimensions of grave political importance. But a bitter attack in the American Congress on the topic of the dinner hour would scarcely be listened to, and would certainly relegate its champion to the realms of crankdom and ridicule. So, too, any uneasiness on the part of legislators lest they should not get away to the country for the grouse shooting, a common enough failing in England, is so far beyond reasonable probability in America that it is impossible to characterize what would happen to an agitator on such a subject.

Americans staying any time in England, whether men or women, are impressed by the fact that it is the country of men. Likewise the English, both men and women, who visit America are impressed by the fact that America is the country of women. Possibly we might deduce from this that Americans make the better husbands, and the English the better wives. But this is much too subtle a subject, and one providing too many exceptions to discuss. One may perhaps say tentatively, without much fear of contradiction, that English women take it for granted that their husbands' pleasure and comfort, and even amusements, should take first place; while the American man rather delegates the part of pleasure, comfort, and amusement to his wife, and she, perhaps, has come to look upon this often as her privilege, and sometimes, alas, as her right. Whatever the reason, the general average of home life is more comfortable in

England than in America. Whether it be a matter of political economy, of free trade for example, or not, all the requirements for comfortable living are indubitably cheaper in England than in America.

People having incomes varying from $1,500 to $15,000 a year can and do live more comfortably in England than with us. In the view of the Frenchman, however, the English require more than the French. Taine writes that where a Frenchman eats a sheep and a half in a year an Englishman eats four sheep; and goes on to say: "Possess £20,000 in the funds here or else cut your throat. Such is the idea which constantly haunts me, and the omnibus advertisements suggest it still more in informing me that Mappin's celebrated razors cost only one shilling." This gives the other side of the picture, but to the American, the opportunity for comfort and economy on the same income is far greater here than at home.

In the case of people with say less than $1,500 a year, or more than $20,000 a year, they do not profit so materially by the difference in prices, for the reason that luxury is everywhere expensive, and genteel poverty everywhere equally distressing; or even more distressing in this country where for so many months in the year the landscape looks like a charcoal drawing over which a damp sleeve has been drawn.

Nothing gives more conclusive proof of the truth of these comparisons than to notice how the English and the Americans respectively go about it to economize. In a large establishment in England the horses for the wife's brougham and victoria would go before the husband's hunters, while the reverse of this would be true in an American establishment compelled to make similar sacrifices. It is the husband, rather than the wife, who is looked to to advertise the family prosperity in England. It would be a very rare case indeed in America where the wife would not have more and greater variety of clothes than her husband, but this is much less true in England. Even poor men in England have more clothes than well-to-do men in America. An income of $5,000 a year in England would mean four times the amount of clothes that the possessor of the same income in America would think necessary. On the other hand, the percentage of any given income, from $3,000 to $20,000, expended by the wives and daughters for clothes, would be half to two-thirds less in England than with us. A man servant of some kind in the establishment is far more common in England than with us, and he among other things takes

care of the master of the house, who is thus
more easily capable of dealing with a large
wardrobe and has more leisure to employ as he
prefers.

Both for the reason that such service is much
cheaper here, and also for the reason already
given that the man is the important person, the
men are more cared for than the women, and a
man servant is a common appanage of men in
this country whose incomes would be deemed,
and would be, as a matter of fact, quite inadequate
for such an expense in America.

The last things that an Englishman willingly
parts with are the appurtenances and conveniences which permit him to have his friends
around him at his own table, or at his club;
and this applies up and down through all but the
lowest class. With us, on the contrary, the great
mass of my countrymen, outside of a comparatively few dwellers in our large cities, would
scarcely miss not having people to dine with
them at their own table. An Englishman forced
to economize would move out of a big house into
a small one in order to keep certain conveniences,
such as servants, a certain standard of living and
a certain personal dignity, which make for his
personal comfort; while an American would try
to the last to stick to his big house, but cut down

the number of servants and other personal conveniences by which he does not set so much store.

If one were training a race-horse to win an important event, the last thing one would economize upon would be comfortable stabling and the quality of his grooms and his feed. One is continually reminded of "training," in seeing how the hard-worked Englishman, whether in politics, business, literature, the civil service or in a profession cares for himself, and is cared for in his own house. Everything bends to make him and to keep him "fit."

Such men as the leading statesmen, diplomats, barristers, journalists, bankers, business men generally, and prelates; in short, the dignified, responsible and great ones of the earth are, so to speak, regularly groomed, and kept in condition physically, and mentally, for their arduous duties. They take frequent holidays; everything that paid service can do,—and such service is astonishingly cheap here, — from keeping their clothes to attending to their correspondence and their engagements, they are relieved of.

Gladstone was a fine horseman in his early days and a widely advertised performer with the axe later; Balfour plays the piano, plays golf and writes on philosophy—all pastimes in their way;

Rosebery is the most charming occasional speaker in England, and a racing man besides; Chamberlain is a grower of orchids, Grey is an authority on fishing, Salisbury was a chemist and in his early days a journalist, and countless others are sportsmen and writers upon sport and travel; while Sir Charles Dilke is the only man I have ever met who seriously impressed me with the idea that a man might be omniscient after all. They make a business of recreation, in order that in its turn business may be in some sort a recreation. A good wholesome doctrine.

It is not venturesome to say that public opinion in America would not permit a member of the Cabinet to keep a racing stable, and it would not help him politically and would certainly serve as a text for much ridicule were it known that he were a crack golf or racquet player. Such a man with us, with complications of immense importance in Siam and in South Africa on his hands, would be considered to be either mad or a traitor should he hurry off for a day or two's journey to a race-course to see one of his horses run in one of the classic races.

In England these engrossing avocations are deemed to be a wise economy of power; with us they are still looked upon by the great majority as a frivolous waste of energy. Such an innocent recreation as a translation of Virgil probably carried little weight in our national legislature, even though the perpetrator was as popular as our ex-Secretary of the Navy, Long, of Massachusetts, was and deserved to be. On the other hand, the fame of Gladstone's unscholarly Homeric heresies produced an undoubted effect both in and out of Parliament, upon both his followers and his opponents. They have been at it longer than we have, and hold with Plato that the man is not the body, but the fellow who has the body, and also that change is rest.

We are not concerned for the moment with the comparative merits of these methods of life; they serve merely to illustrate the dominant theme. They all go to show that domestic economy in England is devised for, and directed to the aim of making the men as capable as possible of doing their work. The home is not a play-house for the women and their friends; nor a grown-up nursery for the mother and the children, but a place of rest and comfort in which the men may renew their strength. It is possibly fair to deduce from this that house-keeping as a rule in England has a more definite aim and consequently more system, and less waste of energy, and money, than is the case in the majority of American houses.

However awkward and flamboyantly dressed the Englishwoman may appear upon the boulevards of Paris; however dull she may appear when ranged alongside of her American cousin in a drawing-room, in her own house she has few superiors—unless it be in France—as a domestic business manager.

She gains this ability by previous years of training. It is the exception, rather than the rule, where both the boys and girls in an English household do not receive an allowance. It is true that nothing permits of so many shades of meaning as the word "allowance" when thus used. It may mean anything, from a good-natured paternal promise to pay, which is irregularly fulfilled, to a light advance fund for gloves and bon-bons, to be followed each month, or each quarter, by the infantry and heavy artillery of dressmakers' and milliners' bills. Those who have suffered in adolescence from the one, and in maturity from the other, know what a multitude of interpretations lie between these extremes. The British interpretation is, however, serious and fixed. Girls and boys alike are held pretty strictly to account and are obliged to live upon a certain fixed sum. Women coming into the management of establishments of their own are already trained to the business aspect of the situation. They have also a tremendous advantage over their American cousins, as an aid to wise expenditure, in public opinion. Nobody, from the King down, is either ashamed or afraid to be economical. Here either a man or a woman is thought to be a fool or a vulgarian who is not careful of expenditure; while in America our Negro, Irish, and other foreign servants have been clever enough to make it appear that economy is mean, and as a nation we suffer accordingly. We are fools enough to be fooled by these underlings who, driven from their own countries, come prepared to exploit ours.

Not so in England. Money is not so easily made, nor has it such earning power in England as in America, and as a consequence it is much more carefully cherished. And money buys more in England than in America. It is by no means true, as prevalent opinion leads one to believe, that money plays a greater rôle in America than in England. The "almighty dollar" receives no such obsequious homage in its native lair as does the "sovereign" in its own house of worship. Everybody takes tips in England, from the Prime Minister to whom an earldom is given, or the radical who is made a knight, down to the railway porter content with threepence. The typical American boy abroad, described by Mr. Henry

James, whose frequently repeated war-cry is, "My dad's all-fired rich!" has many even more vulgar prototypes in England. The methods English men and English women will stoop to, and the humiliations they will suffer, in order to make or to get money, are not merely not practised in America, but are quite unknown there. For the very reason that money gives so much of comfort, and standing, and opportunity here, the struggle to get it is unparalleled anywhere else in the world. To have money here, no matter what the other advantages of birth or ability may be, is to add a thousand-fold to their value, while to be without it is a heart-breaking handicap.

A great soldier, a great sailor, a great ruler over one of the English colonies is rewarded for his successes not only by a title, but by a large gift of money. Lord Roberts, Lord Kitchener, Lord Cromer are all cases in point. They were not only promoted in the social scale, but handsomely rewarded by gifts of money.

There are few Americans of a certain standing who cannot tell extraordinary tales of the humiliating proceedings of needy aristocrats from England; from the men who are out and out blacklegs to the women who exploit their American hosts for the purpose of gambling in the stock market.

But this is not by any chance to be a chronicle of gossip. We have our social fringes as well as the English. It is intended, in recalling the misdeeds of some of our visitors, merely to illustrate the fearful temptation people of a certain class are under in their endeavor to keep up appearances, and to note to what extremes they will go to keep themselves even ostensibly afloat. A Mississippi steamboat captain maintained that his boat drew so little water that she would float wherever there had been a heavy dew! A needy Englishwoman will float her financial social craft or try to do so on even shallower water than that; and no spectacle is more inexpressibly pitiable. To have been somebody and to become nobody; to have had and not to have, are more appalling changes here than with us. The successful here are rewarded as in no other country in the world, and the strong train and fight for the prizes grimly; and the weak hang on to the shreds of prosperity in a painful and humiliating way. In a country therefore where money is so potent and so difficult to acquire, those who have the disbursing of it must be trained to, or acquire wisdom in, its use, even in the affairs of the household.

The fact that the English house is so ostensibly, and first and foremost, conducted with the aim of making the men comfortable, makes it easy to understand and to give the reasons for the greater economy practised therein. Men suffer from a far more severe strain of competition in England than with us, and economy always, whether it be economy of method, of time, or of money, is just so much saved from the imperative, for the voluntary. There is no possibility of great exertion without frequent periods of rest. This is taken into account here. In England men have more avocations, more amusements, more interests outside of the daily round of pressing business than with us. These avocations demand leisure, and economy is the mother of leisure. The percentage of men—although much less than it was twenty-five years ago—who aside from their engrossing pursuits of business or profession, devote themselves to some hobby, if one may call it so, is overwhelmingly greater than with us. And one may say unreservedly that this is a good thing. "You'll get no good from all your runnin' and sparrin', sir, without plenty of rest!" was the oft-repeated injunction of an old trainer of athletes. The hour's complete rest after the eight-mile spin was what made the muscle.

The employment of man's leisure hours has most to do with making or marring him. "Le

temps le mieux employé est celui qu'on perds!"
The number of men who raise horses, or dogs,
or pigs, or sheep, or cows; who are players at
cricket, golf, tennis, or rowing; who collect books,
prints, or autographs, Japanese curios or odd
bits of porcelain; who are studying an ancient
or a modern language; who make a business of
doing a bit of travelling every year; who climb
mountains, or explore new countries; who go in
for hunting, shooting, fishing, botany or geology;
who study some branch of archeology, or dig for
the roots of a genealogical tree, is astonishingly
large. Indeed the man of even moderate means
who is without some such, more or less important,
recreation is, one may almost say, the exception.
Of course I am speaking now of men of serious
pursuits. The idle club lounger is no more a
stranger here than with us, and even less worth
classifying. To know something about many
things, and everything about something, is a
good educational ideal, besides giving breadth,
variety, and a saline interest to life. An Englishman's holiday is looked forward to, planned for,
and provided for with some care; while all too
often in America a holiday to a busy man over
thirty-five is a white elephant, which he ends by
turning over to his wife and daughters as a
mount.

One is in no danger of exaggerating here, at least, for the intense competition of English life to-day, which makes it necessary that men should "train" in order to achieve success, or even so much as hold their own, is everywhere manifest.

In so far as these Englishmen take better care of themselves, they are younger for their years than our men. I am controverting the received opinion about the English, both on the Continent and in America, when I say that Englishmen laugh and smile and "lark" more than other men of mature age. I have noted how men of different ages play together; so, too, they get on comfortably and happily together in all sorts of ways. This may be due to the fact that priggishness is so abhorred here, and, consequently, serious matters are not much discussed, intellectual differences between men of different ages are not so marked, and men in their conversation as well as in their games are more on the same level. Any assumption of superiority is frowned upon, and both young and old make a mild form of "chaff" the conversational medium of intercourse. At the club, in the country house billiard room, over their cigars and coffee after dinner, the conversation seldom drifts beyond the understanding, or the easy participation therein of those most mildly endowed intellectually.

The young and the old are much more together than with us. At a dinner in town, at a house party in the country, there is no dividing people by their ages. Fathers and sons, uncles and nephews, are much more at home with one another than with us, and see much more of one another, and have apparently more in common. In the Row of a morning, at the cricket games, at the shooting and fishing and racing, at the billiard table after dinner, the youngsters between twenty and thirty not only mingle with but are the boon companions of their elders. It is generally noted how much more a man of the world the English boy is than the American boy. He probably does not know as much, he certainly is not so sharp and quick, but he is far more of a man, speaking of course very generally and leaving room for exceptions. This is due to the fact that the English boy spends so much of his time with his elders. A common ground of meeting and conversation is of course sport, and in that realm prowess and experience, and not age, mark the differences between men. Here a man is merely as old as his handicap at the games he plays; and the number of "scratch" men over forty is greater than in any other country in the world.

They love sport, it is true, for its own sake;

but they realize that youthfulness is a valuable asset in affairs, in politics, in social life, and so make a business of keeping young.

The Englishman at home on his own little island and amongst his own friends is, contrary to the opinion almost universally held abroad, a very cheerful and boyish person. He has nothing of the feline flavor that almost always pertains to the indoor man. The cleverest amongst them conceal their cleverness, and the race as a whole are rigid abstainers from all forms of intellectual meat and drink as such. The rule of thumb and common-sense methods are good enough for them, and thus far their national preeminence has not forced them to question their value.

Nature comes down hard on those who go too far in the development of the brain. We are more cheerful, younger, better tempered, and saner, most of us, the more we live out of doors, eat and drink without thinking of it, and give the brain no more than its fair share of work to do. This is the attitude of the Englishman toward life. One can breed to physical, but not very successfully to mental, type, and the English by intuition have neglected any attempt to do so. The boulevards of Paris swarm with mediocre intellectual celebrities, all too many of them, of a most unwholesome odor; even we Americans are still more or less obsessed, at any rate in politics, by the haranguer, the mountebank, and the wire-puller. The Englishman will have none of them. He refuses to consent to the burial of Herbert Spencer in Westminster Abbey; he proclaims in the House of Lords by the mouth of a cricketing peer that: "Lord's Cricket Ground is one of the most sacred spots in England," a statement received with loud cheers by that assembly when it was proposed to cut into the grounds for a tram line, and he goes his way through the world quite convinced that he is right in his estimate of the comparative value of mind and matter. Even their formally intellectual professions are filled with men, in the church, in the law, in medicine, and the like, who openly exalt the material rather than the intellectual and spiritual side.

That fine fellow, the Church of England parson, is one of the most useful persons in England, but it is because he is generally an outdoor rather than an indoor man. A small boy here was asked what he would like to be were he grown up. He hesitated a moment and then said: "I think it would be rather jolly to be a sporting parson!"

It is this attitude toward life that makes the

Frenchman and the American cry, "dull," when the Englishman is mentioned. I should phrase it differently. He is very young, and he is sane and seldom mentally finical, but he is a very sophisticated man of the world in the best sense of the phrase for all that. It is not dull to succeed, and as the world stands to-day he is still first in the race.

I emphasize this trait of youthfulness, and this habit of theirs of the young and the old living more together and having more in common than do we, because this is distinctly the Englishman as he is at home, and distinctly not what he is held to be abroad. With us, "young people" are often enough spoken of, and treated by their elders, as though they were a class by themselves, bounded by eighteen on the south and by, say, twenty-five on the north. This is the absurd fiction of a shallow and a provincial civilization. It makes boys and girls silly, and it often makes their elders shy and pompous. Neither old nor young profit by such exclusions. Every man does his work better, and every woman lives her life more serenely, the more of youthfulness and vigor and optimism there is in the atmosphere. There is not only the good fellowship, not only the experience of age and the daring of youth, but a saner tone all round. A man is not dead at forty, nor infallible at twenty, and it is well that Forty and Twenty should rub up against one another and make the discovery frequently. It is good for both. The importance of this is well understood here, where only the "fittest" and the "most fit" survive.

There are more than 1,200 ordained clergy of the Anglican Church without parishes, not to mention some sixty-five who were actually, at last accounts, in the workhouse; 85 per cent. of the barristers have nothing to do; 80 per cent. do not make $1,200 a year. The agricultural depression of late years has been such that incomes from land have been sadly reduced all round. The great increase in the last twenty-five years of facilities for gaining something of an education at small cost has flooded the market with both men and women who are ready to sell, or rent, their small intellectual equipments at almost starvation prices. Even when one goes further up the ladder there are many more men in England than in America who feel this pressure of competition, and who prepare themselves, and look after their reputation and their health, with scrupulous care lest they be shoved to one side.

A certain moral stability in matters of business and finance is partly due to this. A man cannot afford to fail, cannot afford to make a mistake here, for there is little chance of his ever getting back if he does. The swarms of Englishmen in South Africa, Australia, New Zealand, China, Japan, Canada, South America, and the north-western parts of our own country attest the fact that only the best equipped and the very strongest can hold their own in the tight little island itself.

At this moment a gentleman with a fair income has his oldest boy, of nineteen, at work with the village blacksmith; and the next, a boy of seventeen, in a neighboring carpenter's shop; and some months later they will leave home to try farming in Manitoba. These are not isolated examples. They happen to come under immediate observation. There are hundreds of gentlemen's sons who are obliged to leave England to find occupation and a living. They cannot be supported, or support themselves, at home. The strictness with which these matters are arranged and carried out here is unknown in America and would be deemed cold-blooded indeed by the American parent. The younger children of wealthy parents soon learn that they must fend for themselves. To be second, third and fourth sons of a great house is often enough to live upon a pittance, and there is no redress either at law or by appealing to sentiment. It is the law of the land, and anyone at all acquainted with England's social life is soon aware of the hardships of the noble and gentle scions who happen to be born too late. It is this arrangement, of course, which explains two things which are at first puzzling: First, that so many Englishmen must seek in other lands for position and a living, and, second, that there is so little virulent class feeling in this nation of class distinctions. A duke's grandson is only a commoner; an earl's second son's children may be, to all intents and purposes, poverty stricken — not infrequently they are. But they are of the same blood and very nearly related to the great ones of the country, and, therefore, in spite of the disparity in worldly goods, they still remain, out of pride, supporters of the classes rather than the masses.

Since the days when political places, commissions in the army, and fat livings in the church were in the gift of a feudal aristocracy, the straits to which the younger sons and daughters are put are illustrated by the countless amateur wine merchants, shopkeepers, servants' agencies, millinery shops, tobacconists, brokers, jobbers, agents for estates, and the like, in the hands of gentlemen and ladies, trying to make a living.

One man born two years before another comes in for title, wealth, position, and opportunity; the second son comes in for a beggarly income grudgingly given, while the grandchildren of the eldest son and the grandchildren of the second son may be poles apart in wealth and status. But it is exactly the same blood, and if blood tells, then these descendants of the nobility, but without title, ought to make themselves felt for the general good of the nation. And they do. This is economy indeed. Economy even of blood and family. The eldest gets practically all, the younger sons a pittance. The softly sheltered American girl, of a family only moderately well-off, would be amazed, if she could be induced to believe the truth, at the small incomes of many a nobleman's sisters and daughters. This, too, is economy in a still larger sense. It is the economy of concentrating even the money power in a few hands. The vast amount of capital in the hands of comparatively few people has been one of the great factors in enabling England in the last hundred years to become the landlord of the great industries of the world. That time is fast passing away, but England's unprecedented prosperity from 1815 to 1875 was to some extent due to that: She was the only country in the world with large supplies of liquid capital ready for investment in those days, and she has profited enormously from the situation. Her dividends pour in from every corner of the earth to-day as a consequence of this. The concentration of her wealth and the dispersal of her younger sons have been features of her economy of management and prime factors in her empire making. It is harsh domestic doctrine, this, of all to the eldest and little or nothing at all to the younger ones, but when one looks about and sees the seedy, out-at-elbows *noblesse* of France, Italy, Germany, and Russia, without leadership, without wealth, without power, and often merely the anæmic transmitters of foolish faces, the system appears to have something to be said in its favor. England is a commercial country and her aristocracy is still held, or holds itself, at the highest price. The foolish American mother, and the ambitious American girl, find that titles on the Continent may be bought by the dozen, while in England they still command a fair, though declining price, for each one.

One does not wonder then, at the domestic economy, or, on the other hand, at the applause, the obsequiousness, almost the servility, which greet success in England. The prizes are fewer, they are far more difficult to win, and they are splendidly rewarded. A really great man in

England is rewarded as in no other land, while the failures suffer in proportion.

Of all nations in the world, with perhaps the exception of our own, England has had the reputation, at least, of demanding that success should be accompanied by virtue. At any rate since the days of those torpid Teutons, the Georges, this has been the case. But the strife has become so keen that even this imperative consideration is sometimes lost sight of. So long as a statesman keeps within legal bounds, he is judged rather by the power he wields than by his reputation at the club, or in his house. It may be said of course that genius always, everywhere, has been permitted a certain license, but that is not the point at issue here. The English people would never consent to be ruled by a genius, or to permit genius to be in power amongst them. Anything that is not ostentatiously, and plainly to the naked eye, commonplace, they distrust to a man. There is an easily recognized difference between power and genius; the one representing the result of organization, the other the result of temperament; and even to the former there is to-day accorded a liberty in the realm of morals, which the great mass of the English people permit, because they are forced to do so by the exigencies of this keen competitive strife. They are driven to employ their able men both at home and abroad without too much scrutiny of their private morals. There have been, and are, great soldiers, sailors, statesmen and pro-consuls in England whose private lives would not endure examination. I forbear illustrating this point. Only an Englishman would criticise the statement, and, if he be well-informed, there are too many examples to make it worth debating.

It may be said, without fear of successful contradiction, that if the private life of every public man in England were submitted to the same scrutiny that follows his public performances, there would be more reversals of judgment than would result from the same kind of criticism applied to public men in America. A country which is preëminently a man's country must necessarily suffer from a man's code of morals. Divorce is bad to be sure, but no one who knows England and the Continent and the arrangements — often enough open — which take the place of the American divorce-court, would for a moment wish to exchange the latter for the former. No man could hold a position of supreme public trust in America whose private life has been of the character of the male sovereigns of England for an hundred years. And be it remembered that they give the lead to their subjects.

It is the fashion in America — and it may be doubted whether it is a good one — to sneer at politicians and politics, and to start movements, and to form societies every now and again for the propagation of the gospel among them. Just as professional philanthropy is so often merely benevolence seeking an audience; so the professional reformer is often failure posing as a critic. It is all too often the case after each of these ethical rebellions that the so-called, and self-styled, good men, reveal weaknesses which interfere sadly with the millennium that they propose to introduce. There is such a thing as being so occupied with the shielding of one's own virtues that one has no courage for a more robust form of usefulness.

The English are rarely deceived in this way. A strong and efficient man is kept in his place so long as he abides by a man's code of morals. It may be expected, but it is not required, that the woman's code should be applied to him. It is fair to say of this particular question that public men, at any rate successful public men in England, share in the honors, the emoluments, the privileges, and in the *pardon*, granted to every kind of success here. High rank, great power, great wealth, are it is true bound by the supreme law of *noblesse oblige*. They must give their blood, their wealth, and their power on every occasion when their country needs them; and one is only doing England bare justice in saying that right royally they have always done so; but beyond that, into other ethical realms the discussion had best not go. No man who seeks only to tell the truth and to be understood would willingly irritate his audience into an attitude of defiance.

The mention of these apparently disconnected points is necessary, because in reality they are the matters which most deeply concern and do much to make English home life what it is. In a country where the competition is excessive; where money has unwonted power to purchase comfort, distinguished consideration and even charitable judgment; where success is greeted and rewarded with an enthusiasm and generosity almost unknown elsewhere, and where failure and mediocrity are forced to play very small rôles indeed, the men are worth training to win the prizes. Only a man of gigantic abilities can be uncomfortable and miserable at home and at the same time successful in the world. This is understood here. Whether it is the English woman who appreciates it, or the English man who forces this view upon the woman, let some one else say, and let me keep my opinion to

myself and be silent. At any rate the English
woman knows that she can prevail only through
the honors and distinctions of the man. *Ubi
Clodius, ibi Claudia.* The proportion of English
women who are satisfied — or appear to be,
whether they are or not, who knows ?— to make
men comfortable, is very large.

No man knows just how much tiresome routine
and minute supervision go to make that sum
total of comfort in his home of which we are
writing. But every man knows that economy
and system are the elementary principles which
must underlie any such happy consummation.

The economies practised in very many English
households, both great and small, would almost
be called — and wrongly — meannesses, with
us. To begin with, houses are less extrava-
gantly, though quite as conveniently furnished in
those regions not entered by the public or one's
friends. The furnishings of the living rooms and
sleeping rooms are curtailed, not however to the
point of discomfort, in order that the general
average of comfort throughout the house shall
be higher. The servants' quarters, whether in
big houses or small ones, in town or country, in
inns or private houses, are incomparably less
convenient, and less comfortable, than with us.
The linen room, store room and wine cellar de-

partments are guarded by lock and key, and managed with a scrupulous nicety of calculation. Soap, candles, tea, sugar, coffee, trifles for the stable and kitchen, in short all the minor details of house-keeping, are looked after as carefully as are the minor expenditures in a great business house. The fact that a saving in candle ends, persisted in for a year, amounts to something is taken into account. Just as I have heard a young officer say that he found he could keep another hunter by giving up smoking and drinking, and had promptly done so. This economy which pervades the management of the household machinery, influences the servants as well. The cost of the butter provided each week by a cook, whose name for reasons of charity we forbear to give, in a city house in America, equalled almost exactly what was paid in an establishment on a similar scale in England for all the vegetables and fruit for the same length of time. It is, however, to be noted that a cook of Irish extraction in an American establishment occupies an autocratic position which has no parallel in England. As compared with America, servants are plenty and good. This is a subject in which the personal equation plays so predominant a part that it is not open to debate. There are good and bad servants, and good and bad masters, everywhere; only it is worth noting how very often the good masters and mistresses and the good servants, and vice versa, happen to come together.

In this matter of servants, competition is the dominant influence. Men and women servants are a recognized and self-respecting class in England. The King gives the medal of some inferior order to the butler of a house he visits, or has done so on one occasion at least. This marks his notion that servants are a recognized order, of a certain grade, in the State. Domestic service and politics are not considered here the sole employments requiring no preliminary and no special training. They enter the service and devote themselves to it and work to rise in it, not to escape from it. Much is expected from them, and, comparatively speaking, much is received from them. Servants' wages, even including beer money and other perquisites, are much lower than in America, though it is claimed that English servants specialize and consequently one needs more of them. A cook in England receives from $125 a year in the country to $200 a year in London — more of course, much more, in large establishments. Housemaids receive from $80 in the country to $120 or more in London. Of men servants it is not so easy to speak in figures. A good all-around man servant, where only one is kept, may not cost more than $200 a year in the country, while in London wages vary. One distinguished nobleman with a house in Park Lane, and a large establishment in the country, remarked that he knew he paid his head man, or butler, too much, but that he liked him, and therefore kept him on at $450 a year. Men servants are sometimes paid fancy prices where they are endowed with six feet of height, beautiful calves, and good complexions. Tall parlor-maids fetch more than short ones, and not long ago we saw an advertisement in the London *Daily Telegraph* for a man servant who was expected to look after a pony and make himself useful in the house, and also to sing in the choir of the parish church; the wages offered for such a domestic Admirable Crichton being $120 a year. An advertisement for a governess for two little girls, the wages offered being $125 a year, brought 162 replies in two days. It may be seen at a glance without going into more facts and figures in relation to a wearisome topic that in England servants are cheaper, better trained, more numerous, and better satisfied with their positions as servants, than in America. This state of things below-stairs lessens materially the difficulties of house-keeping economically, although as

a final word one may say that there are some men
and some women who would have good and faith-
ful servants in Seringapatam, and others who
could not keep a cook in Paradise. We have no
desire to enter the arena of flying adjectives and
bitter adverbs of the Servant Question. As in
religion and politics it is, far oftener than is admitted, a matter of temperament rather than anything else. This explanation is not generally wel-
comed, because few people are willing to damn
their failures and themselves by accepting a
simple explanation of what they deem to be a
complicated problem. It concerns us here merely
to state that servants' wages in England are,
roughly speaking, fifty per cent. less than in
America.

The reasons why economy is more general in
English than in American households are scarcely
more important than the results of such economy.
The best and all-sufficient result is that economy
gives leisure. System and regularity and lack of
worry give men more time to sleep, more time to
eat, more time to play, and more time and a
better preparation for work. In America our
first distinguished men were from the South,
where men had most leisure; and after that from
prosperous New England. And, say what one
may — and there is much to be said — in praise

of the hard taskmaster; poverty, it must be granted that the larger part of the distinguished work of the world has been done, and is done, by men who have had, or who have made for themselves, leisure. The man who voluntarily permits, or who is forced by circumstances to permit, things to get into the saddle and ride, necessarily lacks the confidence and the mastery which marks off the men who ride from the men who are ridden.

Mr. Buckle, after his manner, might deduce from these facts that the saving of candle ends in English households results in the colonizing of the globe by Englishmen. One need hardly go to such lengths as this, and yet it were unfair to English women, whose reputation for formless taste in dress and for hobbledehoy shyness of manner is already a sufficient handicap, not to say that the efficient ordering of their households has much to do with the working power of their men at home, and the influence and valor of their men abroad. It may be said, too, in this connection, that English women do not make such demands upon the time, and the engagements, of their men folk as do women in America. Englishmen have far more occupations, and many more pastimes and uses for their leisure, apart from their wives and sisters, than do American men. This is not meant as suggesting a less happy, or a less high standard of home life, for that would not be true. It means merely that English men spend more of their time with men, either for business or pleasure, or the occupation of their leisure in other ways, than do Americans. The American woman expects more, demands more, receives more attention, from the American man, than does the English woman from the English man. It begins in the nursery, and continues through the school age; the male animal is the favored one. More is done for him, more is expended upon him, and the household focuses its energies upon his development rather than upon that of the female. The result is the assumption of rights and privileges by the male, as over against the female, from childhood to, and through, maturity. This is a delicate thing to define, but all the more valuable as a contribution to the study of the English, because it is subtle and not easy of definition. There is an atmosphere in every household which predisposes the girls to look up to the boys, and most English women never recover from it, even where the one to whom they are expected to do reverence is openly unworthy of it.

As over against the French methods of bringing up their boys, as though they were girls, the results are in themselves sufficient comment upon which is the better system. An American may approve of the results in the bearing of the men themselves, but he is none the less tempted to wonder sometimes if the English woman is not here and there deprived of a little of all she has a right to inherit. But, to put it bluntly, this is no affair of ours. The American girls are marrying English men, and the English women are not marrying American men; and therefore comments upon the situation may be looked upon as acts of supererogation. To state the case at all demands the explanation that this is one of the prime factors in the development of the English man and in making him what we find him.

England is not only a man's country, but the English man is preëminently a man's man. The prizes here go to the soldiers, the sailors, the statesmen, the colonizers, the winners of new territory and the rulers over them, the travellers and explorers, the great churchmen and successful schoolmasters, to those in short with masculine brains and bodies. The feminine, the effeminate, and the Semitic prowess, is rewarded it is true — more of late years than ever before, be it said — but it is not the ideal of the nation. It has been wittily said that a statesman is a dead politician; but in England this does not apply. The great statesmen, or the leading politicians, as one may please to call them, receive their rewards early and often. As a consequence, England has had for hundreds of years an honor-roll of mighty men at the helm of her affairs.

England has never had a social upheaval which has driven out her old families, and in consequence the public service commands an ability, and on the whole is conducted with an integrity, due to the fine feeling of a class long trained in genuine patriotism such as no other country can boast of.

Spain drove out the Moors and the Jews. France expelled the Huguenots, and later indulged in orgies of indiscriminate murder of her aristocracy. Italy has emasculated her great families, leaving England alone the possessor of gentlemen of race and character with pedigrees of responsibility.

We have dared to note here and there throughout this volume certain signs of decadence in the England of to-day. Not the least ominous of these is that those who are leaving England are Saxons and Celts, while those who are coming in are Teutons and Jews.

The old sturdiness and independence of character seem, at least to the outsider, to be deteriorating somewhat rapidly. Under the flimsy academic disguise of socialism, sops of sentiment are more common than they were. Trade unions, workhouses, free schooling, old-age pensions, shorter hours of work, endless public and private charities, have inadvertently set up a standard of sloth which must prove disastrous to the former and better traditions of the race. It is not the first time in the history of the races of the world that the forerunners of decay have been distaste for steady work, craving for excitement, a mania for gambling and loose-minded willingness to look to the State for the solution of personal problems by general and generous legislation. Public men confronted by the cry for bread and games are tempted to sell their political souls for place and preferment.

A man with ability, ambition, money, rank, knows that the best the world has to give in the way of power is his if he succeed here in politics, as does the man without rank or wealth, and one and all are tempted to go into politics, rather than tempted to keep away altogether.

At the bottom of this is the feeling, scarcely realized by the English themselves fully, that the individual who can do and does most for England, is the one to whom the great prizes belong, and to him rank and wealth are given without stint. England is a small island, scarcely bigger than the State of New York alone, and her very geographical position is an overwhelming demand for men, men, men! Without them she is starved, shorn, humiliated, lost. This is true of every country to be sure, but it is the essential truth about this great Empire with its heart in a small island.

When we emphasize therefore certain peculiar features of their home life here, it is seen now at a glance not only that certain facts are true, but that they must be true. There would be no England without them.

That Englishmen are such hardy explorers, such persistent settlers of the waste places of the earth, attests their love of home. They go, not because they wish to go, but because they hope to return with enough to establish a home in England.

Neither English men nor English women like the unattached and nomadic existence of the hotel and the boarding house. The proportion of Americans who could have a modest home, but who prefer the flat and stale unprofitableness of hotels and boarding houses, is, as compared with English people of the same income, vastly greater. And perhaps no one cause of the stricter economy of English households is more potent than this.

To have a house and a bit of garden of one's own, an English man or woman will submit to the utmost economy of expenditure, and the most rigorously accurate system of accounts. It may be a social prejudice or an ingrained habit of the British stamp of mind, but whatever it is, there can be no doubt, that the Englishman's ideal of life is to be a free man and master of the castle of his own house.

To a greater extent than is commonly appreciated this domestic economy throws light upon the larger questions of British politics, whether domestic or foreign; and, conversely, British politics both at home and abroad are focused upon the maintenance in freedom and comfort of thousands of British householders. Home Rule for Ireland, the Education Bill, the Abolition of the House of Lords, the Employers' Liability Bill, the Licensing Bill, which are now the gist of political discussion are, one discovers on closer inspection, argued for and against on no theoretical grounds, but ever with an eye to their probable or possible bearing upon British domestic economy. The severest stricture that can be passed upon a man's political course by his opponents is that he neglects Imperial interests in his desire for a mere party majority. The translation of that is, that it is considered the most fatal thing to be said against even the greatest statesman, that he subordinates the safety of British commerce and consequently the security of British possessions and incomes, and thus necessarily the peace and comfort of English homes, to his own ambition.

V

ARE THE ENGLISH DULL?

THIS title for a chapter might be considered unnecessarily impertinent, not to say insulting, were it not that it must be promptly answered in the negative. Why then put the question at all? For the very sufficient reason that it is a common misapprehension in America, in France, and elsewhere, and because in explaining this misapprehension we shall light upon interesting characteristics of Mr. John Bull and his family.

The slowness and steadiness of the race tempt the superficial critic to call them dull. But the people who have produced Chaucer, Shakespeare Swift, Sterne, Sydney Smith, Charles Lamb, and Robert Louis Stevenson, may well laugh at any accusation of their lack of intellectual humor; while the people who have gobbled the wealth and commerce of the world for a century may look on with some amusement while other nations call them dull.

On Sunday, June twenty-fourth, 1906, there appeared in a reputable London newspaper a communication to the effect that if America were in earnest in her expressions of friendliness toward Great Britain she should at once take steps to redeem the Confederate bonds! There is no lack of grim humor here, and this is a typical illustration of the lack of dulness of this race who never for a moment lose sight of the main chance. The insolent impertinence of this suggestion at this stage of the game, when the English powers that be are well aware that our friendship is a valuable international asset, and when an alliance between, say, Germany, America, Japan, and France would spell ruin to the British Empire, is proof enough that whatever the circumstances, no sentimental haziness veils the keen, commercial, selfish vision of the English. The Pecksniffian ethics which raises hands in horror at our insurance scandals, our trust methods, at the disclosures of immorality in Germany, on the part of a nation which sells its Indian opium in China under the protection of British guns, and keeps twenty-five thousand Chinamen in the mines of South Africa, points to a very highly developed sense of humor.

Be it said therefore in this connection that this question of dulness though it is not an enlivening

quality in society, is nature's resource for pre-
serving steadiness of conduct and consistency of
opinion.   It enforces concentration, which is the
necessary and fundamental mental quality pre-
ceding all others, no matter how lofty or how
rare they be, and a people who learn slowly do
not learn much, and then only what they must.
The Englishman might say, with not a little in
his favor, that the best security for a people's
doing their duty is that they should not be dis-
tracted from doing it by knowing much else.

Perhaps what the American calls dulness, the
Englishman calls steadiness.   Indeed "steady"
is a much used word among the English.
"Steady, men!" you hear on every parade-
ground, and no doubt hundreds of times in every
battle where Englishmen are fighting, and they
are fighting somewhere, in big or little fashion,
much of the time.

> "Quand Italie sera sans poison,
>   Et France sans trahison,
>   Et l'Angleterrre sans guerre;
>   Lors sera le monde sans terre."

"Steady lad!" "Steady girl!" you hear from
every horseman, whether he be riding or driving.
The English genius is not for analysis, but for
action.   He seeks to act, to do, to accomplish,

and the first necessity is to get people, or things, or horses, or ships, or balloons, or motors, steady. They cannot start, they cannot be controlled without steadiness. They demand this quality above all others in their statesmen, their soldiers, as well as in their horses. There is no talk of glory as in France; no constant vision of self-advertisement, and of self-advancement by means of the reporter's pen and camera. England expects every man to do his duty, that's all. The glory and the advertisement may take care of themselves. In the naval fight between an English and an American ship, during the war of 1812, the American vessel appeared, flags flying. A young officer on the English ship asked his captain (Captain Broke, of the "Shannon") if they, too, might not put up more bunting. "No," was the reply, "this has always been an unassuming ship!" Such people keep the chief end in plain view, and are therefore not dazzled, not turned aside and tempted by side issues. Diversity of interest and desultoriness — this last word in its nice etymological sense — are not characteristics of the English. We sometimes think them dull for this reason.

Some of their great men would probably appear dull at our after-dinner festivities, alongside of certain American publicists we might mention,

who have been renowned principally as "orators"
and story-tellers; but what man, however much
he loved his country, would mention them in the
same breath with Cromer, Milner, Kitchener, as
public servants and patriots? Disagreeable as it
may be for the American to say so, it is the difference between mastiffs and monkeys! In the
long run, which of these two types of men is dull,
the for years hard-working, unheard of Cromer,
or the ceaselessly chattering simian public men
we all have in mind? At least we must give
credit where credit is due. When we take this
superficial view of dulness, the Englishman shines
by comparison with the oratorical flippancy and
the ready acceptance of the part of after-dinner
clown which have made so many reputations in
America. Not that we have not our own type of
self-sacrificing public servants in men like Wood,
Magoon, Taft and scores more, but how shabbily
do we reward them!

There are three kinds of more or less intelligent
men nowadays who encumber the earth: men
who talk for the sake of talking; men who write
for the sake of writing; men who read for the
pleasure of reading. But they do nothing. They
incite no one else to do anything, either by voice,
pen or example. It is worth while remembering
that this so-called dull race has produced the

greatest literature since the days of Greece. I believe that the secret lies here: their great men have had things to *say*, instead of trying to *write* things. French literature is notable for trying to write things, phrase things elegantly, or saliently; attempting to put little thoughts in very fine clothes.

We in America have had no time, no energy to spare for literature. What we have produced is of the second-rate order—with perhaps the exception of Poe and Hawthorne—with one piece of prose however, unsurpassed in the English language since the King James version of the Bible, Lincoln's address at Gettysburg. Lincoln, no more than these Englishmen, was a man who wrote, or talked, for effect. He concentrated his energy and his brilliant powers, — powers unrecognized at the time by his fellows — upon one object, and he saved his country by his success.

It is not strange that the people who believe in action should produce a great literature. All penmen envy men of action not only their deeds but their phrases. Raleigh, Cromwell, Clive, Hastings, Nelson, Roberts, Grant, Lincoln, Lee and "Stonewall" Jackson have written phrases of memorable prose. "Trust in God and keep your powder dry!" writes Cromwell. "I stand astonished at my own moderation!" says Clive.

"We'll fight it out on this line, if it takes all summer!" and "Unconditional surrender!" are phrases of Grant. It would be a mockery of life if the men of deeds and daring did not write better than those who study them. Great literature has never been born inside four walls. It is tossed up from the sea, wrung from war, found by running streams, fed in pastures green, and heard best in the clash and clamor of the opposing forces of men in earnest for life and liberty.

People think it strange that England's reputation in the world rests so largely on her aptitude for poetry and politics. Chaucer, Spenser, Shakespeare, Milton! It is not far from the truth to say that every poet of the small first class is an Englishman, save one, Dante. Goethe and Schiller can hardly be classed with these, much less Corneille or Racine. But it is not strange. The nation of great deeds must of necessity be the nation of great words.

So little do these English believe in mere talking and writing and reading as such; so little do they trust those superficial attributes that are generally classed under one head, as brilliant, that they have given astonishingly little attention to the education of the masses. While the rest of the Western world has given itself up to the fetish of universal education, they have been quietly giving themselves to the task of conquering, colonizing, and governing a fifth of the habitable globe. Consciously or unconsciously, they seem to realize that the asylums for the insane are peopled by those whose brains are too active or too morbid; not by those who are slow and dull. The dangers of modern civilization are mostly for the swift, not for the slow.

Ten years after the beginning of the reign of the late Queen Victoria, not only the children of England, but practically one-half the adults, could neither read nor write. The marriage register is a good test of education, in England, at least, because the married must sign the register. At the time of which we are speaking, roughly fifty years ago, only sixty-seven men in an hundred, and fifty-one women in an hundred, could even sign their names. "This leaves little doubt," says the report of the Registrar-General of that date, "that thirty-three in one hundred of the men, and forty-nine in one hundred of the women at the marriageable age, are quite unable to write." We all know very well that the first thing one learns to write is one's own name. In addition to this large percentage of those unable even to write their own names, there must have been a large number who had learned just enough to sign their names and nothing more.

To write is to read, and it is not stretching a point, therefore, to say that as late as fifty years ago at least one-half of the *adult* population of England and Wales — not to mention Ireland, where the proportion was, and is, much larger — were in primitive ignorance.

We in America had public schools before we were a nation; while England had won an empire before she had given a thought to the education of the masses. It was long after the beginning of the nineteenth century before any attempt was made to break through the matted sward of ignorance of the laboring classes in England.

To this day the Englishman is quite indifferent to this state of things. Their unobtrusive but virile self-confidence satisfies them that they must be right, that they must be superior. Those of the better class still assume that their use of the English language, for example, whether as written or spoken is the only proper use thereof. *Punch* and the *Saturday Review* still write of Americans as they were wont to do half a century ago. If you have your *Punch* volumes at hand, turn to the year 1844 and read the article on "Etiquette for American Congressmen," or to the year 1846, pages 19, 71, and 82, or to page 104 of the year 1860, and from these opinions the Englishman in the street has not changed.

At the high table at Trinity College, Cambridge, sat an American dining as the guest of the Vice-Master. During the dinner his neighbor discovering that he was an American remarked with both flattery and surprise in his voice: "You are the only American who has ever dined with us whom we did not know to be an American by his speech." This is merely a typical instance of the never-ceasing surprise of these insular people to find an outsider using the common language with a delicacy and purity equal to their own. What is the surprise, then, of the American, on his side, to find that England is the home of all those vices of speech of which he has been accused for so long of having the monopoly!

Our slang and profanity, picturesque though they be, are constantly noted as peculiar to us. From the days of Elizabeth down, these people have been and are more coarsely profane than we. Elizabeth herself swore "By God's Son." In a letter to Bishop Coxe she wrote: "Proud prelate, you know what you were before I made you what you are; if you do not immediately comply with my request, by God I will unfrock you!"

Shillingford, the Mayor of Exeter, wishes to make a present of fish to the Lord Chancellor. For some reason, the fault of the treasurer or of

the carrier, the fish do not arrive, so he writes:
"Christ's curse have they both and say ye Amen
non sine merito, and but ye dare say so, think so,
think so!" After the Restoration "the new
breed of wits and fine gentlemen never opened
their mouths without uttering ribaldry of which
a porter would now be ashamed, and without
calling on their Maker to curse them, sink them,
confound them, blast them, and damn them."
The tendency to coarseness of speech still obtains. Their appeal is usually to the physical
and fleshly. A charming English lady returning
from the golf links on a wet day remarks that she
is "in a nasty mess!" The Englishman of a
certain class uses "bloody," "beastly," "rotten,"
"bloomin'" and "Go on, you brute" he murmurs
to his short puts at golf, while in commendation
he expresses himself by the hesitating, unimaginative "goodish," "not half bad," "useful,"
and so on. Where the Englishman uses "cheeky
beggar," the American's imagination supplies
him with "too previous." The vulgar Englishman after eating heavily is "full up," while our
Western American, accustomed to the over-
loading of the old-time stage coach, replies to the
invitation to have more under the same circumstances, "ef I dew, I guess I'll hev to hang it on
the outside." Both these replies are Bœotian if

you please, but the latter is imaginative, a product of the intellect, the former merely a porcine grunt.

The American vulgarities of speech have a touch of Homeric exaggeration, as when it is said of anything very old that "it was old before Adam was a rag-baby," or of a well-beaten adversary that you "wiped up the floor with him." Analogous with these are the Psalmist's "he wept rivers of tears," or Virgil's:

"Primus abit, longeque ante omnia corpora Nisus
   Emicat, et ventis et fulminis ocior alis."

Mr. Chamberlain in a speech in the House of Commons speaks of a "put up job." The *Spectator* even writes of the evidence proving "that no man over forty can 'stand the racket,'" and when one finds "chestnut" in the sense of an ancient joke, "bulldoze," "highfalutin" "Tammany methods," "not in it," and "caught on," in the pages of reputable English journals, one begins to wonder if these verbal prodigies of a riotous rhetoric are after all so distasteful as is pretended.

Nowhere in America does one hear so constantly the nasal twang as in England. The New Englander says "teown" for town, "keow" for cow, "neow" for now, "yew deon't sai" for

you don't say, and so do many of the old Eng-
landers. "Baiby" is the cockney for baby,
"plaice" the pronunciation of place, and these
and the millions of orphaned aitches are far
more common in England than in America,
where at least every aitch is given a good
home.

If it be true that the test of pure English speech
is that the speaker should give no indication by
colloquialisms, or by peculiarities of pronunciation of the place of his birth, or the university he
has attended, or the class to which he belongs,
then the best speakers of both countries are about
on a par. Lord Rosebery, Mr. John Morley,
now Lord Morley, Mr. James Bryce, and other
less known Englishmen I can mention, speak as
well as President Eliot of Harvard — the best
speaker of English I have ever heard — and the
late James Russell Lowell, the late George
William Curtis, and the late Charles Eliot
Norton, but no Englishman speaks better, and
very few as well.

The most defencelessly objectionable English
now spoken on the face of the globe is spoken
by Americans — Americans who are attempting
to speak like the English, for they speak neither
like cultivated Americans, nor like the well-bred
English. And let the American admit it to his

shame that while there are such epicene fellow countrymen and countrywomen there are none such among the English. At any rate, however ridiculous his affectations, no Englishman tries to speak like anybody but an Englishman, and let this be said to his credit. They have their eccentricities of speech, but they indulge in no such folly as that. "Yes, skatin' would be charmin' if it weren't for the freezin' stoppin' the huntin'," says the smart lady, and Lord Adolphus replies: "Yes, and ain't sleighin' toppin' fun, except for the snowin' spoilin' the skatin'?" The English in certain smart circles make a rank affectation of careless speech, probably to prove that their position is such that they may speak as they please, but also because the English as a race have never given much thought, much credit or much reward to culture. The governing classes of England have governed by self-control, by common-sense, and by personal authority or superior character, but not by erudition or mental brilliancy.

We in America perhaps overrate the value of education. We have been too busy for much culture, and so we exaggerate its importance. *Ignotum pro magnifico*. Mr. Carnegie, who is an uneducated man in the academic sense of the word, litters his own and other lands with libraries. With no disrespect to him, he probably thinks he would have been a more useful man had he been born to schools and libraries. I doubt it. To know things makes one less afraid in the world, just as in the case of a man in his social relations, the more at home he is the more readily he gives what he has to give, but the at-homeness does not produce what he has not got. So with education, it facilitates the use, and even exploits the use, of what one has, but it produces little. Education is a good training for nascent ability, and a good test of whether such ability exists at all, but it never of itself creates ability.

The world has never been educated, so we in our ignorance are trying to convert man by training his mind. Laws were codified, and libraries, and art, and culture, existed before Moses. Indeed there was a code of laws in Babylonia eight centuries before Moses. One sometimes hears education spoken of in America as though it were a discovery, somewhat like the discovery of America itself by Columbus. It may be indeed, that we are preparing a disappointment for ourselves as a nation, in depending so blithely upon universal education for our salvation. That a good deal can be done without it the history of England proves. Even the most perfunctory and the most elementary education is something of a novelty with them, and dates back not many years.

Charity schools, as they were called, existed as early as the beginning of the eighteenth century, but they were founded and controlled by a private Society for Promoting Christian Knowledge, and were undoubtedly conducted on narrow lines, with the specific object of teaching the children the catechism.

Early in the nineteenth century two individuals, one Lancaster, a Quaker — who, by the way, afterward died in America — and a Rev. Dr. Bell, started schools on their own account. The Quaker, Lancaster, though an enthusiast, was impracticable, and soon brought down upon himself, and his schools, the violent opposition of the church; and the Dr. Bell schools, under the title: "National Society for Promoting the Education of the Poor in the Principles of the Church of England," now known as the "National Society," were started as a result. This quarrel between the Nonconformists and the Churchmen, which began at that time, has continued to this day. Indeed it is this same controversy which is even now, in this present (1908) Parliament, making the passing of a satisfactory Education Bill so difficult.

In 1833 the first Parliamentary grant was made "for the purposes of education," and was only a meagre hundred thousand dollars, and even this was cautiously and specially limited to the building of school-houses.

In 1870 an act was passed establishing School Boards. These Boards were to be elected by the rate-payers, were given power to levy rates, and to compel the attendance of the children. The Voluntary Schools, schools largely supported by the Church of England, went on as before. Finally in 1903 the Act of 1870 was superseded, the School Boards were abolished, and District Local Education Authorities were established to take over the management, both of the Board Schools and the Voluntary Schools, the former being now termed "provided," and the latter "unprovided" schools. From this brief summary it may be seen how very recently has England deemed it a province of the State to control, and to compel, national education.

This is not the record of a nation given over to the things of the mind, or greatly impressed by the advantages to be derived from universal education. It is this attitude of constant and satisfied indifference to such matters which has often exasperated such men as Matthew Arnold, for example, who maintained that the fundamental reason for many of England's errors, "is our preference of doing to thinking."

Indeed Arnold went so far as to describe the English social system as landing "modern communities in the possessorship of an upper class materialized, a middle class vulgarized, a lower class brutalized." This was the superficial, not to say the parochial, judgment of a man, who leaned so far toward culture that he became a prig. Education, trained intelligence, a wide range of reading, are not in and of themselves moral or efficient, or productive of comfort or contentment. "Nine-tenths of the calamities which have befallen the human race had no other origin than the union of high intelligence with low desires," writes Macaulay. Education may engender sins of the mind, which are quite as dangerous as sins of the body. A forger is quite as dangerous to the community as a wife-beater.

Many people look upon the question of education as though there were but one answer to it. This is by no means true. It is still a very open question whether or not the over emphasis of the intellectual side of the animal man is good for the individual, or profitable to the race. The shovel, the hoe, the pick and the plough are, after all, not only the necessities for the foundation of civilization, but experience has not proved that their employment is not also the most wholesome exercise for the vast majority of the human race. We have yet to see an educated race which can survive and hold its place in the world. Greece to-day is represented in the world by an island covered with crumpled monuments. However that may be, there is no doubt, on the other hand, that thus far England's superiority rests also upon her grounded preference for doing rather than thinking.

Voltaire maintained that: "On étudie les livres en attendant qu'on étudie les hommes." But the English have made man and men and the best methods of controlling them their study without bothering about any preliminary bookishness. Apparently they are not only proud that they do not understand, but also proud that they understand that it is better not to understand. They have no patience with, and no belief in, the restless intellectual activity of the French, for example. A profound instinct arms them against intelligence, which they recognize as the greatest foe to action. Their predilection for action and commercial enterprises has been so lucrative that at the present moment the British Empire is fifty-three times the size of France, fifty-two times the size of Germany, three and a half times the size of the United States of America, and thrice the size of Europe, with treble the population of all the Russias, and embraces four continents, ten thousand islands, five hundred promontories and two thousand rivers. "Lud" was the god of commerce, who was worshipped in England in Pagan times. Ludgate Hill is a remainder, and a reminder, of "Lud." The Welsh still call London, "Caer Ludd," or Lud's Town. Thus it is seen how deep are the roots of their commercial supremacy.

As in their political affairs, so in intellectual matters, they leave it to the few to govern and to guide, reserving themselves to act behind them when called upon, just as their ancestors the Saxons did fifteen hundred years ago. If Mr. Pierpont Morgan were an Englishman, it would be impossible to imagine him as not in the House of Lords, and also in the Cabinet, if he would consent to serve there. England would compel a man of such signal abilities, a great financier, a Christian gentleman, and over and over again a self-sacrificing patriot, to serve her as a counsellor. How is it in America! What President in our history thus far, except perhaps Washington or Lincoln, would imperil his popularity by asking him into his Cabinet!

Why not? Simply because he is a rich banker. Is England dull, or is America dull, in this case?

It is manifestly impossible to arrive at any exact statement of the quantity and quality of the reading-matter of a whole people. The likes and dislikes, the hopes and ambitions, the secret strivings and the mental processes of men, cannot be represented by numerals. It is none the less interesting to attempt to discover what the English read, as a commentary upon this reputation of theirs for dulness. It is by no means impossible so to collate facts and figures, and to bring to bear subsidiary matters upon the subject, as to arrive at a fair general impression.

There are, to begin with, a percentage of people in every country who do not read at all, or very little; there are others whose incomes and employments indicate that they probably limit themselves to a certain very light kind of reading; while more useful still as a factor in such a problem, every nation has a certain personality of its own, from which one may judge that this or that special form of literature would be best suited to satisfy its literary appetite. There is, too, in England, a large proportion of the actual readers, who read as a pastime, or as a soporific, or as a dissipation. Their reading amounts to little either one way or the other.

> "Who reads
> Incessantly, and to his reading brings not
> A spirit, and a judgment equal or superior,
> Uncertain, and unsettled still remains
> Deep vers'd in books, and shallow in himself.'

When we come to divide up the population of England and Wales, for the purpose of discovering, even roughly, the number of persons whose reading is of little consequence, we find that something over fourteen millions fall into this class, including over six million school children under fourteen years of age; over a million paupers; a million nine hundred and fifty thousand domestic servants; three million laborers in the agricultural, fishing and mining industries; two millions engaged in textile manufactures or employed as tailors, seamstresses, and shoemakers; to say nothing of over one hundred thousand lunatics, and one hundred thousand bar-maids. Although, even here, it is unsafe to say that what these thirteen or fourteen millions of people read has no influence upon themselves or upon others, it is at least fair to conclude that whatever that influence, subjective or objective, may be, it is of small consequence.

This condition of things is due: first, to the lack of free education facilities for children over fourteen years of age — until very recently there have been practically none; second, to the almost entire lack of free public libraries, of which later; third, to a well-defined, and to an American strange, but widely held opinion that the secular education of the masses does more harm than good — an opinion held by many among the masses themselves; fourth, to the discouraging lead of the classes in all matters of education over the even now heavily handicapped masses, which leads these latter to look upon their past and present condition as necessary and permanent; fifth, to the profound national instinct, which from highest to lowest, prefers doing to thinking; which always, everywhere, shaves down the ideal to the practical, and seeks a working hypothesis.

The total number of schools receiving annual grants is twenty thousand six hundred and fifty-six. The number of children on the register of the education department is six millions, of whom five millions are, on an average, in daily attendance. Of these only some fifty thousand are over fourteen years of age. The reason for this remarkably small number of children above fourteen years of age is that this is the limit of age when a child is required to attend school, and also because, as has already been shown, there is no school machinery, and very little encouragement in England, for the education of poor children who wish to go on beyond the provided curriculum of children of fourteen. The American system of compulsory free education, by means of which a lad may go on from primary school to grammar school, from grammar school to high school, and thence to college, without any expense for tuition, and very little for text-books, does not exist in England.

The Budget for 1907–8 estimates the revenue at £144,190,000 and the expenditure at £140,757,000; of this only £200,000 was set aside for educational grants, although in the Civil Service items, under the general head of "Education, Science and Art," is set aside the sum of £17,495,237. During the year 1904–5 the public expenditure on elementary education is estimated at £11,065,496 from the Imperial Exchequer; £8,464,555 raised from Local Rates; £1,100,000 from Church of England and other Voluntary School subscriptions; £988,723 from Ragged and other charity schools. The distribution of this fund is such that only a small percentage of the population of Great Britain are even in the way of fitting themselves to read anything but the most lamentably light and elementary literature. As a consequence of this policy, the percentage of adults who are, at least for all purposes of this discussion, practically illiterate, is probably very high. There are, unfortunately, no figures in the census returns which enable one to say exactly what that percentage is. But exact figures are not necessary. This is not a problem of mathematics; it is a problem of temperament. Overwhelming evidence is enough, without nicety of computation. The Home Office in 1893 reported that of four and a half million total votes polled one hundred and thirty-five thousand were illiterate. If one voter in every thirty-four is illiterate, one may be quite sure that, including the remaining women and children and non-voters, the percentage is very much higher; and these figures would be still further borne out did one care to make a calculation from the facts already given in this chapter, concerning the signing of the marriage register; and also from the fact that even now ten men in an hundred, and twelve women in an hundred in England and Wales; and twenty-three men in an hundred, and twenty-five women in an hundred in Ireland, can not sign the marriage register. How many more are practically unable to read and write!

A phase of the subject, that from an American

point of view deserves repeated notice, is, that a large number of intelligent people in England are altogether opposed to free general education. They are the Conservative, not to say the Tory Old Guard in politics and religion, who hold that the children, as of old, in each parish, should be taught to read and write, and to say their catechism, in the schools, under the supervision of the clergy, and then earn a living as did their forefathers. This system, which to all intents and purposes, in spite of the strides in the last few years, is still in vogue, explains why so many well-educated German youths are employed in London, to the dismay of their English rivals. One may lay aside for the nonce the ever-present bugaboo of the statistician, which is the fear of generalizing from incomplete details, to assert without reservation that it would be difficult to find an American who is utterly opposed to free education for the people, so long as it is not carried to a foolish length. In England, on the contrary, there is almost a party of reactionaries, with many of whom I have discussed this question, who scout the very idea that the education of the lower classes has benefited either those who have received it or those who have bestowed it. They point to the situation, as well they may, of a nation which, while paying little attention to technical education, and much attention to character and religious observance, has beaten out all rivals in the race for supremacy and respect among the nations. They hold to the Old Testament view, that corn, wine and children are the fruit of the formal, God-fearing people, with which education has nothing to do.

This attitude of mind, it must be emphasized here, is not one of arrogance. It has no flavor of superiority in the sense that these people feel that the lower classes are unworthy of notice, and incapable of becoming like themselves. We have already seen, in our discussion of the make-up of the House of Lords, that this is not the English spirit. At the bottom of this feeling is the thoroughly English instinct that what a man cannot earn, or get for himself, he does not deserve. They are not believers in any of the modern nostrums for the artificial stimulating of the body politic, under the generic title of socialism. The socialistic section of the labor party makes more noise than progress. On the other hand, no people in the world give more heartily or more generously to those who succeed, no matter from what social layer they come, than do the English. They have no weakness of logic and principle to prevent their worship of God and Mammon at one and the same and all the time. The Jew, the fop, the novelist, the cynic Disræli, becomes Prime Minister and Earl of Beaconsfield. The able man may be what he will, come from whence he may — if he can serve England, he always has of her best. There is no false, no foolish, pride in their attitude toward this question of education. It is purely practical; all a matter of personal efficiency.

The following figures show better than any expression of opinion the difference between England and America in this matter. The census of 1891 counted 606,505 men and 765,917 women of sixty-five years and upward in England and Wales, or a total of 1,372,422, of whom 401,904, or nearly one-third, received parish relief. Over against this set the other statement, that in 1874 in a House of Commons of 658 members, 235 of them were Oxford or Cambridge men, and 100 of them, or six and a half per cent. of them, were old Etonians. In the last Parliament of 670 members, 371, or more than one-half, were graduates of the two great universities; while in the United States Senate, at the same date, there were 14, and in the House of Representatives 22, graduates of our dozen more prominent colleges, or 36 in all.

It would be difficult to put it more clearly if one piled facts and figures upon facts and figures for page after page that in England the classes are educated and rule, while the masses have little voice in administrative matters, and fall toward the end of their lives into helpless and rheumatic dependence; while in America the general average of prosperity is higher, though men of first rate ability are fewer. To put it in another fashion, if we lined up man for man, our American standard, whether physical, moral, or material, would be immeasurably higher than theirs; but if we lined up our million best men against the million best Englishmen, we should not reach their standard, nor, for that matter, would a million men from any other nation in the world. In physical courage and pluck we should be their equals, but in all-round efficiency they are superior. Let us not forget, however, that they are a thousand years old, we are an hundred years old — we are in our first youth, they are in their prime.

We have noted the influence of the climate upon other features of English life; it has also a notable influence upon this matter of reading. The mild and equable temperature of England, which permits one to be out-of-doors, and consequently to take part in some form of sport or labor all the year round, lessens materially the time given to reading. Other things being equal, the inhabitants of a mild climate will read less than people who are perforce kept in-doors many weeks of the year by great heat or intense cold.

No country in the world has such a never-ending round of sports in which so large a proportion of the population take part as has England — bicycling and motoring all the year round; hunting from October to April; racing of a kind all the year round; golf, which has developed from a game into a widely prevalent disease, all the year round; cricket and tennis from April till October; shooting from August till January; foot-ball, played, alas, by professionals, but as many as two hundred thousand people in attendance at one game, from September till May; and, besides these, coursing, fishing, boating, and a long *et cœtera* of other pastimes. Nor are these sports confined to the rich and idle, or even to the well-to-do alone. Again I repeat, England is the most democratic country in the world, where the rights of the individual are more respected, where the individual has more of personal freedom, and where the individual is less trammelled by artificial barriers of birth or class jealousy, in his efforts to rise, than anywhere else in Christendom; for to miss this characteristic is to lose the explanation of many apparent anomalies. Aristocracy exists only where few people are free. Where every one is free, where every one feels himself to have aristocratic privileges, there is no aristocracy.

It is, strange to say, in America, not in England, that one hears much talk about the tailor grandfather of A, the shoemaker grandfather of B, the washerwoman grandmother of C, and so on. In England his lordship, the parson, the squire, and the butcher, the baker, the candlestick-maker, go galloping across the fields together after the hounds, and the best man among them is he with his head and his heart up, and his hands and heels down, and a good one under him. The meeting-place is advertised in the local papers, and it is not necessary to wear pink to join in the sport; and one may see such a mingling of classes on terms of purely horsemanship equality as one seldom sees in America, and never in any country on the Continent of Europe.

The same is true of the cricket field, where the county magnate, the parson, the young squires of the neighborhood, play under the captaincy of some local tradesman's son, proving again that the genuine aristocrat is the best democrat and that the snob and the prig lack something, if not everything, of being gentlemen. A man must always be much more what he is than what he has. The danger in a prosperous and commercially active civilization is that we may forget this, and begin to see men with distorted vision as *having* much, rather than as *being* true. England has somehow escaped this. Indeed, practically the only people either in England or America whom one hears talking much of what it is, or what it is not, to be a gentleman, are they who secretly suspect their own claims to the title. The very first requisite of the gentleman is that he should have forgotten at least an hundred years ago that he is one.

It may give some idea of the part played by out-door life in England to say, that it is difficult to find an Englishman between eighteen and sixty-five in fair health and not supported by the rates who is not a performer at some kind of sport or interested in some phase of it. Of the nearly seven hundred reviews and magazines of a non-religious character printed in England, one in six is largely devoted to some form of out-of-door sport or pastime. Between 1880–85, according to a private index kept in the British Museum, there were 266 books published on the one subject of sport and athletics, and between 1885–90, 412. During the ten years ending 1907, there were published 2,024 under the general head of Travel; 569 under the general head of Geographical Research; 5,498 under the general head of History; and 1,059 Biographies, and over 1,200 books dealing with questions of Trade. This shows the general trend of thought and action. Their serious literature deals largely with men and the doings of men.

In a word, John Bull loves the fresh air. He is a sportsman, an athlete, a soldier, sailor, traveller, a colonist rather than a student, and all the figures bear one out in making the statement. During those trying days in the Crimea these sport-loving "young barbarians" were "all at play" when they were not fighting; racing their ponies, playing cricket, and off shooting such game as there was. One family in England, the Pelhams, have hunted the Brocklesby pack of hounds for more than one hundred and seventy-five years.

While Italy has twenty-one universities, Germany twenty, and France fifteen, England has only seven. On the other hand, the value of the sea-borne commerce of Great Britain and her colonies is double that of all European countries combined, or a total of imports and exports for the year 1906 of $5,344,120,960. Of the immense possessions, and the enormous population, over which they exercise control, we have already written. In addition, it is calculated — though

I mention these figures diffidently as more or less guess-work — that they own foreign securities to the amount of over $3,000,000,000.

A nation of students does not exploit itself along those lines. These people are the Romans of modern times, slow, vigorous, law-loving, law-abiding, and colonizers of the best type, but not students. They are contented, confident. Their disregard of philosophy proves their happiness. What they are, and what they have, satisfies them. It is the unhappy man, who indulges in thought, and dreams himself and others into non-existent situations, only to come back to be disappointed by the real world. These people live always in the real world.

When it is said that the English are, as compared with the Germans, or even with the Americans, a non-reading race, we have still facts and figures to give concerning the reading population. To begin with, the census of 1901 for England and Wales groups under the heading, Professional Class, 972,685 persons, and of these, it may be supposed, that all are readers. Most startling of all, despite the fact that there are over a million more women than men in England, there are under the head of Unoccupied Class 1,977,283 males and 9,017,834 females in England and Wales; 264,893 males and 1,198,618 females in

Scotland, and 786,097 males and 1,708,861 females in Ireland, or out of the total population of Great Britain and Ireland of 43,219,788 there are 14,953,586 persons who have no occupation, or one-third of the population. It goes without saying that "unoccupied" here does not mean "idle," since it is precisely from among the unoccupied classes that the rulers of the Empire come. This large unoccupied class in England, larger than that of any other country in the world, is due to the overcrowding, 445 persons to the square mile in 1881; 497 in 1891; and 558 in 1901; to the competition, which forces people to be conservative, and to be satisfied with a small but secure income; to the willingness of the Englishman to live on a small but secure income, if he may be independent and hunt and shoot a little, and play games; to the fact that there are so many idle men in England for companions; also because there is nothing derogatory as with us in having no imperative occupation; and to the civil service system which pensions off the servants of the various departments of the State, there being some 175,000 persons in England living upon State pensions.

In this connection it is suggestive to find that there are more than 140,000 members of London clubs alone, and we are not far wrong in guessing that one man in every thirty of voting age and upward is a member of a club, not including workingmen's clubs, free reading-rooms, and the like. These, and many more besides, are the devourers of the newspapers, sporting papers, and the magazines. And this brings one to the subject of the position held by the newspapers in the national life of England.

The newspaper is a member of the family in every reputable household in England and regularly comes to breakfast with them. Already in 1854 the circulation of the *Times* was nearly 52,000; of the *Morning Advertiser* 8,000; of the *Daily News* 4,000; of the *Morning Herald* 4,000; of the *Chronicle* and *Post* each 3,000. The London *Times* was until lately a sort of eldest son among newspapers, and *Punch* the jolly bachelor uncle who made occasional visits. But the number and influence of other newspapers have vastly increased. The *Times* no longer carries the weight that it did, and party newspapers are playing a larger and larger *rôle*. The sensational, "up-to-date" newspaper still finds it difficult to make headway in England. No one cares apparently to devour the happenings of every hour, whether true or false. It is easier and cheaper to wait till to-morrow and get the truth. The English are lacking, too, in that nervous obsession of occupation which drives the American to read trash in the train rather than to do nothing.

Just as men have been obliged to adapt themselves to life in great cities, so whole populations to-day are striving to adapt themselves mentally to the omnipresent, omniprinting newspaper. The dust and turmoil and excitement of great aggregations of population, the constant strain on eyes, and ears, and throat, and nerves, have changed the physique of mankind. The dusty chatter of the newspapers is working upon the mental make-up of mankind in much the same way. Too much comes pelting upon minds untrained to analyze and incapable of sifting the grain from the chaff. The more generally educated, and the more generally curious mentally, are those who suffer most from this dust-cloud of the newspapers. Men who are only intelligent enough to keep in one way, and to do one task, and to serve one master, are diverted, excited, made discontented, and led astray, by this enormous variety of news, which comes to them every day, but which concerns them not at all. How true this is is seen in the curious temptation to murder, suicide and crimes of all kinds which follows upon the prolonged and detailed discussion of such matters in the newspapers. Many peo-

ple are like children, to whom it would be a mercy
to keep them in ignorance of many of the grosser
happenings which fill the newspapers. Here
again the duller, less curious people have an
advantage. They are not diverted, they are not
excited, not impelled hither and thither to disconnected action and thought, which leads nowhere, and tempts men to the discussion, and to
the handling, of matters for which they lack both
experience and capacity. Some great statesman
may have the courage in these democratic days
to say, or perhaps some great physiological
psychologist to demonstrate, that certain occi-
dental peoples are suffering from having been
educated too fast! They are trying too many
remedies at once, like a child in a sweet-shop; or
they are glorying in political panaceas which
were tried and found wanting centuries ago, but
they do not know quite enough to know it. This
alert intelligence working in a cloud is more
dangerous than ignorance, where the real progress of a people is concerned. Here again, the
English, consciously or unconsciously, have suffered less than any other first-class modern
nation from this distracting power of the press,
and for the reasons we have outlined.

Englishmen, however, still take their newspapers into their confidence and have a naïve way

of writing to them on all sorts of subjects. If an Englishman rows down the Thames and stops for luncheon at an inn and is overcharged, he promptly writes to his newspaper, and later on, his first letter is followed by others, in which the comparative merits and cost of light luncheons on the Continent, in Canada, in Central Asia, in Seringapatam, in Kamchatka, and everywhere else where Englishmen have eaten and drunk — and where have they not eaten and drunk? — is discussed at length. This goes on till we have a complete international history of mid-day gastronomics. Then the editor writes at the bottom, "We cannot continue this correspondence," and the affair is over. Very often it is delightful reading.

If a horse stumbles and falls in Rotten Row, there are letters on the subject which go into the matter of road-building, modern horsemanship, best methods of shoeing horses, and the like, with quotations from Xenophon — who by the way wrote some of the best pages ever written on the subject — from Virgil, and anecdotes of accidents that happened half a century ago, and so on.

Half a dozen Englishmen go to Homburg. Finding that the golf course there is not to their taste, they sign a round-robin on the subject, and send it to the *Times*. They write letters on the lynching of negroes in our Southern States, on the subject of our banking system, our methods of finance, our presidential candidates, our hotels, our iced water, our over-heated trains, our lack of swift justice to criminals; some of them good, some foolish, but all with that ponderous sense that the Englishman is responsible for the contemporary auditing of the accounts of the Day of Judgment. The world belongs to him who takes it, and the Englishman takes it with a confidence and nonchalance that one cannot help admiring. This habit results in a sort of signal system to all Englishmen everywhere. This is condemned, that is praised. The Englishman is warned against this, and recommended to do that, and so he swings around the globe noting everything, criticising everything, telling his countrymen about everything. He feels somehow that his supervision keeps things in order, and makes things easier for every other Englishman. Perhaps it does!

On the other hand, the better class English newspapers do not indulge in rash suppositions, hasty generalizations, uncertain guesses at probable future happenings, and the daily exploitation of the personal affairs of notorious nobodies. And one may say diffidently that this is distinctly preferable to the methods of certain of our own journals, which have dropped into miscellaneous meddling, in their rage for news.

If Mr. Balfour, for example, were to go abroad for a holiday, it would be considered contemptible to chronicle his doings and dinings, and absolutely brutal and boorish to write particulars of the dress and behavior of his sister, or his wife, if he had one. The sense of fair play of a nation of sportsmen would not permit an editor to torment even his enemy from behind a woman's petticoats.

So far as possible the newspaper maintains a strictly impersonal point of view. There is plenty of discussion and plenty of criticism of men and measures, but rarely any attributing of mean, or dishonorable, or interested motives. There is no attempt, as in the French journals, to be epigrammatic, smart, to make a hit, no matter what it costs in dignity and truthfulness.

These Englishmen fight one another sturdily enough in the press, and on the floor of the House of Commons, but personally they are friendly. They never dream of disgracing journalism or politics, or of making their country ridiculous, just for the momentary pleasure of planting a barb where it will rankle most in an opponent's body. "My brother and I quarrel,

but it is my brother and I against the world!"
It is ground into them that no private affair, no
hurt of their own, no enemy whom they wish to
punish, can for a moment excuse any harm they
do their country, in indulging personal spite. I
do not maintain for a moment that this high
code of breeding is never broken, but it is to their
honor that this is their code at all, that this is
their ideal.

It is amusing to see their stupefaction, their
serious open-eyed wonder, when such a politician
as Keir Hardie breaks away from their traditions,
and foments, or is alleged to foment, discord in
the ranks of the English possessions. They are
studying the problem now, as I write, but with
no solution in view. An Englishman who is an
enemy of England, as England has always been,
is a strange creature, and as yet they have settled
upon no plan for dealing with him.

The women, who at the moment, are asserting
their right to the ballot, and who are using fantastic methods to advertise, and to bring to the
attention of the public, their demands, are treated
both by statesmen and policemen with a bored
kind of patience. It is annoying, but hardly
worth while taking seriously, they seem to think.
Englishmen generally, but secretly, hold the
opinion of their greatest living novelist: "The

last thing man will civilize is woman!" The average Englishman would add, particularly foreign women. He knows, too, by an unique experience of conquest, that the last resort, the final tribunal, in the settlement of questions between men, or between nations, is force; and that therefore women have no right to a final voice in questions that they are physically debarred from settling, in the only way that they can be settled, in a world such as it is at present. Here again he refuses to be led astray by either theory or sentiment. He knows the fact, and by hard experience; that is enough.

So fundamental is this feeling about England wherever her flag floats, about Englishmen wherever they are; so imbued are they with pride in themselves and their country, that even recognized evils are handled gently and circumspectly, and, above all, slowly, lest harm be done. There are of course flippant, careless journals in England, but the bulk of them mirror the sentiments above described, and are, even though they differ widely politically, always an aid to the State, and champions of their brothers, right or wrong, against the world.

Although there is no way of knowing with exactness the comparative amount of newspaper reading in England and America, the fact of the wholesome and patriotic influence of the British press must pass unquestioned. Though the best of the English journals assume an attitude of fair play, there is always a tinge of superiority in their comments upon foreign affairs, particularly when the foreigner chances to be a political or trade rival. They choose as news from America, or from Germany, the less flattering happenings, and give them, whether with or without comment, in a way to suggest inferiority. This is the gentlemanly way of causing irritation, but it is none the less effectively exasperating. In spite of an assumption of friendliness, there is no press in Europe which does so much to humiliate America and the Americans as the English press. It may be intentional, or it may be merely the feeling that between friends one may be more frank than with other people; but the fact remains, and can be easily proved by copious quotations, were it worth while. I make no affirmations as to motives, since these pages are written that we may understand, and distinctly not to further misunderstanding.

The Englishman takes his newspaper much more seriously than does the American, first, because his newspaper is as a rule more accurately and seriously written, — certain of their journals, the *Spectator* and *Times* for example, are unimpeachable in their style and temper — and notably because of the wider sweep of interest, and the broader horizon offered to the English newspaper reader, due almost wholly to the fact that all the news, and every interest of the vast British Empire, is centred, not in forty-eight different states, but in London.

Such a newspaper as the *Observer*, which appears only on the Sunday, is one of the best newspapers I know. It is well printed on good paper, its news is carefully chosen with an eye to the greatest variety of interests, and its editorial matter is sane and well informed. As a model of brilliant editing it ranks with one of our own best newspapers, the *Sun*. On the other hand, there is no newspaper, French, German or American, so thoroughly vulgar, so grossly, sometimes even so licentiously, coarse, as one English newspaper devoted mainly to racing. It is with astonishment that one sees it for sale on the public news-stands, and on the tables in respectable houses. In Paris one sees illustrations and reads paragraphs in the papers which at first make the Puritan-bred gasp, but one says to oneself, this is Paris! But to see a newspaper whose front page blossoms with the most disgusting allusions and the most lascivious jokes sold in England on all the news-stands leaves one bewildered. Does this prudish England not understand these jokes, or does she not care, or is it possible that the English at bottom enjoy this lowest form of stable-boy humor?

The English newspapers are, therefore, to be taken seriously into account when one estimates what, and to what purpose, English people read. Their ephemeral intellectual provender is heavier than ours, and, be it said, more instructive and less exciting.

Englishmen are easily the most numerous, and the most careful, travellers in the world. Men who hope to make journalism their profession, or men training themselves for public office, look upon a trip around the world as a necessary part of their curriculum. This reacts upon their newspapers and magazines, which receive weighty communications from experts wherever a British interest is threatened, and whenever the British lion's paw is suspected of being used to roast somebody else's chestnuts. Nothing does more to keep up the tone of the daily press than this intimate and serious interest that so many Englishmen take in their newspapers; while the wide and varied interests of Imperial control — there is seldom a month when the British army, or British diplomacy, or the British navy is not actively at work in some part of these wide dominions — give to the newspapers an heroic cast, and a dramatic concern, which in themselves supply the place of other literature. It is the policy, too, of many of them to maintain correspondents in the various capitals, who are not only men of sound training, but men of breeding and culture. They have, as a result, unusual facilities for keeping Englishmen at home well posted. It is a pity that our great journals do not do the same. An intelligent, well-bred correspondent abroad is better than countless cables. Therefore it is that, in casting about to discover what the English people read, one gives great weight to the fact that they are a nation who take their newspapers seriously, and, in reading them, become possessed of a great variety of information, and in the main accustomed to a sound style of writing and thinking. There are something under two thousand newspapers published in England and Wales.

Judging, then, from these diverse facts brought to bear upon what the English read, what are we led to conclude? What would such a fellow as John Bull read? Newspapers, magazines, novels, particularly novels of sport, adventure and travel; and next travels, history, biography, exploration, and then, because the bulk of the English are Puritan still, books of a religious character. An analytical table of books published in London in a given year shows the following—

	NEW BOOKS	NEW EDITIONS
Theology	459	74
Novels and Fiction	518	104
Political Economy and Trade	71	14
Voyages, Geography	247	74
History, Biography	269	65
Poetry, Drama	197	37
Belles Lettres, Essays	96	11
Sport	75	..

Out of the list of books published this same year, 1,435 of them were devoted to fiction, travel, biography, history and sport.

To an American, particularly if he live in be-libraried Massachusetts, it must seem strange that in writing of what John Bull reads no use is made of library statistics. When it is said that the first rate-supported library in England was opened to the public only in 1852, and that there are now only some two hundred such libraries, it becomes apparent how small a factor this is. In the state of Massachusetts alone 248 of the 351 cities and towns have free public libraries, and there are besides 23,000 school libraries in the United States, containing 45,000,000 volumes. A careful calculation made some few years ago showed that in 106 of the total of 165 lending libraries in England there were 389,698 net borrowers, and of them, on the average, nearly 80 per cent. called for fiction and juvenile literature, and therefore what some 78,000 readers in the free lending libraries read, even if one could know, would be of small service in showing what the English people read. Mudie's Select Library and Smith's Lending Library have over 60,000 subscribers and probably 250,000 readers, but here again one-third of the books they distribute are novels.

In short, the only method which results, or can result, in anything like a satisfactory answer to the question as to the reading tendencies of the English people is the broad method of dealing with the nation as a whole. Doubtless there is here or there a governess writing a "Jane Eyre"; or a school-boy wasting his time in preparing to write a "Vanity Fair"; or a dull boy at his arithmetic who will some day be called The Grand Old Man and make poetry of future budgets; or a young fop in Piccadilly who may seem to belong to the class of non-readers, and wear his rings outside his gloves, and yet who is destined to receive £10,000 for another "Lothair," and to make his Queen an Empress — who knows? At any rate I am not so enamored of my figures that I am not willing, like Luther's school-master, to lift my hat to these possibilities.

The countless exceptions to any and every rule, the undoubted prowess of English scholars and statesmen, and the maintenance of an uncommonly high average tone in matter, manner and method of the English newspapers and periodicals, prove fairly enough that, though the English nation is not a nation of readers, there must be a percentage, by no means small, who demand and who succeed in getting a high class of reading for their daily consumption.

On the other hand, it is equally fair to say that the 38,000,000 inhabitants of a small island, who offer next to no facilities for the higher education of the poorer classes, who have over a million paupers, over a million and a half of domestic servants, three million out-of-door laborers, two million and a half working in mills, factories and shops, and who yet have conquered and rule a population *in partibus* outnumbering them twelve to one, cannot be spoken of as a nation of readers, students, thinkers.

In short, the great bulk of the English people read nothing, literally nothing; he who knows something of rural England will agree to this; the casual and occasional reader reads, as we have shown, fiction, biography, history, travels and no small amount of theology in a diluted form; the large middle class read and trust their periodical literature and their newspapers; the students and real readers, who feed their minds as other men feed their bodies, read with more thoroughness and patience than any men I know. The preliminary examinations for any college at Oxford, Cambridge, Edinburgh or Dublin are trifling as compared with the entrance examinations at Harvard, but, on the other hand, both the classical and mathematical men who take the highest rank in England go through an amount of reading that our men hardly dream of. In America there is a very widespread education of the hare; in England there is, confined to narrow limits, a very thorough-going education of the tortoise.

But here again, what does this prove? Who has not known men with enough university sheepskin to make a wardrobe, who were sterile critics, or vacillating incompetents! Who forgets how small were the libraries and the early opportunities of Washington, Lincoln, Grant and Cleveland! This silent, non-gesticulating, steady non-reading race, who have given, until very lately, almost no attention to general education, are very often spoken of as dull. On the surface, to quicker, more responsive, more genial peoples, this seems true. But beware of believing it! It is one of those boomerang errors that does harm to a rival when he least, and where he least, expects it.   Their orderliness, their respect for law, their genius for give and take, and their national solidarity, which thus far have kept them well to the fore among the peoples of the earth, are not the result of dulness in any intelligent use of the word.   It is one of those widespread misapprehensions well worth a chapter by itself to explain, and to contradict, for the benefit of both the enemies and the friends of England.

Indeed, the most interesting and the most notable commentary upon this phase of English life is the present attitude of both the German and the French better class parents.   It is astonishing to hear a group of well-to-do German fathers stating that they intend to send their sons to an English public school.   Why, one asks. Out of the mass of reasons given one disentangles the fact that the Germans are beginning to see that they educate their youths, but they do not train them.   The English public school-boy is governing all over the world, while the German boy serves him as a clerk.   The Englishman has a way of gaining the confidence, the affection even, of stranger races, and of handling them and governing them with least friction.   As one German said: "We must produce men who can govern, if we expect to colonize successfully."   The

German schools do not do this. The same is true of the French schools. Recently I have been travelling by road in a leisurely fashion through France. One sees school-houses everywhere, games, sports, evidences of private wealth, nowhere. The English boy would be as a child in an examination room compared to French or German boys of his own age. But he is far more to be depended upon, a far more companionable person, and much more at home in the world. The French and German youths are stuffed to the brim with book-learning, while the English lad is in many respects a man. If the three of them go out to the colonies we all know what happens. The French boy keeps the books, the German boy attends to the foreign correspondence, and the English boy manages both. A great German manufacturer who has a number of Englishmen as heads of different departments said naïvely: "Somehow these Englishmen seem to get on better with the work-people."

The same thing is true of the Englishman in India. The India Babu, or educated native, is intelligent, often brilliantly educated, but he is hopeless as a governor. He lacks initiative, he fears, and wilts under responsibility, and is unfit to deal out justice. I have no brief for the Englishman, but one must give him his due in this respect. The secret of his success is, in part at least, due to his training by men in his public schools; in the rough welding he gets from his school-fellows, which hardens him, and at the same time softens him in his treatment of others, and which knocks any idea of bumptiousness or boasting out of him, and makes him test himself and others by deeds and trustworthiness rather than by words and book-learning. He may well say to the German and the Frenchman, if this be dulness, make the most of it!

Nonetheless, one must answer the question categorically, the question which is the subject of this chapter. To the average foreigner, the average Englishman and Englishwoman is dull. This dulness, as has been explained, is their safety and their success. You may call the chess-board black, you may call it white. It resolves itself into a question of taste. To the American, to the Frenchman, to the quick-witted of all nations, the English are distinctly dull, but out of this root of dulness has grown an overshadowing national tree.

VI

SPORT

IF one were writing of France, of Germany, of Italy, of Russia, of Spain, no one would notice the omission of a chapter on sport. A few pages upon hunting and shooting in France, of which there is still a certain amount; upon the students' duelling, and the hunting of the wild boar in Germany; upon the shooting over the enormous preserves in Hungary; upon big-game shooting in some parts of Russia, and upon bull-fighting in Spain, would suffice to give an idea of the relative importance of sport in those countries.

It is very different in England. The first thing to attract my attention on this my latest visit to England was the announcement on all the newspaper bulletins: *England's Big Task*. I happened to know that the Prime Minister was seriously ill, that there was fierce debating in the House of Commons upon the estimates for the navy, and upon the new licensing bill just brought in by Mr. Asquith, and that there was fighting upon the frontier of India with a certain

tribe of natives. But England's big task had
nothing to do with these trivial matters. An
English cricket eleven was playing in Australia.
The Australian eleven in their second innings
had made an unexpectedly big score, and England's big task was to beat that score!

Though England may be fighting somewhere
in her vast dominions all the time, she is also
playing somewhere all the time. Unless the war
is a very important one, there is more interest
taken in the playing than in the fighting. They
are verily a nation of game-players and out-door
sportsmen.

If we could know just what circumstances, and
what environment our children would be born to,
and what tasks they would be set to do, we could
in time do as well with them as with horses and
dogs. The trouble lies not in heredity, but in
the haphazard of what awaits them. A horse is
bred to run, or to trot, or to draw heavy loads, and
we know exactly what we expect of him twenty
years before he is born. With ourselves it is
different. Few parents know what a son will be
called upon to face at the age of twenty-one.
Whether there will be a war and he must serve
his country in arms; whether family fortunes will
be on the ebb and he must make money; whether
a friend will offer him a start in anything, from

a machine-shop to a newspaper office. It is impossible even to train him for a pursuit, or a profession, that is still in the hazy distance. Civilization is the great disintegrator. As we become rich we dissipate our energies, we think of our dinners, our horses, our dogs, our friends, our books, our clubs, our travelling. A little strength and power goes to each. The peasant, the poor man, must perforce direct all his powers to one end, and often he becomes master there, while the rich become weak and small in scattered interests. So families cannot and do not keep their places. The rough and poor and strong come in and take them. Simplicity easily beats out complexity and dissipation in a few generations. Hence the constant redistribution of wealth and power. Until we can overcome this ever-present obstacle to the successful breeding of human beings, socialism, it would seem, is an unnecessary philosophy. Nature beats socialism hollow at her own game.

The English common-sense comes to the fore again in an attempt to solve this problem. She is old enough to know from experience that the world is still ruled by men, and in all probability will be for a long time to come. She breeds men therefore as strong and simple as she can. In these islands sport is not a dissipation for idlers, it is a philosophy of life. They believe in it as a bulwark against effeminacy and decay.

A Congregational minister makes a speech in which he confesses to "a feeling of bitter humiliation" when he reads that the Prime Minister is the owner of a Derby winner, and stands to win or lose thousands of pounds on the race. Lord Rosebery's attention having been called to this speech by a political opponent, he replies as follows: "Sir, I am desired by Lord Rosebery to thank you for your letter and its enclosure. He will offer no opinion on the latter, for these matters should be dealt with according to the good taste, Christian charity, and knowledge of facts possessed by each person who touches on them." The letter is signed by the Prime Minister's secretary. Lord Rosebery is one of the most accomplished Englishmen of the day. He considers it lacking in *Christian charity* to abuse him for owning and breeding a great race horse. So do probably more than nine out of ten of his countrymen. From top to bottom of English society, from the Prime Minister to the Yorkshire foot-baller, sport is almost as much a part of national existence as eating and drinking.

Harvard University, not many years ago, conferred the honorary degree of Master of Arts upon a young Englishman, who devotes a good deal of his time to studying and furthering the interest in wholesome sport. It was Mr. Lehman, a graduate of Cambridge University, England, who received this distinguished mark of his acceptability to the powers that be at Harvard, and this in spite of the fact that the crews he coached were wofully beaten by Yale. He was recognized as typical of one very prominent feature of British civilization. And so he was.

An accepted authority upon all matters of sport in England has compiled some figures as to the investments and expenditures upon sport, by the forty odd millions of inhabitants of Great Britain. His estimates, when they have been criticised, have been criticised mainly because they were too low.

His estimates are as follows:

	INVESTED	SPENT ANNUALLY
Fox-hunting	$78,035,000	$43,790,000
Shooting	20,335,000	40,640,000
Fishing	2,750,000	2,945,000
Racing	41,610,000	52,965,000
Yachting	28,000,000	15,160,000

But even these sums are not the whole of the budget, for he adds:

	INVESTED	SPENT ANNUALLY
Coursing	$2,600,000	$1,587,000
Coaching	1,451,250	1,188,975
Polo	435,000	552,500

Golf, there are some seven hundred and fifty golf links in Great Britain, counts for $2,625,000 invested in laying out of links, building club-houses, purchase of clubs, bags, etc., etc., and $3,627,750 annual expenditures for labor, up-keep of club-houses, and for caddies, professionals, and other necessary expenses, including travelling.

	INVESTED	SPENT ANNUALLY
Rowing	$1,420,000	$2,871,500
Foot-ball and Cricket	53,815,000	58,560,000

These figures have not been seriously questioned, except to add to their totals, so that we may conclude that some $233,066,250 are invested permanently, and $223,887,725 spent annually for sport. There is, in short, an investment in sport of some five dollars and twenty-five cents for each man, woman, and child in the United Kingdom, and a slightly smaller sum spent each year for sport. When aggregate investments and expenditures reach such figures as these, we may be sure that the people who tax themselves thus heavily have, or believe they have, satisfied themselves that there is a valuable equivalent of some kind that justifies the expenditure.

The London County Council give in their report an analysis of the athletic games played during the past twelvemonth in parks and open spaces of London. The following table is of interest:

GAMES	PLACES TO PLAY	GROUNDS PROVIDED	GAMES PLAYED
Bowls	15	74	24,749
Cricket	35	452	28,904
Croquet	22	31	1,535
Foot-ball	35	231	16,228
Hockey	23	39	2,246
Lacrosse	5	7	120
Lawn Tennis	40	476	102,649
Quoits	20	36	2,063

Travel by train or motor anywhere in England and you see games being played — particularly if it be a Saturday — from one end of the country to the other. The open spaces of England seem to be given over to men and some women batting, kicking, or hitting a ball. The attendance at games on a Saturday is very large. Even in these days of distress in the ship-building and cotton industries, when the problem of the unemployed is a serious one, there is no lack of sixpences and shillings to gain entry to the foot-ball games. Even at the beginning of the foot-ball season the gate receipts show an attendance of more than 200,000 people. When the big and final games take place, I have calculated that out of the male adult population of England and Wales on a great foot-ball Saturday one in every twenty-seven is in attendance at a game of some sort, and this leans to the error of being too few rather than too many.

The domestic exports of the United Kingdom in 1905 were slightly over thirty-eight dollars per head, while the expenditure and investment for sport are about ten dollars per head, or a little more than one-fourth as much. Excluding troops and expenditure on troops serving outside the United Kingdom, England spent only the paltry sum of $75,000,000 on her army in 1907, and the cost of her naval armament in the same year was only $167,500,000, both together considerably less than was spent for sport. The capital value of the sporting rents advertised by a single firm of land agents one season not long ago, reckoning the letting value at four per cent., amounted to $43,750,000. The licenses to kill game bring in a revenue to the State of something over $925,000 per annum.

In a territory of some 19,000,000 acres in Scotland, 3,481,000 acres are preserved and devoted to deer forests alone.

It is not to be wondered at then that England has been described by one of her more irascible sons, who was probably not interested in sport, as: "The paradise of the rich, the purgatory of the poor, and the hell of the wise."

We are not convinced that the writer of this description is right. The bookish man is probably disheartened by the size of the sport budget of his country, and by the enormous amount of time and energy thus expended. On the other hand, when we examine the results, and gather together the threads of what Englishmen have accomplished all over the world, nobody but a blind man can conceal from himself that certain virile qualities of character have thus far in the world's progress dominated the more intellectual and philosophical traits.

Not only are muscles and sinews strengthened and hardened, but the temper and the will are trained as well. The man who learns to spar, for example, not only schools his eye and his hands and his feet to respond quickly when called upon, but he learns also, and what is far more important, to keep his temper under control, and to take a pounding cheerfully; and if a man can translate these lessons to serve in the larger affairs of life, where temper is often tempted, and where poundings are meted out to all of us with even impartiality, he has learned a valuable lesson. As Stevenson puts it: "Our business in this world is not to succeed, but to continue to fail in good spirits."

Every sport has the valuable effect of diverting

both mind and body. A sharp gallop, a round of golf, a week's yachting, a day's shooting or fishing, changes the current of one's thoughts, and rests the mind as well as the body. All the benefits to be had from sport group themselves under these two heads, of training and diversion. The lad at his rowing, his foot-ball, his cricket, or his tennis, needs the training more than the diversion; while his father, riding, shooting, golfing, or yachting, needs the diversion more than the training.

The first settlers in America, indeed all the inhabitants thereof, until very recently, needed no sports for their training or their diversion. Building roads, and bridges, and houses, and railroads, and canals, and defending the same from their savage neighbors, were enough. Civilization in those rough years was hard training enough, and every citizen was obliged to play the game whether he liked it or not. But increased prosperity, and, above all, steam and electricity, not only in America but in Europe, have done away with the necessity for constant physical exercise, or for daily deeds of daring. The best of mankind, however, know intuitively that luxury is the most insidious of all foes. If we are no longer obliged to ride, or to walk, in order to see our friends or to attend to our business, then we turn to and make a business of riding, walking, shooting, fishing, climbing mountains and hunting wild game, in order to keep alive in us the hardier virtues, which, in the beginning, made our forefathers capable of winning a place for us in the world. As the necessity for self-defence and great exertion to provide food lessen, field sports become more popular.

It is often said as an objection to this argument that a man can learn self-control and show high courage just as well by doing his duty, whatever and wherever it happens to be. It is not necessary that we should have wars, or rough games, like foot-ball or polo, to steady the nerves of men, to give them courage, and to teach them to take care of themselves. The controversies and temptations and hard tasks of daily life are enough. This is true in a way. Taking care of a peevish child who is ill is a tremendous test of patience and gentleness. Bearing the frowns of fortune with cheerfulness and in silence shows courage. Keeping oneself well in hand through the various worries of daily life, in business, profession, or in the home, is a constant schooling of the nerves. Riding a horse over a five-barred gate, or across a water-jump, is a test of horsemanship, but before these can be successfully negotiated it is necessary to have some training at simpler feats of riding. It is the same with these other matters. He who has learned self-control, fair play, and good temper at his games, finds it easier to exercise these same high qualities in the more complicated emergencies of daily life. There is a German proverb which runs: " When the devil cannot go himself he sends an old woman." There is just enough truth in the old woman argument against rough games and sports to lead one to believe that the devil sends it. The nation which presides over the destinies of one-fifth of the inhabitants of the globe spends over two hundred millions annually for sport, and has invested something more than that besides.

Perhaps there is no severer test of a man's all-round abilities than his power to govern wisely; at any rate the governing races of to-day are races of sportsmen. The peoples who are inheriting the earth to-day are the peoples who play games, perhaps because their contests make them meek! France, with her violent attempts in the last hundred years to reduce all life to a philosophical system, has a decreasing birth-rate, and has become of second-rate importance as a world power. In fact, every fresh compilation of statistics helps to show that this declining birth-rate is not a passing phase. The latest figures available for Paris, those of 1907, show that an actual shrinkage of the population is a fact. In spite of the fact that the marriage rate has been on an ascending scale for the last twenty-five years, and that the death-rate has had, on the whole, a tendency to lower, the population does not increase. Last year there were 50,811 births against 50,499 deaths, a margin of only 312 to the good. But even this is not accurate, since some 30 per cent. of babies born in Paris are sent away to the country to be nursed. Their *births* appear in the Paris registers, but if they die in infancy, their *deaths* are recorded in the provincial commune where the death takes place. Thus Paris escapes having to record nearly one-third of the infant mortality which might reasonably be expected in the city's death roll. Whether it be the lack of the sporting instinct or not, there is no gainsaying this proof of lack of breeding power. And when it is added that only recently France was obliged to dismiss her Secretary of Foreign Affairs, at the demand of the German Emperor, her situation as a world power becomes pathetically inferior.

The traveller in Spain sees that the salient characteristics of the race are overweening personal pride, untrustworthiness and cruelty. The sordid stealing on all sides by Russians during the war with Japan needs no repetition here.

The Chinese despise unnecessary physical exercise, and can scarcely be driven to fight, and they are no more capable of defending their country than an enormous cheese to prevent itself being eaten.   On the other hand, Japan is a nation of athletes whose prowess has only lately been discovered, and they are the more dangerous accordingly.   Indeed, it is an open question whether England's hypocritical and short-sightedly selfish alliance with these varnished savages has not done more to menace Saxon civilization, both in Europe and in America, than any diplomatic step that has been taken for centuries.

We have seen something of the origins of the English race in another chapter, and we have seen, too, something of their almost universal desire to be let alone, and to be governed only up to that point where individual freedom is least interfered with.   Their love of the land, and their out-door life, have prevailed through all the centuries since they became possessed of what is now Great Britain.

There is a rational philosophy back of this interest in sport.   Only a race of strong men, fighting men, can keep themselves free from enemies abroad and enemies at home, as they have done, and conquer the world to boot. Sport is merely artificial work, artificial adventure, artificial colonizing, artificial war. It is shooting at a mark because there are no enemies to shoot at; it is keeping the muscles hard and the nerves steady, and the head, heart and body under control, by a subterfuge, now that the real necessity has passed. And though there are, perhaps, higher and better tests of patience and self-control and courage than are required at football, hunting, or golf, there is certainly no better preparation to bear those tests than the schooling one gets by playing these games.

There is, of course, another side to this question, that no one can afford to overlook. There is a marked difference between a game played for training or diversion and a game played as a business and for a salary. That is no longer sport but business, and there is nothing more degrading than to give all one's time and energy to the lighter, or to the physical, side of life. That is not training or diversion, but merely a debauchery of brutality. Society is good, sport is good, novel reading is good as a diversion or a rest from more serious matters, but any one of them taken up as a business, as a vocation, makes but a sad return to its devotee. Sport as a profession, I quite agree, breeds more bullies, boasters and tricksters than anything else I can name.

Sport, too, even in the hands of amateurs, may

produce these same vulgar qualities. England has suffered severely along these lines, because here sport has so many more participants. The gentleman sharpers, welshers, and blacklegs at racing, pigeon shooting, and cards are too largely recruited from the English. Only within the last few years a turf scandal, involving two gentlemen of high rank and another of no rank, either socially or morally, disclosed a degree of infamous chicanery unworthy of a Chinese gambling hell. Race horses have been poisoned, pigeon shots have sold themselves to the book-makers, and so on. This indeed is the grave danger to sport among a people whose tastes are predominantly physical. An hundred years ago you might have seen in a certain English village the village idiot taken out on fair days, and chained to a stake on the village green, that he might have an airing, there, in all probability, to be teased by the local loafers. A subscription for Tom Sayers, the prize-fighter, was headed by Lord Palmerston, and subscribed to by most of the members of the House of Commons of the day. Prize-fighting cock-fighting, bull-and-bear-baiting, rat-hunting, dog-fighting, fights between men and dogs, and the like, were favorite pastimes not only of the masses, but also of the gentry, not an hundred years ago.

The great Prime Minister of the early days of Queen Victoria, Lord Melbourne, remarked that he liked the Order of the Garter, because "there is no damned merit connected with it!"

There are people in the world who are of a very coarse-grained moral fibre, of a very animal make-up, people who do not realize that it was not the absence of costume, but the presence of innocence, which made the happiness of the Garden of Eden. A disproportionate number of these peope are inhabitants of the British Isles. There are many fortunate results due to their predominating animal characteristics, but there are also disagreeable features of that same temperament, that even the most friendly critic may not overlook. The intense love of sport is founded upon this virile temperament, which must, of course, have its bad side. Fortunately for them they have been the nation who have undertaken, and, be it said, accomplished, some of the greatest feats of conquering and governing that the world has known. These adventures over-seas, and their untiring devotion to sport at home, have subdued and kept within bounds the animal side of them, though it has and does still crop out at times in evil practices.

A people of this type, somewhat indifferent to intellectual interests of any kind, are almost driven to exercise in some form, and their climate is a still further incentive.

Possibly the greatest foe to an orderly and useful life is monotony. The human mind and the human body wear out easily if they are subjected day in and day out to a steady repetition of the same thing. The brain worker must change from his mathematics to a novel, or from history to the study of a new language, or he finds his mind getting rusty. The man who goes from house to office and back again, seeing the same faces, doing the same duties, conning over the same figures; or the teacher going over and over again the same tasks; or the judge hearing every day the same round of quarrels, definitions and criticisms, grow restless and tired. No one of these may recognize that monotony is at the bottom of his troubles, but the drip, drip, drip wears the stone away. Drink, dissipation, wickedness of various kinds are put down to various causes — to disappointment, to failure, to lack of self-control — but in reality, back of all these is monotony. These failures and shipwrecks could not stand the deadly strain of such a life, and did not realize that change was the medicine they needed. For the great mass of men, to go away, to travel, to change the whole environment of life, is impossible. Just here is where sport

comes in, in our artificial civilization, to help us
out. In Great Britain, for example, there are
some thirty thousand cricket and foot-ball clubs
alone, the members of which come from all classes
of society. Hands from the factories, clerks in
small shops, tradespeople, and the lesser professional men, all take a hand. All through the
English provinces there are no distinctions of
class at their games.

This rather heavy, muscular people keep their
health, and their heads, and their happiness, by
this almost universal participation in some form
of sport. It is their way of letting off steam,
which every individual and every nation must
have for safety's sake, in some form or other. If
one computed the amount of wealth and territory
brought to acknowledge the British flag by
travellers, explorers, sportsmen, by adventurous
botanists, fishermen and the like, the two hundred
odd millions spent for sport annually would seem
a small sum indeed.

Newspapers of the most conservative bias
devote columns every morning to the doings of
the sportsmen. Cricket, foot-ball, racing, hunting, in all their details, are chronicled and discussed, and advertised, with the same seriousness as are speeches in Parliament, dispatches
from the seat of war, and international diplomatic

affairs. The classic races, such as the Derby, the Oaks, the Grand National, are the theme of long newspaper articles months and months before they take place; and the betting odds against this and that horse are published each morning six months or more before he is to run, as regularly as the stock-market quotations.

If the King's horse or the Prime Minister's horse wins the Derby, or any one of the great classic races, the owner, as he leads the horse back to the paddock, is received with tumultuous cheering. This is true of any owner fortunate enough to win such a race, but for the King, or a popular statesman, the ovation is almost frenzied. There, at any rate, the whole population is unanimous to a man, a good sportsman is universally popular.

Prowess at any sport is counted upon as a telling factor in the availability of a candidate for office. A candidate for Parliamentary honors lets it be known as widely as possible that he is an old "Blue" of either Oxford or Cambridge; or that he has played for England at cricket or foot-ball, or won honors in some one or other of their many games, or been an adventurous traveller, or a great hunter or fisherman. These things help his candidacy, if not more, quite as much, as any qualities of intellect, unless he be a statesman who has already won his spurs.

The stranger, whether American or other foreigner, is at a loss to understand much of the workings of the political and social life of England until he has become thoroughly imbued with the idea that sport is a much more serious and much more widely distributed interest here than anywhere else in the world. In England, some form of sport is either the reminiscence or the avocation of practically every man who has been, or is physically capable of, playing a game, or taking part in some form of field sports.

It is the only country in the world which supports not only a number of weekly and monthly periodicals devoted to sport, but also two, if not more, daily journals exclusively given over to the chronicling of racing and game-playing. The *Sportsman* is a recognized and well-edited daily paper, to be found at every club and in many houses. The betting odds, present and prospective, the official starting prices, appear daily, as well as columns of news dealing with the exercise from day to day and the comparative merits of all horses in training.

The King breeds and races horses, and is the conspicuous and, be it said, a long way the most popular, person present at all the great race meetings. The Prince of Wales is one of the half-dozen best shots in England, and I am not far wrong in saying that his prowess as a shot does more to endear him to Englishmen than any other ability he may have. The Speaker of the House of Commons fences, and shoots, and rides to hounds. Lord Brassey is a yachtsman of reputation, who has devoted himself to the service of the navy as an editor, and has ruled a distant colony with distinction. Lord Onslow is an authority on harness horses, and a big-game shooter of long experience, as well as a valuable servant of the State; and so one might go on with an interminable list of distinguished Englishmen who are as well known for their prowess at some form of sport as for their ability, uprightness and self-sacrifice as political servants of their country.

The very speech of the Englishman savors of sport. "He did it off his own bat." "He put his money on the wrong horse." "This is a painful game." "Let us," or "we had better change the bowling." "I don't think he can go the distance." "It is an odds on chance," or about anything the Englishman is apt to express his feelings in the words of the bookmaker and say: "Oh, I should call it a three to one," or "a five to one," or "a six to four chance." "It isn't cricket," or "it isn't playing the game" refers to any underhand or not quite straight conduct.

These and countless other expressions serve to express distinctions and differences even of a subtle kind. If you have hunted in Ireland for a winter you come away convinced that most of the stock phrases in conversation are invented by the horses themselves. The universal use of "fit" to express one's condition, and of "feed" for eat, are constant reminders of that habitation, dearest of all to the hearts of so many Englishmen, the stable.

I have never forgotten the slovenly grooms, the staring coats of the horses, the bad smells, and the generally unkempt appearance of the stables of the King of Spain in Madrid. They spoil their children in the Latin countries and neglect their horses; while in England the stables are in many cases better and more comfortably furnished than the nurseries. As a result, both the English children and the English horses are superior! There is a kindness which is cruel and a harshness which is kind. This nation of sportsmen make this subtle distinction unerringly. Why? one asks. They are not philosophers. No. They think little of the intricacies and niceties of living, and discuss such matters even less. It is God's air, and life on the land, and wholesome bodies which guide them aright in such matters. It is only of late, when the population is shifting from the land to the towns, that they seem to be losing the sterling qualities that are their heritage. They are the last race of all to be fuddled and disturbed by new religions, new theories of government, new solutions of the problem of existence; in short, that effervesence of semi-education which is posing as the interpreter of God and man all over the democratic world. We in America are so much older, so much more weary than they are, and it is with some regret that one sees nowadays that England and the English are not as boyish as they were. The greatest Englishman of letters now living, Rudyard Kipling, writes of

> "The flannelled fools at the wickets.
> The muddied oafs at the goals."

He is much too sure an interpreter of all things English to mean that quite as it stands. His writing is the incarnation in words of ever youthful England. Like other wise men, he is incensed sometimes that his countrymen play so much. If I were an Englishman I should pray God that my countrymen might never play less so long as they played the game. It is the men in the closets, not the men in the fields and on the seas, who breed sorrow, suspicion and envy; and the Englishman is not so dull as it might appear when he pins his faith to the out-door man. **He** is not far wrong in his belief that: *Ceux qui manquent de probité dans les plaisirs n'en ont qu'une feinte dans les affaires.*

Englishmen look upon sport as a part of character, as well as a physical developing factor in civilization; while the interest of the majority of Americans is confined to the excitement expected from a contest. Many Americans look upon the international yachting and other contests almost as though they were serious battles, and are elated or depressed accordingly; while the English take these matters much more calmly, and, while eager to win, welcome these contests as being good for the sports and games themselves, and bear always in mind that the genuine sportsman:

> "Sets his heart upon the goal,
> Not upon the prize."

Let me put it even more clearly by saying that the proportion of the spectators at Lord's on the days of the university or public school cricket matches, who have themselves played the game, is very much larger than the proportion of spectators present at a base-ball or foot-ball game between Harvard and Yale. Or again, out of the Eton and Harrow "elevens," the fathers of twenty, and possibly the grandfathers of fifteen, of the boy players, have themselves been cricketers — some of them even of sufficient prowess to be on their school eleven. Of the last year's Harvard and Yale base-ball and foot-ball teams and 'varsity eights, not one of the players had a father and grandfather who had both distinguished themselves along those lines, and there were, with two noticeable exceptions that I recall, almost none whose fathers, even, had been expert at these games.

Though we Americans believe, or pretend to believe, with Cicero, that every man begins his own ancestry, one is forced to admit that a game with a long ancestry of tradition will differ in all probability from a game with little or none. It must be admitted, too, that a boy whose father and grandfather, whose uncles and brothers, all play some game, or take an interest in some form of sport, will grow up to look at the question very differently from one whose relatives take little or no serious interest in any game. Englishmen practically never realize that sport lacks entirely this atmosphere of almost sacred tradition in America, while, on the other hand, few Americans understand the very serious and unassailable position of sport in England.

It is only two centuries and a half ago that the

settlers of New England ran away from sport in England, to found a commonwealth, where one of the names for the devil was diversion, and another amusement. It was said of these people, the Puritans, that they believed hell to be a place where every one must mind his own business. At a time when English parsons and school-masters were some of them playing cricket on Sunday afternoons, and others of them hunting two or three days a week in the season, their representatives in America, who should have attempted to imitate such enjoyments, would have been ridden out of their parishes on rails, or confined in a mad-house. In America to-day it would be difficult to find a clergyman over sixty years of age who had been a distinguished athlete in his college days; in England even the stranger can count such by the score.

This ancestry of sport marks the difference in the way we Americans look at sport, and it also marks the very great difference in the auspices under which we practise it. In America boys play with boys almost exclusively; even a professional coach for the crew, or the ball nine, is a source of much discussion and dissension. English schools have not one, but several, professionals, and what is most important of all, English boys play their games, a good part of the time at

least, with men. Old Carthusians, old Etonians,
old Wykehamists, go back to play their school
eleven, or their school foot-ball team; old university men play the youngsters; country gentlemen have house parties of cricketers and polo
players; and the writer had the pleasure to play
against a team, at a certain country house, where
the host of fifty kept wicket, and captained an
eleven, no member of which was under thirty-
five; and it is with mingled feelings of pleasure
and pain that he recalls that they won. This
fact alone, of the participation of the adult and
middle-aged element so generally in English
sport, accounts for the wide difference in the way
in which sport is regarded and the way in which
games are played. Where boys and youths are
accustomed to play their games, cricket more particularly, with grown men, it introduces an element of sobriety, courtesy and reticence in their
play and behavior, which are lacking to some
extent among boys and youths who play exclusively among themselves. Games played in such
auspicious surroundings assume their relative
place and receive their proper value, for men do
not feel defeat so keenly, nor do they look upon
such victories as the greatest of all achievements.
Men play for the game's sake, while boys are apt
to play exclusively to win. In England games

and sports receive their status and character from men; in America it is the boys who give our games their status and character.

In England, as a result of this, there is a very large and mature public, thoroughly conversant with the rules, precedents, and traditions of their games and sports; and the English press following this lead, differs from the American press in its comments, criticisms, and descriptions in much the same degree that the English players differ from the American players; that is, in their sobriety, courtesy and reticence.

All good Americans were at one in condemning the blatant and puerile excuses and accusations of a portion — happily, a small and easily recognized portion — of the American press, in regard to the defeat of the Cornell crew at Henley a few years ago. And when there were added to this letters to the newspapers from trainer, and parents, and the boys themselves, the condemnation became disgust. Americans could not help feeling, about these underbred and unsportsmanlike people, as one would feel should his own son go to visit at a friend's house, and behave like a vicious stable-boy, and thus throw discredit upon his home. Here was a most unhappy example of the result of leaving the whole domain of sports and pastimes quite too much in the hands of professionals and undeveloped boys. On the other hand, the visit of a Harvard crew to England two years ago, to row against Cambridge, made every American proud that he was so well represented, and marked the great stride that the genuine sportsmen has made in America. They were good sportsmen, good fellows, and gentlemen, and it was worth while to have them come three thousand miles and suffer defeat, if only to show the Britisher something first rate of our own breeding.

It is true that, to some extent in these latter days, the college contests and their arrangements have had the great advantage of the superintendence of an advisory board of college officials, and college graduates, but even then one must realize the difference between advice from the outside, and the more forcible influence of example by actual participation in the games themselves, by older men. It is just therein that the English games and players have an advantage over our own. The masters at the public schools in England play with the boys every day; during their holidays, these same boys play with their elder brothers, with their fathers and their fathers' friends, and I recall one instance of a grandfather who plays cricket with his sons and grandsons, and no doubt there are many more.

Only the other day a certain family composed of grandfather, father, sons, and one daughter, challenged their local golf club to a match of eight a side, and won. In America, with the exception of a few of our boys' boarding-schools, modelled somewhat upon the lines of the English public schools, there is almost no active participation in the boys' games by older men.

The results of this difference between the English and American method are many and manifold. Seldom a year passes with us but there is friction, discussion, and even displays of puerile bad temper about the arrangements for, and the carrying out of, our intercollegiate games. Harvard will not play Yale at foot-ball; or Princeton declines to play Harvard at base-ball; the smaller colleges grumble at the arrangements made by the larger colleges, and they quarrel among themselves to boot. What men can fairly represent the college, and what men cannot; whether this man or that has been bribed by having his expenses paid at this or the other college merely that he may be eligible to play on the base-ball or foot-ball team or row on the crew; which teams shall play on a given date, when most gate-money is expected; these and many other matters of a most unsportsmanlike character come up for acrimonious discussion, which ought not to arise between gentlemen at all.

The games themselves are played during the exciting and decisive moments, amid a yelling, howling, and cheering, backed up by a brass band, that would do credit to an Omaha dance among Sioux Indians. Worst of all, this pandemonium is methodically let loose under the direction of certain leaders, at a time when it is intended that it shall seriously disconcert opponents. Decisions of the umpire, if they are in the least doubtful, are received with jeers and howls, and the players themselves express their dissatisfaction, by grimaces and gesticulation, which would be unbecoming and punishable in infants deprived of their toys. It is true that it was some score of years ago, and possibly would not happen now, but the writer playing foot-ball against one of our prominent universities, on their own ground, was with the rest of the team hooted at, jeered, and almost interfered with during the game by the members of the university whose present supremacy at the game in question makes such behavior unnecessary.

One may say that such behavior is never, certainly rarely, seen among amateurs in England. Fathers would be ashamed of their sons; schools and universities would lose not only caste, but revenue and reputation, if such things happened, and the head-masters and masters would root out such evils at any cost. If the playing of games resulted in this veritable delirium of excitement, they would no more permit it than they would countenance the taking of dangerous stimulants by the boys. They would consider the two on the same plane of harmfulness.

One must add, in this connection, that games as played in America are not more difficult, nor are the points to be decided nicer, than in English games. An illustration of how we in America try to obviate all possible causes for dispute is found in the fact that the batter is not out now, if he is caught off the bat by the catcher, at our game of base-ball. It was difficult to decide whether it was the snap of the catcher's gloves, or some like-sounding noise, or the actual contact of the swift ball and the bat; hence the change. But at cricket there is even a more subtle point still left to the judgment of the umpire. Indeed, this latter is worthy of emphasis because it stands quite alone, I believe, as being the only question, not of fact but of hypothesis, left to the decision of an umpire in any game now played. The point in question is known to cricketers as "leg-be-fore-wicket." Here the umpire is called upon to decide whether a ball pitched at a certain spot *would have* hit the wicket, if the batsman s leg had not been in front of the wicket at the time. It is a very nice question of eye and judgment at the best of times. In scores of games of cricket, at which the writer has been either spectator or participant, he has seen many men given out "leg-before," men from all classes of society, from the member of his university eleven down to the butcher's boy on his village eleven; but in no single case has he seen the player make a gesture or open his lips to question the decision of the umpire, or to make a comment. Granted that one is even a prejudiced American, one may well question whether so very delicate a decision as this would pass unchallenged, by both players and spectators, in a match between two American colleges, upon which great hopes were placed— and probably some dollars.

It is fair to say in this connection that our spectators are largely at fault in this matter. To the uninitiated the prime, not to say the sole, interest of a game is, who wins. Our spectators are despondent, or elated, according as their favorites win or lose. All the accessories and fine features of a well-contesed game are swamped for the majority by this one all-embracing interest. They appreciate little else, because they understand little else, and they therefore put the emphasis much too strongly on the one feature of winning. An English audience is not only much less excitable, and much more experienced, but a technically educated audience, and the spectators get their enjoyment from a multitude of nice details, and therefore do not have the same baleful influence upon the players.

In this matter of the influence of the spectators I must repeat, even at the risk of saying the same thing over and over again in these pages, that neither the English nor the Americans appreciate how much more democratic in these matters, as well as in many others, is England than America. Englishmen who know America only at the long range of theory cannot understand what seems like a contradiction; and Americans, who are mostly but birds of passage in England, do not recognize the truth of it. There cannot be the slightest doubt in the mind of the man who knows both countries, and who has played the games of both countries, that the Englishman is a far more democratic sportsman than the American. I mean by that definitely that all classes come far oftener in contact with one another, especially in the provinces, than with us, and are on more friendly and less awkward terms of good fellowship. Trades-people, school-boys, the squire, the parson and the noble play together.

interest themselves together, and get on together in the most wholesome fellowship at cricket, boating, hunting, and the like. Almost more than anything else this has made England so homogeneous a nation.

This custom is an advantage in that thus a very large number of both players and spectators, of whatever class, have not only seen, but have participated in, games, with players playing for the love of the game, and with a respect for, and a courteous obedience to, its best traditions. The butcher and the ironmonger would be as quick to see and reprehend such a trick, let us say, as knocking a man's bails off when he accidentally steps out of his ground, as the young gentleman from Eton. The rule is that a man may be thus put out for stepping out of his ground, but unless he persists in stealing ground, there is a higher, though unformulated, law, which says this advantage shall not be taken. In America, at baseball, on the contrary, the habit of running inside of second and third base, thus shortening materially the ground covered by the runner, became so frequent that now two umpires are employed, when, if the players could be trusted, only one is necessary.

The large proportion of the general public in America who interest themselves in the playing

of games labor under the overwhelming disadvantage of seeing only our game of base-ball, and
that played by paid professionals who are managed by stock companies, whose sole desire is to
make money out of an exhibition of ball-playing.
Nothing could be worse. These players are not,
as the stranger might gather from the names of
the clubs, as the Chicago, the New York, the
Boston, the Washington Club, men from those
particular cities. On the contrary, there is a
regular traffic in players by the managers of the
clubs, without the least attention to what part of
the country they hail from. They play purely
and simply for their salaries, with no more sec-
tional loyalty than a race horse which runs to-day
for one owner and to-morrow for another. As
their living depends upon their success at the
game, one can readily understand their attitude
toward the umpire, toward one another, and
toward the game. They care no more for the
best traditions of the game, or for a sportsman-
like attitude in their play, than a terrier hunting
rats. Nothing could be more debilitating to the
morale of sport than the state of things as above
described. It is true that cricket in England
includes many professionals, but no county
eleven is without its contingent of gentlemen
players, one of whom is always the captain, and

the standard of behavior demanded of, and acquiesced in by, both players and spectators, is very high. A row on a base-ball field is not uncommon, and a graduated scale of fines, to be inflicted upon players by the umpire, is a necessary weapon of defence in his hands, against insult and even assault; while a disturbance at a cricket match is practically unheard of. Football in England, played by professionals and attended by vast crowds, suffers much as our base-ball, and rows and assaults are not uncommon.

I have gone at some length into this matter because the American in the West, Southwest, and South, indeed the American, generally, has little interest in sport; and the influential portions of these and practically all communities, except in Massachusetts and the neighborhood ot New York, where the college graduate is beginning to make his influence felt, cannot from any similar experience of their own, in the least realize what a predominating factor sport is, and has been, in this English civilization. The Duke of Wellington's dictum about Eton's effect upon Waterloo sounds in American ears like an exaggerated flattery of sport. As a matter of fact, it is a commonplace. There is not the smallest doubt but that the education, moral and physical, of these Englishmen through sport, is one of the most saliently distinct features of their civilization. You can see it in their 'bus and cab-drivers in the management of their horses, and from thence all the way up to their management of the large variety of races they control in their colonies. What you see at Lord's you can see in Egypt and in India. They play more than they pray, and they spend more upon sport every year than upon either education or religion. There is no false shame about it. On the contrary, there is enthusiastic and unabashed interest in all forms of sport, by practically the whole population, from highest to lowest. It is looked upon, in short, as part of the curriculum of education. One might search a long time to find an English cabinet, one or more of whose members was not an authority at racing, or fishing, or hunting, or cricket, or rowing, and the like. The few who do not take an actual part, live surrounded by, and steeped in, this atmosphere.

As we have seen, they are not by origin or by temperament a pugnacious race. Their fighting is done generally to preserve the peace, to keep themselves and the land in quiet, however selfish their aim may be.

It is a far cry, perhaps, from playing to painting, but I never stroll through an English art gallery without noting the quiet, the homeliness, the innocence of the scenes their native artists choose for their studies. Fred. Walker, Dicksee, J. C. Hook, Luke Fildes, Wyllie, Constable, Poynter, Farquharson, Orchardson, Millais, Holl, Frith, Watts, Linnell, and many others; go look at their work, whether a landscape or a study of a situation, like Fildes's pathetic painting "The Doctor," for example, and see how simple, how quiet, how pathetic are the scenes that appeal to them. It was to these people first that landscape appealed. There is no enthusiasm for mere land and sky, in Greek, or Roman, or Renascent art. It was born here, that particular love of the land, lifted into poetry and painting, through the brush and pen of Englishmen. The animal virility, which will out, and which finds its vent elsewhere in political excitement, in pornographic literature, and suggestive art; which unsteadies and excites, and culminates here in Napoleon, there in Zola; or here in a revolution, and there in a morbid philosophy; seems to be dissipated and calmed in this moist island, and to lose its feverishness among these hard-playing islanders.

The bulk of their art leans to the mild type, as does their literature, and their statesmanship. The effervescent politician or demagogue, whose denunciations are suspicions, whose promises are dreams, and whose actual achievements are mere rhetorical promises to pay, seldom makes much headway here, and rarely lasts long. The turbulent and spectacular journalism, common elsewhere, pecks at the heart of public interest here largely in vain. Men of whatever class cannot be coached to believe that noise and fury, personal attacks and impudence, are to be trusted, or that bombastic oratory means real business and level-headed leadership.

The reader has quite mistaken the meaning of this chapter, however, if on reading it, he concludes that the writer intended a eulogy of sport and game-playing, and in particular of English sports and games, and nothing else. This is not at all the object of the chapter. The intention is to emphasize, strongly, the very large, one might even say the disproportionately large, place they occupy in English life, and to show also that what good they do, and the comparatively little harm they do, are due entirely to the fact that they give in some sort a training for life, because, as a rule, they are conducted on sounder lines of fair play, sanity, and uprightness than anywhere else in the world.

It is not the business of this chapter to discuss the question as to whether a hard-drinking, hard-riding, game-playing, out-door-loving people will continue to hold their own against such rivals as America, Germany, and Japan. Personally, I believe we stand at the parting of the ways, and that the student of England and the English is looking on to-day at the first indications of the decay of, in many respects, the greatest empire the world has ever seen. The sun that never sets is setting. Nothing but a tremendous, almost miraculous, wrench can turn our stout, red-cheeked, honest, sport-loving John Bull away from his habits of centuries, to compete with his virile body against the nervous intelligence of a scientific age. His game of settlement on the land, there to raise his crops, there to play, there to live in peace, there to expand himself till he occupies his present large proportion of it, he has played to perfection. But the nations are playing a new game now, and some of them seem to play it more brilliantly, and more successfully, than he does. Though one may praise, and praise honestly, the game he has played, and the manly way, upon the whole, he has played it, this need not interfere in the least with the conviction that he is being caught up with — which means, of course, ere long left behind — in the far more scientific game that Germany, Japan, and America are now playing.

That pleasant physical fatigue which lulls the

nerves to sleep, and which is one of the most beneficent effects of physical exercise, may be at work in this case, leaving Mr. Bull as confident as ever, and pleasantly unconscious of his own danger. That this worship of, and training of, the body by playing games seriously and taking sport seriously, has provided them with a calmness, steadiness and fearlessness of character all their own, no one can doubt. That these characteristics have made them ideal governors of inferior races, no one but perhaps a jealous German will deny; nor can it be denied, either, that it has kept the peace at home, leaving them unharmed and practically untouched by the class wars, and modern political philosophies, which have caused grave unrest among the masses of the people all over the world.

England, at any rate, has kept in view the laudable ambition to bring up her rich with the hardness and resourcefulness of the poor; while we in America have dropped into the vulgarity of bringing up our poor to be rich. Not a few of our social sorrows in America are being fostered by a widely advertised, though fortunately small, class, diligent in making themselves conspicuous, who, having been recently poor, are trying to appear anciently rich. At least there is no such thinly veiled hypocrisy, no such self-conscious social awkwardness in England. That, at any rate, is not their weakness. On the other hand, the easy unconsciousness, born of great physical vigor and great national success, is apparently consoling them with a blind belief that theirs is the only type of manhood, theirs the only road to national health and prosperity. Alas, there are many indications just now that, though this is a brave and comfortable creed, it is not comprehensive enough.

VII

IRELAND

TO write of England and the English
without a chapter devoted to Ireland,
would be to omit a phase of English
social and political history which throws much
light upon the English character. There have
been many things said and written about Ireland,
sad, pathetic, insulting, vituperative, in praise
and in blame. Not being either English or
Irish, the present writer deals with the tangled
and perplexed subject, not from choice, but from
necessity.

The English-Irish divorce case has been in the
courts now for some seven hundred and fifty
years, and is apparently no nearer a settlement
to-day than at any date during those centuries.
A vivacious, emotional, law-ignoring Celtic lady
is united, not altogether of her own free will, to
a rather dull, self-centred, law-worshipping Saxon, and their domestic troubles have been unceas-
ing ever since. They have murdered their
children; they have stolen one another's household effects; they have made love, and been

made love to, by strangers; they have committed every offence known to the law; they have patched up a temporary peace, only to fight the more fiercely afterward; and they have called one another every name in the vituperative dictionary. It is the *cause célèbre* in the annals of the divorce court of the nations of the world. The robbing, plundering, snubbing, bribing and beating that have a part in their riotous and unlovely domestic life make a story unique and unparalleled in history. For seven hundred years and more this has gone on with the result that to-day, at the date of this writing, a prominent English statesman says that the condition of lawlessness in Ireland is "a scandal to civilization." England sighs with pity at the lawlessness in other lands; she dispatches missionaries over the world to bring the peace and charity of Anglican Christianity, and she often follows these with the sword, but her own spouse, Ireland, is as irreclaimable, as lawless, as vindictive, as unloving as ever:

> "Wid charmin' pisintry upon a fruitful sod
> Fightin' like devils for conciliation,
> An' hatin' each other for the love of God."

This island, with its 32,531 square miles, with its present population of something over four millions, separated from England by a narrow strip of sea, was given to Henry the Second of England by Pope Hadrian the Fourth in 1155. Nicholas Breakspeare was the only Englishman who ever occupied the papal chair. To show his affection for his native land, and perhaps also to bring this island more immediately under papal control, he presented it to Henry the Second. If ever a nation was presented with Pandora's box it was done then and there.

History in this case for seven hundred and fifty years reads like romance, if not like rather vulgar melodrama. An Irish King, the King of Leinster, runs off with the wife of one of the Irish chieftains, there follow war and riot, and the King of Leinster, getting the worst of it, flees to England and appeals to Henry the Second for aid. Henry, seeing in this request an opportunity to take formal possession of the pope's gift, sends some of his nobles over with an army, and followed himself in 1171 with a still larger army, and, after much resistance and bloodshed, received the submission of most of the Irish kings. Then having given away nearly the whole of Ireland to his followers, he leaves a chief governor behind him, and returns to England. Then begins the long drama of opening, shutting, slamming down the lid, and sitting on the lid, of this Pandora's box. Probably the seeds of the land league, of boycotting, of cattle driving, of obstruction in Parliament, were sown at that time, and the crops have been continuous and flourishing from then till this very day.

The authentic history of Ireland may be said to begin when St. Patrick, taken as a slave from Ireland to Scotland, and then returning to Ireland after completing his studies as a priest, converts Ireland to the Catholic faith early in the fifth century. The Danes overran Ireland, as they did England, in the eighth century, and the Irish fought many bloody battles with them; but it is not until Pope Hadrian the Fourth presents Henry the Second with Ireland that Anglo-Irish history begins, and that history is merely a series of quarrels, disputes and wranglings, punctuated with famine, plague and slaughter.

From this time on the Anglo-Norman barons and their descendants fought among themselves and fought the Irish. Through one reign after another the affairs of Ireland went from bad to worse. After the Wars of the Roses, when Henry the Seventh came to the throne in England in 1485, the English settlement in Ireland was found to be very much reduced in power and size. The first English settlers had married Irish women and had become more Irish than the Irish. Though this was forbidden and punished by the severest, and even the most brutal, measures, it still went on. The Irish were not considered to be even under the protection of the English law. To kill an Irishman was like killing a dog — none the less, while the English had been occupied with wars in Scotland, France, Wales and among themselves, the Irish had recovered something of their power. They went so far as to receive, and to crown openly in Dublin, one of the pretenders to the crown of Henry the Seventh. Then was passed the famous, or infamous, **Poynings's** Act. Henry sent as his representative to Ireland Sir Edward Poynings, who summoned a parliament, and passed the act which goes by his name to the effect that: All English laws have force in Ireland, and the Irish Parliament must confine itself to measures first approved of in England. The English King and his council must be first informed of all bills to be brought forward in the Irish Parliament, and must give their consent.

It was four hundred years from the first invasion of Ireland before Ireland was wholly subdued. As late as the time of Henry the Eighth, England only held possession of some of the seaport towns of Ireland. King Henry the Eighth in his day assumed the title of King of

Ireland, for as much as any other reason that he might not be supposed to have accepted or inherited Ireland from a pope. Henry confiscated the church lands in Ireland, as he had done in England, and began to bring to bear that pressure, which has been insistent ever since, to make the Irish give up the faith of St. Patrick for the novel Protestantism which Henry the Eighth had evolved from the necessities of his personal domestic situation. Nearly all the chiefs in Ireland were brought to acknowledge Henry as the head of the church, but the people refused to do so then, and have refused to do so ever since. We now have clearly before us the two matters that underlie almost all subsequent troubles. Their land had been taken from them, their religion was to be taken from them. Edward followed Henry, and was even more bitter in his Protestantism; then came Mary and a return to the old faith; and then Elizabeth, with years of religious and land wars. There were few years of her reign without war, bloodshed and rebellion in Ireland. If the Irish could not be subdued and converted, there followed the plan of establishing plantations of English and Scotch in Ireland, who drove off the Irish and settled in their place. During these wars of the time of Elizabeth, crops, cattle and houses were destroyed purposely to bring about famine and thus destroy and drive away the people. Thousands of men, women and children perished of starvation. People were fined and imprisoned for not attending Protestant worship, and nearly a million acres of land in the counties of Donegal, Derry, Tyrone, Armagh, Fermanagh and Cavan were turned over to settlers who promised to be Protestants. Large numbers of English and Scotch were thus settled by force, fraud, or cunning on the most fertile Irish land. In 1641 a general rising took place, known as the rebellion of 1641, followed by atrocious cruelties, murder, and misdeeds unmentionable. In 1642 a national convention was called at Kilkenny — ominous name — to proclaim and establish the independence of Ireland. This was aided in a half-hearted way, it is supposed, by Charles the First, then at loggerheads with his own Parliament at home. But a man of different stamp from Charles then undertook the rule of Ireland, and probably for the first time since England came into possession of her Pandora's box the lid was firmly closed and locked. From the rebellion of 1641, till the final stamping out of all insurrection under Cromwell in 1652, out of a population of 1,466,000, 616,000, or nearly half, perished by sword or famine, and the land was again turned over to Protestant settlers.

Cromwell's solution of the problem was simply wholesale murder, to be followed by plantations of English and Scotch, who were to crowd out the Irish. They were driven to emigrate, sold as slaves or for worse purposes in the West Indies, and those who would not, or could not go, were segregated, and kept apart in the province of Connaught, and treated as were the Jews in Europe — driven like cattle into their pens and marked off from the rest of the population as though they were lepers. Of the horrors of this period of Irish history it is not easy to write without giving an effect of exaggeration, and this is to be avoided at all hazards, since these pages are written not to prejudice any one, or to please any one, but merely as one of the pigments necessary in painting our picture. It is not Irish history but English history. "Deeds of murder, rapine, plunder and devastation carried out so ruthlessly in Ireland, and the expatriation of so many millions of the Irish race, must recoil on England's head," writes Corbet. "Such is the past of English government of Ireland: a tissue of brutality and hypocrisy scarcely surpassed in history," writes Lecky. "Such a combination of rapine, treachery and violence as would have disgraced the name of government in the most arbitrary country in the world," writes Benjamin Franklin. "The legislative union between England and Ireland," writes Gladstone, "was brought about by a combination of violence, fraud, baseness, tyranny and cruelty in a degree rarely if ever paralleled in history." These are the comments of different men, of different opinions, at different times, and whatever may be the rights and wrongs of the bickerings of to-day, these are fairly typical of the estimate of practically all fair-minded men.

But the story is not told as yet. Cromwell's iron heel marks indelibly the end of one period and the beginning of another. The Restoration brought little comfort to Ireland. Whether Catholic or Protestant is in power seems to avail the Irish nothing. Under William of Orange a series of new penal laws were imposed upon them, again with the intention of suppressing Catholicism. It may be added here that the natural hatred between the Anglo-Norman and the Celtic portions of the population, between 1172 and 1540, only added to and made fiercer the quarrel between them when Henry the Eighth's religious reforms were made. The English naturally followed the changes made in England; while the Irish held all the more tenaciously to papal supremacy, which, as a sequence, became, and remains to-day, a synonym for hostility to England. Romanism and nationalism became close allies in Ireland for a series of reasons which even this short outline of Irish history makes clear. The Irish Parliament was barred to Catholics, as were the law and the church, and practically all positions of trust and emolument, while under Anne and George the First, the rights of the Irish Parliament were still further mutilated.

The Protestant Parliament of 1695–1709 passed a series of penal laws against Catholics which for well-nigh two centuries kept the land in a turmoil of suspicion, denunciation and sycophancy. "The law does not suppose any such person to exist as an Irish Roman Catholic," said a certain Lord Chancellor. An Irish Catholic might not act as a teacher under pain of banishment, and under pain of death if he returned from banishment. Their children could be educated only by Protestants. They could not hold property in land or take land on lease for a longer term than thirty years. They were forbidden to carry arms. They could not act as guardians of their own children, or marry a Protestant wife, or inherit an estate from a Protestant relative. The law of primogeniture was abrogated in the case of a Catholic so that his property might the more easily be distributed.

These drastic measures against a religion served also as an opportunity for the Protestant to possess himself of the land and wealth he coveted. Here as ever, no doubt, the Englishman found his duty trotting amiably and conveniently in double harness with his selfish interests.

One notes these things not because they are disagreeable, but because they throw light upon both the English and the Irish character. The imperturbable self-sufficiency of the English probably interpreted these doings and this legislation as a duty that they were called upon to perform. Its effect upon the Irish was to make them slaves with the vices of slaves. They grew in jealousy, in malice, and in feline methods of defence, of treachery and trickery. The Irish contempt for law is an unfortunate heritage of the many years when law was tyranny, and prejudice against themselves was not only looked upon as a virtue, but paid for by the ecclesiastical and governing authorities as a professional service. The informer was regularly paid. He received twenty pounds for an unregistered priest, and fifty pounds for a bishop. Even as late as our own day one hears of a Lord Plunket who evicts his Catholic tenants because they refuse to educate their children in Protestant schools; a Lord Leitrim who violates the daughters of his tenants;

a Lord Clanricarde whose treatment of his tenants is such that his own counsellor at law describes it as "devil's work."

As far back as 1665 and 1680 laws were enacted in the English Parliament absolutely forbidding the importation into England of all cattle, sheep and swine, of beef, pork, bacon, mutton, and even butter and cheese. In 1699 the Irish were forbidden the exportation of manufactured wool, lest any or all of these, the natural products of a rich grazing country, should interfere with the profits and prosperity of English merchants.

One may go far afield to find a more typical example of that characteristic of the English of bovinely seeing duty where their interests call them. "Toward the end of the seventeenth century," says Froude, "the mere rumor of a rise of industry in Ireland created a panic in the commercial circles in England. The commercial leaders were possessed of a terror of Irish rivalry which could not be exorcised." As a result of this stupid commercial fear, England set out to paralyze and to destroy the industries and the commerce of Ireland by prohibitory measures. William the Third, shortly after his coronation, said that, for his part, he would do all that he could to discourage the woollen manufacture in Ireland. A Navigation Act of 1663, confirmed in 1670 and completed in 1696, excluded Ireland from colonial commerce. In 1663 and 1669 the English market was closed to Irish cattle which were declared "a public and common nuisance," as also to Irish meat, butter, and like products. In 1699 the Irish were forbidden to export woollen goods, and under William the Third and Anne the cotton industry was ruined by an English import duty of 25 per cent. "One by one," writes Lord Dufferin, "each of our nascent industries was either strangled in its birth, or handed over gagged and bound to the jealous custody of rival interests in England, until at last every fountain of wealth was hermetically sealed." It seems to have been the policy of England to starve Ireland into subjection, industrially and commercially, as the easiest method of keeping her harmless to themselves.

The coming of free trade to powerful England was one thing, to emaciated Ireland it meant merely another blow, another foe, another failure. Ireland was no more fit to compete than a starveling to enter the prize-ring. And a starveling she is still to-day. The death rate in Dublin is 25 per 1,000, the highest of any town in Europe. How deplorable this is may be judged from the comparison with London, 17 per 1,000; Paris 16.1 per 1,000, and approximately the same for New York. In Dublin, out of 59,263 families, 36 per cent. live in one-room tenements. In London the proportion is 14.6 per cent., in Edinburgh 16.9 per cent. It has been said that there are as many as 1,500 houses in Dublin in such insanitary condition that they ought to be demolished. These same houses include 5,383 rooms in which are living 12,926 persons.

During a winter spent in Ireland I often asked myself and others why this beautiful grazing country, with the huge market of London at its very doors, was not made rich by this very opportunity. The answer it appears is a simple one. Eggs from Normandy pay in carriage to London 16s. 8d. per ton; eggs from Denmark, 24s.; and eggs from Galway in Ireland, 94s. per ton. Butter from St. Malo or Cherbourg pays 20s. per ton to London; butter from Antwerp pays 22s.; but butter from Tipperary, where I was living, pays 35s. per ton. No wonder the Irishman replied to an Englishman who asked him why they did not sell their fowl in London: "Do you see that piece of water? If I could sell that water in hell, I could get any money I wanted for it, but the job is to get it there." The chief exports from Russia to the United Kingdom next to corn and wheat are butter and eggs, oats and barley! The chief export from

Germany to the United Kingdom is sugar, refined and unrefined! These, with thousands of fertile acres unused or used for grazing in both Ireland and England. The chief export from France to the United Kingdom next to silk tissues is millinery, so the statistics say, but there is no other proof of the fact! Even were the average Irishman not the shiftless being that he is, it would not be surprising that one Irishman out of every eleven lives on the rates, as is the case. According to the figures of the last "Statistical Abstract of the United Kingdom," the population of Ireland (1908) was 4,363,351, and the number of paupers in receipt of relief in unions was 103,429. The population of Ireland in 1846, or roughly half a century ago, was 8,500,000, and has therefore decreased just one-half in that time. One need read but a few pages of Irish history to discover therein the ancestry of many of the Irishman's faults, weaknesses and vices. We are not blaming, or excusing, but merely analyzing the characteristics of this people who alone in the world have hurled the word Failure at the English race we are dealing with.

While the population of Ireland in 1841 was over 8,000,000, and was in 1901, 4,458,775; the population of Scotland in 1841 was 2,620,184, and in 1901 was 4,472,103. The number of persons receiving poor relief goes on steadily increasing. In 1903 the number was 452,241; in 1904, 488,654; in 1905, 558,814; and in 1906, 562,269.

While 51,462 police suffice to keep the 39,273,-086 population of Great Britain in order, the 4,386,035 population of Ireland requires the enormously disproportionate number of 11,144 police for that purpose. Ireland has one constable for every 362 inhabitants; England one for every 541; Scotland one for every 885. Leaving out of count the two capitals, London and Dublin, the cost of the English police is 2s. 3d. per head of the population, while the cost for Ireland is 6s. 7d. While the police in Scotland cost £400,000, in Ireland they cost £1,300,000. They seem to possess an invulnerable elasticity of irritability, at least against England, which, despite poverty, emigration, police supervision, and centuries of severe maulings, crops out again at every available opportunity. During the Boer war they cheered the Dutch victories in the streets and read and re-read with genuine pleasure accounts of defeats of British troops.

Finally, in 1782, when England was busy in another direction in an attempt to tax without representation, and to control and curtail the commercial energies of her colony in America, the Irish Parliament was declared to be an independent legislature. This was forced upon England after years of an agitation led by Grattan and Flood, and at a time when Ireland had a large armed force raised as a defence against England's then numerous foes. The Irish Parliament became: The King, Lords and Commons of Ireland to make laws for the people of Ireland. Following this came the struggle for Catholic emancipation, but at this demand George the Third, who thought, as did many other Englishmen, that too much had been granted already, took fright, became obstinate, and would grant no further privileges. The united Irishmen soon grew into a rebellious organization. The French were inclined to aid them, and a small French force did land in Ireland, but both they and their Irish allies were swept to destruction, and again cruelty and slaughter on both sides, followed by famine, were a repetition of the centuries' old story. This Irish Parliament of three hundred members contained no Catholics, and Ireland was nine-tenths Catholic, and all but some eighty seats were in the hands of a few lords and landowners who returned whom they pleased. The government still controlled, though the Parliament was nominally independent.

It was Pitt who, while Prime Minister, became convinced that, to have peace and quiet in Ireland, Ireland should be united to England as Scotland had been in 1603. To get the Irish Parliament to pass an act of union was very different from merely controlling a government majority, and then, under Cornwallis and Castlereagh as representatives in Ireland of Pitt and the English Government, began a campaign of shameless and open bribery, which was all the worse because acknowledged and condoned It must be remembered in this connection that we are reading of a time when such methods were by no means uncommon in England itself, where "every man," it had been said by a notable statesman, "had his price!" Though the bribers were blameworthy, some one must make them so by taking the bribe, and one must leave it to the Irish to characterize those who took titles and money to betray their countrymen.

> "Still as of old
> Man by himself is priced.
> For thirty pieces Judas sold
> Himself, not Christ."

Owners of boroughs were paid as much as £15,000 a seat, and peerages and patronage were lavishly given for support, These seats in the

Irish Parliament were looked upon as so much property bringing in a large income to their owners, and since the abolition of the Irish Parliament meant the cutting down of the number of members from say three hundred to one hundred, the owners of these seats were paid, bribed or promoted as a compensation.

"The majority of Irish titles," writes Mr. Lecky, "are historically connected with memories not of honor but of shame."

Mr. Frederick Trench became the first Lord Ashtown; Mr. Will Handcock became the first Lord Castlemaine; General Henniker became the first Lord Henniker; Sir Richard Quinn became the first Earl of Dunraven; the first baroness Dufferin was so created at the request of her son, Sir James Blackwood, with remainder to himself and his heirs; Mr. Robert Lawless became the first Lord Cloncurry; Mr. Seeton Pery was himself made Viscount Pery, and manœuvred his younger brother into the earldom of Limerick; Mr. Cole became Earl of Enniskillen; John Scott, of very humble origin, became Earl of Clonmel; James Alexander, a rich parvenu from India, buys a seat and becomes Earl of Caledon; John Hely, afterward John Hely-Hutchinson on his marriage to an heiress of that name, afterward Provost of Trinity College of most unpleasant memory, received for his wife the title of Baroness Donoughmore, with remainder to the male heir; James Cuffe became the first Lord Tyrawley, and carried the impertinent demands, then the fashion, to the pitch of asking a peerage for his illegitimate son; William Tonson became first Lord Riversdale; John Bourke is first Lord Naes, then Earl of Mayo; Mr. Corry became first Baron Belmore, then Earl of Belmore; Abraham Creighton became first Baron Erne, and later a descendant became Baron Fermanagh of the United Kingdom; James Agar became first Lord Clifden; all these and more date their elevation to the peerage from the time at the beginning of the century when England, by open and scandalous corruption and bribery, was buying up the Irish Parliament. In one day eighteen Irish peers were created, and seven barons and five viscounts raised a step in the peerage.

Even the London *Times* in 1860 characterized the history of the relations between England and Ireland with prophetic despair: "Ireland will become altogether English and the United States republic altogether Irish. Yes, there will be again an Ireland, but a colossal Ireland placed in the new world. We must gird our loins to encounter the nemesis of seven centuries of misgovernment."

In our own day the Irishman in America does what he can to fulfil this prophecy of the *Times*. Here is a portion of a speech made shortly before the celebration of St. Patrick's Day in California. The speech was received with a tumult of applause. "I am glad to see the Irish people arming and practising the use of rifles and instruments of war. For centuries they have been borne down under the tyrannic weight of English rule. In every city of the world where a patriotic Irishman lives on Tuesday the green flag of Ireland will be waved. We must make a success of our celebration, for great things depend upon it. It will reflect the spirit of Ireland throughout the world, and some day it will bring about the raising of the green flag where it belongs. The Union Jack of England will be hauled down and torn in pieces, and two hundred thousand armed men will march into the county of Cork and drive the English into the sea."

In July, 1863, during our war between North and South, the Irishmen of New York became enraged at the fearless editorials of the then editor of the *Tribune*, Horace Greeley. They mobbed the office of the *Tribune* shouting: "Down with the old white coat what counts a naygur as good as an Irishman!"

They mobbed and burned to the ground a

negro orphan asylum, but were finally thrashed and brought to terms by local troops. A fearless and patriotic mayor of New York was roundly denounced because he would not permit the hoisting of the Irish flag over the City Hall of New York. If Mayor Hewitt had never done anything else, he deserves a monument for that. I like Irishmen, we all, I think, like them in America, but America is not Ireland, and Americans are not Irish. We fought our fight with England, and Ireland must fight hers, and long suffering as is the busy, good-natured American, the world may depend upon it that he will never be bullied by Irishmen, or any other foreign people, into pulling their chestnuts out of the fire, or listen to the dictates of any knot of malcontents to whom he has given the freedom they could not win for themselves.

The Irish have enough of the English temper in them to bully and to grab, but the thrashings they have received from the Lion would be as spankings to flogging at a cart's tail compared to what they would prepare for themselves did they once attempt to harness the Eagle in the shafts of their political jaunting-car. The Irishman has become far too much imbued with the notion that his business is agitation rather than exertion. The American people have little sympathy at bottom with this rather effeminate view of achieving political, or commercial, supremacy.

America in these days has her own gigantic problems, both at home and abroad, to solve, and she needs all her citizens to bear arms and burdens in the service of America first, last and all the time. The Irish, the Germans, the English, the Swedes, the Norwegians, the Italians, are not in America to exploit America for their own purposes, but to make and keep America for free Americans, and no one who knows the country has the shadow of a doubt but that she can and will keep them within these bounds. Politicians from time to time pander to the Irish, or the German voters, but should these people demand for themselves what is intended for all of us, there would be a veritable earthquake of wrath throughout the country. It is one thing for an O'Connell or an Emmet to lead an insurrection in Ireland, it is quite another for any Irishman to attempt to lead an insurrection for or against anybody in America.

The Act of Union in 1801 was followed by a short-lived rebellion under Emmet. Wellington finally persuaded George the Fourth to grant emancipation, and Catholics were finally admitted to Parliament after a struggle lasting some three hundred years. In 1842 O'Connell started a great agitation to repeal the Union. He counselled no violence, but his fiery followers broke away from his moderate methods and drifted into active rebellion. This rebellion was put down, the ringleaders escaped or were hanged, but the people were again aroused, and national feeling revived, to be followed by the Phœnix conspiracy in 1858, and the Fenian movement in 1867. By 1847 the population of Ireland, through starvation and emigration, had fallen from eight millions to less than five millions.

Gladstone and Bright endeavored to bring about many much-needed reforms in the administration of Ireland. Gladstone carried through his bill to disestablish and disendow the Irish church, and passed a series of measures tending toward a better distribution of the land. Later a Land Purchase Commission was created to assist tenants in buying their farms from the landlords. Meanwhile the struggle, punctuated as usual by battle, murder, sudden death and other horrors, between the peasantry and the landlords, continued. Parnell and the Home Rule Party are familiar history to this generation, and the story of how they forced the claims of Ireland upon the attention of England by a system of persistent obstruction of all business in the House of Commons needs no repetition here.

On the surface it looks as though all the great struggles in Ireland had arisen from the attempt to impose a system of land tenure by foreigners, and the confiscation and reconfiscation, under the Normans, James the First, Cromwell and William of Orange, of the land for seven hundred and fifty years; and the imposition of a religious faith abhorrent to a majority of the inhabitants, aggravated by laws passed to crush out Irish rivalry in various branches of trade and manufacture. But this is a superficial reading of the facts of the situation.

England has made herself the greatest empire the world has ever known by defects and qualities of which something will be said in these pages, but wherever she has colonized she has dealt with an inferior people, or with those of her own race for whom she has a respect that mitigates the bullying temperament, or, where she has persisted and bullied her own children, she has found them too much for her. Ireland, after one immigration piled on another of English, is largely English to-day, and England is mistakenly attempting to curb in Ireland that vigorous insistence upon personal freedom which is the all outweighing quality of these Saxons, whose Alfred, whose Magna Charta, whose beheading of Charles the First, should have taught by now that, when this

is eaten out of their blood, there will be little of
iron left in it. There is no more peaceable
gentleman in the world, when he is allowed to
mind his own business, than an Englishman;
but whether socially in his club, or domestically
in his house, or commercially in his affairs, when
he is meddled with, his rudeness, his harshness,
his pugnacity and selfishness are open and in-
comparable.

I have taken some pains to dig out and to make
clear this short outline of Irish history, because
the relations of these two throughout all these
years is a suggestive commentary upon the Englishman and his ways. He thinks that his steadily progressing bulk must push any and every
thing out of his way; he thinks his courage will
cleave a path; he thinks his honesty will inspire
respect, and his sense of fair play, confidence.
So they do in India, so they do after a few spankings of the natives, in Africa, so they do throughout his many settlements all over the East; but,
among those of his own blood, these matters
are taken for granted, and not looked upon as
god-given virtues of a people, whose patronage
and whose rule should be accepted as a blessing.
Nevertheless the Englishman goes on just the
same, loses his colonies or lets them alone, but
still poses his great bulk at Ireland, one century

after another, with calm disregard of the fact
that these Celtic Englishmen are no more impressed, no more afraid of him, than is the
American. The Irishman is enraged, the American is amused. Apparently he knows no other
way. The Englishman was permitted until quite
recently to beat his wife, or to lock her up. If
she is not impressed by the good qualities he has,
and be it said he has good qualities, then he is at
his wits' end, and has recourse to a stick. He
knows no better now.

One grows to feel that Ireland is not an island
of England, but a characteristic of England. All
the obtuseness, all the blindness to other qualities
than his own; all the cold stubbornness, all the
inability to change his ways, or to adapt himself
to another temperament; all his complete help-
lessness when he is not respected and obeyed
from the start; all his awkwardness when he
attempts kindly compromise or cajolery, become
exaggeratedly patent in his national failure to
live at peace with Ireland.

Though this condition of affairs is most noticeable in the case of Ireland, the same social
awkwardness exists elsewhere. Ireland is audible and voluble, and the world has not been left
in ignorance of her grievances; but one now
begins to hear a faint rumbling from that hitherto

dumb, dark race in India. The complaint is along exactly the same lines, what one hears of it. The Englishman must govern, must govern alone, must be supreme, must not be meddled with by an inferior race, and, mark you, all other races are assumed to be inferior. A distinguished French publicist and traveller, just returned from India, and writing as distinctly a friend to England, has this to say:

"En somme, ce qui manque le plus à l'administration anglaise aux Indes, c'est la souplesse: tous ses agents sont de parfaits gentlemen, honnêtes et justes, d'une forte trempe, plus que personne capables de résister à ce climat amollissant, possédant au plus haut degré le *self-control*, la faculté de se dominer. Mais ils croiraient faire preuve de faiblesse s'ils ajoutaient à tout cela quelques grains d'amabilité. Ce ne serait pourtant pas un crime de condescendre à gagner les sympathies des indigènes, de l'élite tout au moins. . . ."

It is plain that other observers, friendly though they be, cannot escape the impression that we have emphasized in the foregoing pages. It is fair enough, then, to write that nothing is more characteristic of England than her seven hundred and fifty years of failure to get on with Ireland. Her strength and her weakness are admirably and plainly held up to view for him, even who gallops, to see and to understand. England simply cannot get on with those who do not trust her, and obey her, except by drubbing them into submission, hoping meanwhile that they will grow to appreciate her. The individual Englishman is not unlike this. He can turn away from you, ignore you, go and live by himself without you, or if it is worth while, he can try thrashing you, but as to winning your regard through any except his negative virtues, he is as helpless as a sullen child. What then do you expect a man like that to do with a wife like Ireland? These Saxons

> "Who live by rule,
> Grave, tideless blooded, calm and cool."

I am of the old-fashioned opinion that the best men ought to rule, and that when necessary to bring this about an appeal to force is justifiable. This has been also the pith of England's philosophy on the subject. It applies well enough where there is no question of the superiority of the Englishman, but it fails lamentably where his superiority is open to question. Since 1776 the Englishman has learned that certain colonies populated by his own breed will be self-governing, whether he likes it or not, and by a certain automatic compromise they are little meddled with. But this has not been brought about by any logical sequence of ideas. If logic were a man and lived in England, he would be the loneliest person in the three kingdoms. No theory is ever intended to be carried to a conclusion here, but only to a comfortable working point. The Irish have enough of the Celt left in them to be irritated by this lack of sequence, lack of logic, in their neighbors. They cannot be made to understand why they are still governed much as though they were Zulus. They cannot understand why they are the only parcel of their breed left in the world who cannot govern themselves, and they will not accept the situation on the *ipse dixit* of their brethren across the St. George's Channel. With the rights and wrongs of this question we have nothing to do. It is of interest to us only that, in analyzing the situation, we find a complete breakdown of the Englishman's ability to govern, and to live at peace, with other peoples right at his own door. It is not for lack of experiments that he has failed. He has robbed, starved, slaughtered, bribed, used his whole artillery of colonizing charms, and he is just where he was when he started seven hundred and fifty years ago. It is a very remarkable situation; it is notably what the student physician would call an interesting case. It has been operated upon, it has been drugged, it has had the fiercest massage by sword, and the greatest variety of mud baths and starvation diet, and it is still alive, still kicking, still demanding some successful form of treatment.

If, in addition to some little historical information on the subject, one has lived in Ireland months at a time as I have, the problem is all the more puzzling. There is no better fellow going than the Irishman. No one could be more companionable, more sympathetic, more alive to the opportunities of every and any situation. The more you see of him at home, the more you wonder what there is about him that has made him and keeps him England's imperial and colossal nuisance. It seems easy enough to get along with him. He seems quite as open to the ordinary amenities of life as other men. He is a good sportsman, a fine soldier, and a gallant comrade.

> "And there isn't a weddin' at all,
>   A funeral or a fair,
>   Or any sort of fun or sport,
>   But me and the shtick is there,
>   Impatient to have our share."

His hospitality, though he be but poorly off in this world's goods, is genial and unaffected, and though he be excitable, and not altogether dependable — except in a row — there are other peoples who are excitable and not dependable — even in a row — who manage somehow to govern themselves, and get on in the family of nations without being kept in a school-boy's condition.

This splendid race of Saxons has been dominant at a steadily increasing pace for a thousand years here, there, everywhere. England cannot live on an equality with any other nation. The Englishman cannot live on an equality with any other man. One need only hear the Englishman, or the Englishwoman for that matter, say: "Oh he is a Colonial!" or "Oh, he is a Frenchman," or "Oh, he is an American," to catch the subtle distinction always made between an Englishman and anybody and everybody else.

"I do not care about the opinion of foreigners," said Mr. Chamberlain in one of his speeches, and he voiced the national sentiment. But it should be borne clearly in mind that this attitude is not one of boastfulness. It is not a conscious or artificial attitude which is purposely intended to be disagreeable. It is not a pose, not conceit; it is far worse than that. It is unconscious. It is the natural condition of mind, born of centuries of dominance. It is thoroughly parochial. England knows no world but England. The Englishman who is the greatest and most extensive of travellers knows only Englishmen. This is very impressive indeed. It makes him very formidable, very impervious to any influence toward intellectual orientation. It is one of the important factors making toward the decadence of the Empire.

What he will not do in Ireland, what he is apparently constitutionally unable to do, he will find it equally impossible to do elsewhere. He has rivals now who will be equals ere long, and who may prove to be superiors. The world that was governed by brawn and bulk, and honesty and fair play — always, be it understood, with the Englishman as umpire as to what is and what is not fair play — has become a wonderfully intellectualized world since the days of his last conquerings.

Commerce is a science, not mere courageous piracy. Finance is a science, not mere loaning accumulated wealth under the protection of British guns. Government is a most complicated manœuvring of men, each one with a ballot in his hand, not mere placating of one party of aristocrats by another party of aristocrats, so that both may live in peace and in power over the people. German students shut up in laboratories steal his trade. Japanese diligence, suavity and cunning steal his Eastern trade and his shipping. He finds it to his benefit, and for his safety, to ally himself with a pagan nation in the East, the Japanese; with an utterly unsympathetic nation, the French, and a still less sympathetic nation, the Russians, in Europe. His attitude toward America in 1860–5, when *Punch* ridiculed Lincoln, and the press generally lamented such an early death for the republic across the water, has changed somewhat in its open expression, but very little in spirit. But these things mean nothing to the average Englishman. He has a hazy notion that either he is not as rich as he once was, or that other nations have grown to be respectable rivals in wealth. He was, I must admit, rather stunned by the South African war, when an inconspicuous settlement of Dutchmen cost him twenty-five thousand lives, and $1,250,-000,000 in gold, before he conquered them. He was stunned because this was something he could understand readily. A fellow who can knock him down is the kind of fellow he can appreciate. These other, more subtle threads, in the shuttle of the civilization and progress of nations, he only faintly sees, and dimly understands.

This is, after all, a fine fellow I have been describing, but it is evident that he has his defects and his weaknesses. Ireland seems to be the hot water bath that brings out the eruptions on the English character, showing the need of a physician and a change. This is the reason why a chapter on Ireland is a necessity in any notes such as these on England and the English. It is a distinctly fair illustration, because it is not a matter of party politics, not a matter open to question by the most prejudiced, not a matter to be excused or explained by any of the usual subterfuges of politics or patriotism, not a matter in which other nations take any great interest and which tempts a foreigner to have a biassed opinion; it is simply seven hundred and fifty years of failure to solve a domestic problem — seven hundred and fifty years of inability to get on with other men, a quality upon which the Englishman particularly prides himself.

One of two things must be true then: either the Irishman is impossible to live with, or the Englishman's superiority must have been shown, in the many cases where he has succeeded, among inferior peoples; or, at any rate, a more amenable, a more conquerable people, than the Irish. There are some millions of Irishmen in America, and though they do lend a certain piquant and saline savor to our municipal politics, they are not altogether impossible to live with. The Catholic population in and around

Quebec largely outnumbers the Protestants, but there is no trouble there. The race and the religion are apparently not wholly to blame. Whose fault is it then? Fortunately we are not concerned with a categorical answer to our own question. Many able Englishmen have tilted at this question without answering it. Our purpose in leading up to the question, and asking it, was only to bring out a characteristic of the English. With them it is dominance or nothing — *aut Cæsar aut nullus*. Dominance by compromise, or dominance by distasteful alliances, or dominance even by bribery — as they bribed the Danes to leave them in peace, or as they have tried to bribe Ireland — dominance by intrigue, or dominance by force, but nothing less than that. They can rule in no other way, they can live side by side with other peoples in no other way. As we have seen in another chapter, they reward success more generously, more magnificently, than any other people in the world. Their House of Lords is, as every one knows, not a chamber of blood or birth, it is a chamber of the chosen successful ones. They have no great ruling nobility of high descent, they have an aristocracy of success. Their peers are brewers, ship-builders, soldiers, sailors, newspaper editors, manufacturers of steel and iron, Jew financiers, mammoth shop-keepers, lawyers, chemists, and the like. More than half of the present House of Lords have been created since 1830. Thus they recognize success, power, ability. Thus they believe that the world belongs to those who take it. Thus they shoulder you on one side, penetrate to the far ends of the earth, claim everything, fight for everything. If they cannot beat you, they let you alone, but as for living with you on terms of equality, never! But they feel bound to live with Ireland. Ireland cannot be allowed the liberty to make friends and alliances with France, or with Germany, or with Japan, or with America. Ireland cannot be allowed to interfere with the Orangemen, the Protestants who live in the north of Ireland. England cannot give up Ireland, and she cannot make Ireland acknowledge her superiority; and one or the other is necessary for peace between them. One wonders why Lord Curzon, or Lord Cromer, or Lord Milner, or perhaps a soldier like Lord Kitchener, is not given a free hand in Ireland for a given number of years. Anything would be better for the prestige, self-respect, and fair fame of England than that she should continue — she the modest, she the moral, she the law-abiding, she the patronizing and preaching nation of the world — that she should continue this squabbling, hair-pulling, scratching, this vulgar domestic vituperation, to the amusement perhaps of the light minded, but to the wonderment and scandal of all serious minded men of all other nations.

Another reason why she does continue is precisely another characteristic of England, and the English, worth noting and keeping in mind. As a race they have no nerves. They are protected from most, I may say all, of the minor troubles, trials, griefs, which annoy, upset, and even drag into their graves, other more sensitive people, by a non-conductor of insensibility. The most amazing thing about the English and Irish embroglio is that the English look upon it as a matter of course! They are constitutionally sure that they are right. Are we not the most God-fearing, the most humane, the most just and the most Christian nation? they say to themselves; then how is it possible that we can have murdered, starved, driven into exile, robbed, bribed, and pompously maltreated our brother Irishman? But they have done it. There is no doubt in any man's mind about that. Think of the callousness, the insensibility to pain and starvation and murder, of a people who for seven odd centuries can live in such relations with a weaker neighbor. Picture the quite impossible situation for the French, or the Italians, or the

Americans, or the Germans. We could not stand the strain of it. It would get on our nerves. It would irritate us beyond all expression. We could not push it on one side and go about our business unconcerned and unpitying. Much less could Frenchmen, or Italians, or even Germans, take such a matter-of-fact view of such a problem.

This has been a very valuable quality to the English in their conquering of, and ruling of, other peoples. In countless other ways one might illustrate this sort of well-fed imperviousness to the common griefs and annoyances of life; but in so doing, one might press harshly upon their social and domestic life, and make these notes assume an air of prejudice or bitterness, which is the last thing in the mind of the writer, and, above all things, to be avoided. This illustration of Ireland is all sufficient to prove the point, and at the same time avoids personalities. One has only to picture any other nation, except perhaps Russia, living contentedly, going about its affairs, superbly unconscious of any wrong on its own part, with this gigantic, centuries old, social sore a part of its social and political body. One has only to picture such a thing to make plain this characteristic English trait of confident and stolid self-satisfaction. This trait eclipses even their rather ostentatious claim to be a distinctly religious nation. The *anima naturaliter christianissima* is a rare thing in England, though the profession of religion is not only a State affair, but practically universal. They wear their religion as a formal garment. It never has, and does not to-day, soften in the least the overbearing temperament, interfere with wars of commercial aggression, or condemn immorality in the highest places. The overmastering qualities of a conquering race are but slightly colored by their religion. It is an affair of the State. One is loyal to it as one is loyal to the King, but, as a nation apparently, the general aims and purposes, and the methods of working them out, are not materially affected by the mandates of giving the cloak also, turning the other cheek, or not worshipping Mammon. The Irish question is in no danger of settlement by an appeal to the Englishman's religious sentiments. Nothing apparently can influence, or mitigate, these prime characteristics, illustrated by the treatment of Ireland: the worship of success and supremacy, and the stolid indifference to anything and everything which interferes with the Englishman's obtaining them.

VIII

AN ENGLISH COUNTRY TOWN

"TO announce too much of what one means to do is the best way not to do it at all," says Tallyrand. We all know how dangerous it is to promise pleasure to others from what has pleased us. Our dearest friend may seem but a dull dog to the stranger to whom we introduce him. The book, the play, the picture, the tour in a new country, the hotel in which we have been comfortable, all these we may praise to another, and he only finds them commonplace or positively disagreeable.

There are, however, two things that I dare announce to the traveller as superlatively beautiful. If he be disappointed the fault is his, and not my praise of them. The pictures of Velasquez in the Prado at Madrid and an English country landscape in May surpass any possible preliminary praise of them. You may announce what you will, but the reality still surpasses the promise.

314

Twenty miles out of London, and the sun is shining, and the train glides along with green fields, hedges of Hawthorn, trees blossoming on every side. England looks to be the huge well-cared-for farm of a Crœsus. The absence of much sunlight, so distressing to the American in London, is an advantage now. True, the country is an old country, and had been ploughed and planted and harrowed for close on to a thousand years before America was even discovered. This gives the country-side a mellowness and well-groomed look, and the vaporous sunlight softens all the outlines, hides the harsh features, and gives the landscape the dreamy, far-away, misty loveliness of a mirage. Just now the fields that are not brown, having been turned up for sowing, are of a delicate green, and hundreds of sheep and lambs scurry about as the train flies by. If I were an Englishman, it seems to me that I should grow positively thirsty for this scene if I were long away from it. There seem to be no angles; field melts into field, and hedge into hedge, with here and there a ribbon of road which seems to join rather than to separate them. The houses, big and little, are all of brick or stone and have the advantage of lending their interstices to ivy and climbing roses, and the older they are the softer the color and outline. Houses of wood look to be dishevelled and shabby as they grow old, while brick and stone are the more dignified the older they grow.

I believe it is true that the midlands of England are as fertile and easily cultivated as any similar number of acres in the world, and to the eye of the traveller they seem so.

But where are all the people? Did we leave them all in London, and Oxford, and Worcester, and Birmingham? All through the afternoon and into the early evening we travel, and I could have counted more houses, certainly more sheep, than men and women from the carriage window. It may be a holiday, it may be the day's work is finished, it may be that the laborers, slow-moving, and sombrely clad in grays and browns, are not so distinctly seen in this soft light. In any case, it seems as though one might step out and take possession of as much of this lovely country as one cared to, and this adds still another quality to the charm. There is solitude without loneliness. It is so well cared for, so gentle and cultivated in appearance, that one feels the centuries of human toil, the intimate companionship of men, but without their interruption.

England is London says one, England is Parliament says another, England is the Empire says still another; but if I be not much mistaken, this stretch of green fields, these hills and valleys, these hedges and fruit trees, this soft landscape, is the England men love. In India and Canada and Australia, in their ships at sea, in their knots of soldiery all over the world, Englishmen must close their eyes at times, and when they do they see these fields green and brown, these hedges dusted with the soft snow of blossoms, these houses hung with roses and ivy, and when the eyes open they are moist with these memories. The pioneer, the sailor, the soldier, the colonist, may fight, and struggle, and suffer, and proclaim his pride in his new home, in his new possessions, but these are the love of a wife, of children, of friends; that other is the love, with its touch of adoration, that is not less, nor more, but still different, that mysterious mingling of care for, and awe of, the one who brought you into the world.

This is the England, I take it, that makes one feel his duty to be his religion, and the England that every American comes to as to a shrine. When this is sunk in the sea, or trampled over by a host of invading Germans, or mauled into bankruptcy by pandering politicians and sour socialists, one of the most delightful spots in the whole world will have been lost; and no artist will ever be able to paint such a picture again, for nowhere else is there just this texture of canvas, just this quality of pigment, just these fifteen centuries of atmosphere.

One cannot describe every country town in England, so I have chosen the one I love best. If it is more beautiful than other country towns, if I am partial, even prejudiced, in regard to it, so much the better. Criticism seldom errs too much on the kindly side.

This particular town had a castle, built by no less a person than a daughter of the great King Alfred, who led his Saxon neighbors in driving off the Danes. This town had a charter granted to it by the King three hundred years before Columbus sailed into the west. It is an old town even for England, its hoary antiquity drifts out beyond the harbor of American imagination into an unknown sea. To an American it is almost too old to be true. One might as well say in an Oklahoma village that Adam lived here! At such a distance of time years are too indistinct to be worth numbering. The town hall stood in the main street, and still stands there, when the *Mayflower* set sail, and one of the local inns was an old established hostelry before we made our first noise in the world, taking pot-shots at the red-coats near Lexington. The members of one family represented the town in Parli for several centuries, and the old corn mill back almost to the days of Charlemagne.

In a wholesome old age the features, the speech, the manners, the opinions soften; thus a gentle old lady has a charm that no youthful maiden, be she ever so beautiful, can rival. As for men, I wonder that any woman is willing to marry a man under forty. So it is with a town. Not Time itself can ever console us for the lack of this long vista back through the centuries. Neither dollars nor energy can manufacture mellowness.

There is no lack of manuals, documents, and erudite treatises on the economic, political, religious and social life of England. The student need only look through the catalogue of any large library to find data for the support of his theories, or theories with which to confirm his data. But when all is known that has been written on the laws and traditions and customs that influence the life of a nation, there still remains the peculiar atmosphere, the social climate, that thermometers and barometers can only register; they can no more describe them than a box of colors can paint a picture. This must be acknowledged in describing an English country town.

Given the differences between a republic and a monarchy; between a new country and an old country; a country where there are still millions of acres of unoccupied land, and a country where the land is in the hands of a comparatively few landlords; a country that has had free education ever since it was settled, and a country where education was for centuries considered undesirable, or, at any rate, unnecessary, for the masses; a nation where distinctions of class are recognized in the constitution itself, and a country where no such distinctions, political or social, are generally accepted; and even then there are still differences which cannot be tagged with names, but which are plants centuries old, and having qualities not to be analyzed, qualities like those of old pictures or old wines, born of age.

The moment the stranger puts questions to his neighbor in this English town — a town, I may say in passing, of about six thousand inhabitants — the first differences discover themselves. The Englishman of Northbridge in England does not know as much, nor does he take as much interest in the affairs of his town, as does the American of Bear's Cove, Massachusetts. The whole machinery of local government, until very lately, was based upon traditions, the origins of which are only known to the antiquary or the student. In England laws are almost always the outgrowth of custom and tradition; in America the laws were made brand new for a particular purpose, easily recognizable by the least profound observer. In England the laws of the land are helped out by the fact that the same customs and habits which made the laws also made the man who obeys them, and he wears them like a well-worn suit of clothes. In America the man made the laws, and feels rather superior to them, as one might feel toward clothes not altogether comfortable in their fit. This is part of the secret of the law-abidingness of the Englishman and the American tendency to law-defyingness. It is not strange then that the American knows more about the affairs of his town than does the Englishman. One would naturally be better informed about one's own children than about one's ancestors.

In England, too, the people have not had the franchise long, and consequently the masses are not yet accustomed to feel, or to take upon themselves, much political responsibility. The middle and lower classes are only just beginning to question the political and social *status quo*. For centuries it has not occurred to them that things could be other than they are. "It has always been so" has been until lately the stupefying reason for letting things alone. America, on the contrary, was born of revolt against the political, social and religious *status quo*, and England was left for two hundred years more of "it has always been so," when her rebellious ones sailed away to Virginia and Massachusetts.

In America, politics ranks as one of the domestic virtues; in England politics has been, and is largely even now, the obligatory occupation of the few who can afford it, though this state of things is rapidly changing in both town and country since the widening of the franchise and the passing of the Corporation Act. In America it may almost be set down as an incontrovertible proposition that no man of Lord Rosebery's wealth and social position, for example, could be elected President of the United States. In England until the last few years no man could have hoped to succeed in politics without a private income; in America nothing is such an awkward handicap as great wealth, while if part of this wealth were spent in the innocent recreation of keeping a racing-stable, political preferment would be absolutely prohibited. The English people as a whole still look to wealth and position to govern them, while in America the people are still jealous, not to say unreasonably suspicious, of wealth and power.

These are the larger, the enveloping reasons why the American in his country town takes more interest in its political affairs than does the Englishman in his. The Englishman's town was made for him, and the centuries have swathed it in customs that are almost sacred. The American's town he made himself, and he looks upon it not as a graven image, but as a model of clay that may be often and easily altered without sacrilege and probably with advantage.

The country town in England serves as well to exploit all these national differences as though it were England under a microscope. The classes are as distinctly marked as though they wore uniforms. At the base of the social pyramid are the agricultural laborers earning from $2.50 to $3.25 a week; fifty per cent. of the laborers in England earn twenty-five shillings a week or less. A fact worth remembering when we revise our tariff! Then the farm servants and house servants of the small gentry, earning, the men from $90 to $250 a year, the women from $60 to $125 a year; then the shop-keepers and their assistants and employees; then the richer merchants, and mill or factory owners, and ranking with them the local professional men, lawyers, doctors, Dissenting ministers, land agents, and the like; next come the gentlemen farmers and landed proprietors, and the clergy of the Church of England; and finally the county gentlemen and the neighboring nobility, with the lord lieutenant of the county, often a great noble, as the official and political apex.

The manufacturer, mill-owner, and the like receives of course both social and official recognition according to his success and his wealth. As we have noted elsewhere, the successful brewer or manufacturer often crowns his career by being made a peer, when he leaves his own class and enters another. The same is true of the great lawyer, the successful politician, and so on. I may be mistaken, but I believe the physician is the only representative of success in the professions who thus far has failed to reach the dignity of the peerage.

In the New England town I have in mind — and very proud I am to keep it in my memory — of about the same size and relative importance as the English town I am describing, the governor of the State, who happens to live there, and the cashier of the local bank, and the shop-keeper, if he chance to be an interesting companion on account of his antiquarian knowledge, and the editor of the small local newspaper, if he be of intelligent proportions, would meet at one another's houses, if their common tastes made it agreeable. But it would be considered the height of social glory in this English town should a shop-keeper, no matter how big the shop, or a bank cashier, no matter what his erudition, or even a physician or small solicitor, or small factory proprietor, find himself on equal terms at the table of one of the county nobility, much more at the table of the lord lieutenant of the county, except on some occasion of a formal function. Though the lord lieutenant of the county is usually a man of rank, he may be in no sense superior in social weight to other nobles in the county; for the time being he outranks them by right of his office.

If you cannot be a duke with a large rent-roll in England, by all means be an agreeable American, for to one and the other all doors are open. You dine with all classes, and all are willing to dine with you. No one is jealous of you, no one envious; no one suspects you of pride or vainglory, because, being a sovereign yourself, you are equally at home with sovereigns or with the people abroad. No one else can have the inestimable privilege of warm friendships with all classes, and consequently an intimate knowledge of the ways of life, of men and women of every social grade.

Just as the wages are smaller, so the salaries and incomes are smaller among these people than with us. The largest house in the town, built of brick, with garden, green-house and small stable, and containing rooms ample for the accommodation of a family of six, keeping a governess and seven servants, keeping two horses and doing a fair amount of entertaining — such an establishment as this can be kept going, without painstaking economy, on an income of $6,000 or $7,000 a year. In no place in America would the upkeep of a similar establishment for such a sum be humanly possible. In the first place, the governess and seven servants would require in wages $2,500 a year, while a similar staff in England would cost somewhere in the vicinity of $900 a year. This particular house was in the town itself, and was far more comfortable than the majority of the houses in the town. People with an average income of from one thousand to three thousand dollars a year live in far more convenient houses in America than in England. The matter of water, heat, lighting, suitable kitchens and laundries is insisted upon with us, and is lacking to an apalling extent in English country or even town houses, and also in the more pretentious country houses them-- selves. The houses of the poorer classes, laborers, clerks, servants and the like are mere boxes, with none of the conveniences to which Americans even of the poorer classes are accustomed. Hundreds of thousands of Americans live in houses admirably equipped as to bathrooms, lighting and heating conveniences and the like, where hundreds are thus housed in England. Indeed America is in a class quite by herself, so far as mechanical contrivances for personal comfort are concerned, as compared with England, or any other country in the world. The average level of comfort is far higher than anywhere else, whatever may be said as to the satisfaction of the rarer and more luxurious and more refined demands of the more cultivated. At any rate, America is easily chief among dwelling-places where mediocrity has nearest approached to its millennium. Rent, clothes, service, wines, beer, spirits, tobacco, all are cheaper in the English than in the American town, and prices of meats, vegetables, bread, butter, poultry, eggs much the same. In this particular town in Shropshire, however, the beef and mutton, though costing about the same amount, or a little less, per pound, are very much better than in a similar town in Massachusetts, are of as fine a quality, indeed, as the very best beef and mutton served in the best hotels and restaurants in New York. As you walk through the covered outer entrance to the door of the local inn, you may taste the preliminary joys of the carnivorous gastronome, for there are hanging the joints of beef and mutton, the beef getting that black-purple look which promises tenderness, and at dinner the visual promise is kept to the full. There is no such mutton in the world as a Welsh sheep fattened on the luscious grass of these hills and valleys.

> "The mountain sheep were sweeter
> But the valley sheep were fatter
> So we thought it would be meeter
> To carry off the latter."

But in the sheep from Wales fattened here one has both the sweet and the fat. Alas! the preparation of food in this town, as in all others I know, and in London itself, except where foreign cooks and foreign methods are used, is by no means equal in quality to the materials provided. The only thing that can be said in praise of English cookery is, that one is never tempted to eat too much! It satisfies legitimate hunger amply, but is never a temptation to gourmandizing. With all these fertile fields, it is a ceaseless source of wonder to the traveller that England should have nothing but potatoes and cabbage, and sea-kale, and vegetable marrow, day after day, and year in and year out, and import millions of pounds worth of eggs — some of them from as far away as Russia — butter, cheese, poultry, salads and small vegetables. On the other hand, the home-cured ham and bacon, at my friend's house in a neighboring county, his beef and his mutton, and his famous band of sturdy children, make one pause to remember that by their fruits ye shall know them. To those who have enough of bread, and beer, and beef, and bacon, and plain vegetables, and to boot plenty of out-door exercise and a somewhat varied social life, this diet is evidently well suited. These English, Scotch, and Irish men and women of the well-fed and well-cared-for classes are the sturdiest of the human race. No doubt my own experience is that of others, that you can bear more physical fatigue on this diet, and in this climate, than in America. The hard work of shooting over dogs in Scotland, of four and sometimes five days a week hunting in Ireland, can be kept up for weeks on end, with only a pleasurable sense of fatigue; while in our electrical climate, I am personally, at least, able to do only, say, two-thirds as much. Our athletic performances bear me out in this assertion. At the hundred yards, the two hundred and twenty, and quarter mile, at the high jump and other contests where rapidity and tremendous momentary exertion are required, we beat the English; while at the mile, three miles, and other tests of endurance rather than speed, they beat us.

Probably the most noticeable difference between two such towns, the one in America, the other in England, is the entire absence of foreigners in the latter. In the house I know best at home, out of a staff of some ten or more people, only one is an American, and he is the gardener, and in all the fundamentals he is a gentleman if there ever was one. The others are from Ireland, England, Sweden, and France; France, of course, supplying the governess. But here in the English town they are all English. In America the rough work of the laborer is all done by the foreigners, the servants are all foreigners, the common schools are filled with foreigners, the paupers are practically all foreigners. I have lived in America in the South, and West, and East for many years, and I puzzle my brains, and prod my memory, but I cannot recall that I have ever come in contact with an American pauper, though I know of course that there must be such. This must account for the fact that pauperism seems to be taken so much more for granted in England than in America. On Saturday, April the eleventh, 1908, there were nearly one hundred and twenty-five thousand persons receiving indoor and out-door relief in London alone, and they were practically all English. One feels differently perhaps about being a pauper if other paupers are of one's own breed, so, too, one feels differently about helping them. They are a recognized class in England, but no American, despite the distress, vagabondage, and poverty in our great cities, has taught himself to accept pauperism as a necessary condition of masses of his own race, and as a necessary tax upon the State. There are hundreds of towns all over America where a confirmed and recognized pauper would be as great a curiosity as the man skeleton or the fat woman of a travelling circus. I question if this be true of any single town in England.

On the other hand, this fact of the homogeneity of the race makes for mutual understanding and solidarity. In spite of the social gradations we have noted, the common grounds of intercourse are nowhere so many as here: witness the cricket, the hunting field; the dog and horse and agricultural and flower shows; the friendly and even confidential relations between the landowner and his farmers, bailiffs, woodsmen, trainers, jockeys, huntsmen, and so on. There are no false distinctions, only real distinctions, so the English claim, and no one but a fool or an ape cares to break them down. On ground where men can meet without self-consciousness, they do meet; but why should men who meet because they play cricket, or ride to hounds, or breed dogs, or love flowers, wish to meet in the drawing-room, or at the dinner-table, where they have not the same experience, the same opportunities, or common tastes?

Nowhere do men of sympathetic interests meet more often and more easily, without thought of social distinctions, than here, and no doubt this is due to the fact that differences of social rank are fixed, and universally recognized and accepted. The general understanding of this rather paradoxical social situation, and the smoothness with which social life moves, is due again to this fact that they are all English. This is a key to the understanding of one another, which, while it defies analysis, must be recognized as important. Peoples who speak a different language never fully understand one another, and even when they speak the same language, as in the case of the Americans and the English, they constantly fail to see eye to eye to one another. We give the same words a different shade of meaning, just as we give them a different intonation. These people, all of one race, from highest to lowest, master and man, have an advantage of mutual understanding and a kind of taciturn sympathy with one another that are priceless in solving many of their problems.

The very machinery of government in the town itself runs more easily for this fact. Going from small to great, the Parish is the smallest unit in England, having a Parish Council, or, if very small, a Parish Meeting. Groups of Parishes form the Union, the Union being the unit for the administration of the Poor Law. Unions again, where a Borough is concerned, are divided into "Borough" and "District," *i. e.* Town and Country. Their respective Councils deal with roads, sanitary matters, etc., etc. Groups of Unions form the County, which deals with main roads, education, lunatics, and so on. In some cases a Union is partly in one County and partly in another; then it is divided for County purposes.

The English town of Northbridge is governed as to water, lighting, roads, sanitary matters and the like, by a Mayor, and a Town Council over which he presides. The Town Councillors are elected by the voters of the Borough, who consist of all property owners, practically all occupiers of any taxable property, and lodgers who pay a certain specified sum for their lodgings. Even the sons in a family, twenty-one years of age or over, and living at home, must become lodgers in their own homes, they must have rooms of their own in the house, which they may lock up against their parents, and they must, as has been said, pay a certain sum therefor, viz., ten pounds unfurnished, to entitle them to vote. Women, too, may vote for the Councillors, but not for Parliamentary candidates. Married women may not vote, and other women, spinsters and widows, must be property owners, or lodgers paying a certain sum, and coming under the same rules as to their right to vote as men. This privilege is exercised in certain places, and in certain political crises appealing particularly to women very largely. In other places and at other times scarcely at all. It is not a matter that can be settled by giving figures, since the numbers differ widely. In New Zealand, where the women may vote, but where they have not been obliged to fight for the privilege, they care very little for it, and seldom exercise their right. To what extent the novelty of the franchise may influence the women voters in England it is as yet too early to decide. For the moment it is evident that the majority make comparatively little use of their right to the ballot. At this present writing there are 1,141 women on Boards of Guardians; 2 on

Urban District Councils; 146 on Rural District Councils; and 615 on Education Committees. The Councillors elect so many Aldermen, and from their own number the Aldermen and Councillors elect the Mayor. In the case of Northbridge, the town is divided into wards for the purposes of elections, but this is not so in all towns. When a Town Councillor is elected an Alderman, it creates a vacancy in his ward, and there follows another election. These elections take place every three years. The Aldermen are elected for six years, and half of them retire every three years. This system, however, only dates from 1882, the year of the passing of the Corporation Act by Parliament.

The Schools are controlled: (1) by Parliament, (2) by the County Council, (3) by local managers. Parliament is represented by the Board of Education, whose inspectors visit and report on all schools, and the government grant of money is only paid to such schools as satisfy the government requirements as to efficiency.

The County Council, through its Education Committee, pays the teachers, fixes their salaries, and provides all equipment, such as books, black-boards, furniture, coal, and so on. The government grant is paid at the rate of so much per child to the County Council, who make up the deficiency by levying a tax over the whole county. The tax in this particular county in 1907 was, for elementary education five pence halfpenny in the pound, and for secondary education one-half pence in the pound, or, for both taxes, twelve and a half cents on every five dollars.

The local managers are six for each school, divided as follows: four Foundation Managers, appointed under the trust deeds of the several schools; one appointed by the Town Council, and one by the County Council.

In Northbridge there are four schools, though one, the Blue Coat School, a Foundation school, is very small and rather an exceptional case. The three schools which practically serve the town are: the school in the Parish of the High Town, the school in the Parish of the Low Town (these are merely geographical distinctions), which are both Church of England schools, and the school of the Roman Catholic Parish. In very many towns there are Council schools directly under popular control, but in Northbridge, which is a staunch Tory town, in a staunch Tory county, there are none.

Practically all of the appointments to the local subordinate offices are made by the Town Council, and are not elective, the auditor being one of the few office-holders who is elective. In the matter of licenses for public houses, a much vexed question just now, the licenses are granted annually by the local justices to old license holders, but in the case of applications for new licenses, or of a refusal to renew an old one, the local justices refer the matter to the County Justices, or the Court of Quarter Sessions, who deal with such questions through the County Licensing Committee. The local justices also grant licenses for buildings where stage plays may be acted and the like.

Justice, in a borough or town like Northbridge, is administered by Borough Justices, who are mostly local tradesmen and professional men; they deal with small offences at Petty Sessions. More serious offences are dealt with at the Borough Quarter Sessions, presided over by a Recorder, who is a barrister and a paid official, with a jury. Still more serious offences are sent up to the County Town, in this instance the Town of Shrewsbury, and tried before a Judge of Assize.

In the County District, the Magistrates as a rule are local gentry. They sit in the town itself for Petty Sessions, and in the County Town for Quarter Sessions, when, in place of a Recorder, they select one of their own number as chairman, who is also unpaid. He is, however, usually a barrister, and I know of one instance where a gentleman studied law merely to fit himself to occupy this position in his own neighborhood creditably. Here again the most serious offenders, as with Borough offenders, are tried at Assizes. The offender himself in some cases may demand to be tried by the higher court. These unpaid magistrates are suggested by the Lord Lieutenant, and appointed by the Lord Chancellor. The Lord Chancellor is an officer of the government which may at the moment be in power, the Lord Lieutenant of the County is not necessarily so. When these gentlemen happen to belong to different political parties, it is hinted that the Lord Chancellor sometimes appoints magistrates without consulting the Lord Lieutenant. This is not often done, and the arrangement on the whole works without friction. To be a County Magistrate is the ambition of many men, and the gift of this distinction is rarely if ever mischievously bestowed. It is not supposed to be a question of party politics, but of personal worth, and there is no complaint that the party in power misuses this privilege. These amateur magistrates make mistakes, and Mr. Labouchère and *Truth* devote many paragraphs to their shortcomings, but the system works so well that there are seldom complaints from the class who are judged by them, and over whom they exercise control. It is generally held by those who come before them that more leniency may be expected from these unpaid magistrates, than would be shown by paid magistrates.

The clergy of the Church of England are State officials, for marriage and funeral purposes, and together with the church wardens, control church property. They are also *ex-officio* chairmen of their respective vestries, but vestry meetings nowadays are of historical rather than practical interest. They are often also, under certain trust deeds, trustees of the schools and Parish charities and not infrequently *ex-officio* chairmen of the Trustees, or School Managers.

The clergy of the time of Swift, Sterne, and Addison were not precisely of the gentleman class. They were placed below the salt, and often mated with the upper servants. There seems to be a falling off again now in the quality of the inferior clergy. I know of a neighbor's nurse-maid who is engaged to a curate, and they no longer occupy the position of influence of half a century ago. This may not be wholly local, for no one can doubt the decreased influence of the clergy of New England, in the last fifty years. Up to, and during the time of the struggle between North and South in America, the Unitarians of New England, and the Presbyterians and Dutch Reform ministers elsewhere were not only the moral, but the civil leaders of the people. One can count such clergymen now on the fingers of one's hands. Such men as President Eliot of Harvard, ex-President Cleveland and Mr. Joseph Choate have carried far more weight in their own local affairs and in the country at large, than any clergyman I can mention, unless it be perhaps Bishop Potter and Rev. Dr. Edward Everett Hale, when in the full vigor of his powers. It is by no means intended to infer from this statement that the bulk of the clergy are not hard working or without influence. In the country districts they are valuable public servants, and, according to their willingness, lend a hand here, there, and everywhere. But, with many exceptions of course, they receive nowadays more of social rank from their position as clergymen than they bring to that position. One often hears the lament that it is not easy to get a curate who is a gentleman — using that word, of course, in its limited technical sense understood in England. The temptation to men of a certain social grade and of moderate abilities to go into the church is of course great, when thereby they can, without much exertion become members of a profession which gives them a standing that neither their birth nor their intellectual powers would have won for them in any other way. This is true also in America, where there are hundreds of ministers of all denominations who owe their position to their profession and who would at once sink out of sight were they not buoyed up by their profession. Though it is both in England and America the noblest calling of the noble, it is also largely used as a refuge by the incompetent and the contemptible. No man has a right there who is not man enough to hold his own anywhere. There are still examples in England of parsons who are only clergymen in name; men who wear the uniform, but who not only hunt, but are masters of packs of foxhounds themselves; men who shoot, and farm, and are what Sydney Smith described as half county squire and half parson, under the name of "Squarsons." One of these died only the other day, who had been Master of Hounds for forty years. Such men may say, perfunctorily, *Benedictus benedicat* before meals, but beyond that their clerical duties are purely formal. This stamp of cleric is dying out, though it may be doubted whether the clerical snob, without public school or university behind him, is an improvement or even an equivalent. There are men in this English town whose fathers well remember a certain rector who went home from the tap-room of The Swan every Saturday night with his legs in a wabbly state of drunkenness, whatever may have been the condition of his head. That type of man has, of course, disappeared never to return.

The fact that the clergyman is in an independent position as regards his parishioners, since he is not looking to them either for his salary or for retention in his place, gives him a freedom that is valuable. However much of a heretic a man may be, he may admit that the Church of England and the Roman Catholics have much to be said in praise of their adherence to the logically sound arrangement that the preacher and teacher should not be obliged to look directly to those whom he teaches, for his means of subsistence. There are numbers of men whom we all know, both in England and in America, who are entirely unhampered by this awkward relation. On the other hand, what is more contemptible than the position of many ministers who know, and whose flocks know, that they are hanging on to their positions for their daily bread, and who are as fearful of the frown or disapproval of the local knot of richer men in their congregations who bear the bulk of the parish expenses as though they were lean hounds in a kennel?

But whatever their faults, the English clergy do a large amount of detail work that no one else is called upon to do in these country towns and villages. Indeed the three marked differences between life in an English and an American country town are: the absence of foreigners, the amount of work done by unpaid officials, and the remarkable dulness, awkwardness, and inarticulateness of the lower classes. The mental difference between the university educated gentleman, who is, let us say a County Magistrate, and the ordinary laborer, is greater, far greater than between any two Americans in similar positions in an American town.

There has been little or no chance for education. In 1870 the age for compulsory school attendance was fixed at ten; it was raised in 1893 to eleven, and in 1899 to twelve. As late as 1901, out of every ten thousand children attending school, the number who remained after the age of twelve was only 4,900, and in 1906 it was only 5,900. As a test of what boys acquired and remembered after leaving school, the head of a large labor bureau submitted all boys between sixteen and eighteen to a simple examination. They were asked to do some perfectly simple sums, and to copy in their own handwriting a few lines of print. The result showed that one-fourth could write moderately, one-fourth fairly, and one-half "wrote in quite a disgraceful manner." As to arithmetic, 10 per cent. answered the two questions, 15 per cent. one of them, and 75 per cent. neither of them. Such people must necessarily leave their governing and their guidance in all affairs of importance to others.

One would go far and search long to find a town in Massachusetts without its free public library, and a good one at that. Similar opportunities for reading are almost unknown in the English towns of the type I am describing, and there is little demand for them. Newspapers and magazines are in every house in the American town, but only in a comparatively few families in the English town is there any continued reading of even such ephemeral literature as that.

There has been no opportunity to take any part in political affairs either local or national. The local tap-room is the laborer's only forum, and the fields he cultivates, or the beasts he tends, limit his experience; and as a result the lowest class of laborers in English country neighborhoods, English though they be, are in a condition of intellectual apathy that positively startles the American when he comes in contact with them. In the town in question, with a population slightly over six thousand, there are some nine hundred voters, but there is a surprisingly large number of men of the proper age to vote who are disfranchised by the provisions already mentioned as to financial qualifications. It may surprise American readers to learn that there is a very large male population in England who are still, despite recent reforms, wholly deprived of any participation in government by lack of the necessary financial qualification. In that sense England is very far from being a free country.

As we have noted elsewhere, the total population of England and Wales at the last census (1901) was 32,527,843. Of these 15,728,613 were males, and of these again 6,697,075 were males of twenty-one years of age or over. At the elections in 1907 the number of registered electors was: Counties, 3,428,721; Boroughs, 2,553,-144; Universities, 19,068, or a total of 6,000,933. There were, therefore, 696,142 males twenty-one years of age and over who were not registered voters. We must, however, add largely to this because the census is of 1901, while the electors are of 1907. No doubt some are not registered through neglect, though very few escape from the fine net drawn through every election district by the professional election agents. It is probably, therefore, not far wrong to say that out of a male population twenty-one years of age and over numbering 7,000,000, 700,000 were not registered as voters, most of them probably because they were not qualified to vote. In the county town of Shrewsbury, for example, with a population of 28,395 at the last census, the number of Parliamentary voters was 4,819, divided as follows: Ratepayers, 4,423; Lodgers, 164; Service, 128; Freemen, 104; with 1,301 women entitled to vote for municipal officers. In the last Parliamentary election there actually voted out of the 4,819, 4,350. This does not weigh heavily upon those who are thus deprived of the ballot. They are quite without ambition — this does not refer to factory towns — and of extraordinary mental lethargy. Even their speech is of the guttural, indistinct kind, that one usually associates with people partially dumb. Their vocabulary is of the smallest, and their mental pace tortoisian. This appeals to the stranger, the American stranger at least, because he knows no such type among those of his own race at home. Where he meets with stupidity and political disability, it is among the lower class of foreigners, but here are families who have lived side by side perhaps for centuries, the one in the squire's house, the other in the laborer's cottage, yet the difference between them mentally and politically is as was the difference between the

Southern planter and the hands in his cotton
fields. There is little fear of exaggerating the
opiumonic dulness and apathy among this class,
although I appreciate that the Englishman who
is accustomed to it may wonder that the stranger
finds it so noticeable. It is one of those national
traits that the fresh eye and ear must be trusted
to describe more accurately than may the eye
and ear of the native long accustomed to it.
The English rustic of this type is uneducated,
inarticulate, inaudible and grotesquely awkward, both mentally and physically. But he has
his small political value for he is always and
unalterably for no change! He grumbles, but
his grumbling means little, and effects nothing,
and plays no more part in the affairs of the world
than does an accidental tap on the big drum in
the music of an orchestra.

There is a fierce controversy at the date of this
writing (1908) over a new Licensing Bill. One
sees on every side placards announcing that
"Your beer will cost more!" At the same time
the bill is called "confiscatory," and that it will
ruin the holders of brewery shares is announced.
In addition to this it is claimed that it does not
promote temperance. I am no political oracle,
but he must be dull indeed who can swallow
these three statements together, viz., that beer

will cost more, that just as much beer will be
drunk, and that the breweries will be ruined!
The rustic is evidently counted upon not to
analyse.

> "All still and silent—far and near!
> Only the ass with motion dull,
> Upon the pivot of his skull
> Turns round his long left ear."

There is absolutely nothing like him in America, and he must be seen, and heard, and watched
in his native lair to be understood or appreciated.
He is useful in doing the heavy work of farm and
field, but politically and intellectually he is more
like one of his string of stout draught horses than
like a modern man of our race. What is steadiness in the upper classes droops into sheer
stupidity in the lower classes. It is their apathy
that accounts to some extent for the entire lack
of feverish excitement over temporary troubles
which characterizes us Americans. One would
suppose that there were no storms, murders,
poisoned food, in this country, while in America
we revel in these and other tragedies. Who in
America, for example, knows of the Derby pork-
pie epidemic in 1902, when two hundred and
twenty-one persons were attacked and four died?
Who remembers the Manchester arsenical beer
episode of 1900, in which over six thousand

persons were slowly poisoned? In the last annual report of the Local Government Board, which relates to the year 1906–7, it is stated that the number of samples analyzed under the Sale of Food and Drugs Acts in 1906 was 90,504, of which 8,466, or 9.3 per cent. were certified to be adulterated. Who in America knows that? But who in all the world was not made to hear about Chicago's canned beef! Our rustic Englishman even heard those mischievously exaggerated reports from Chicago, and probably thanked God he was not as other men are, as he said grace over his poisoned pie and his arsenical beer. We Americans are accustomed to exaggerated retailing of our faults and misdeeds even from public men in high places. Our common-school sophisticated people rather enjoy the excitement. They are not educated up to the point of appreciating its immaturity and lack of perspective, but they are wide awake enough to be interested and even stirred by it. In England the mass of people would not be stirred in the least; while the governing class, trained and disciplined, would ignore such exuberance as bad form. It is quite our own fault, and not a matter for surprise, therefore, if, when we are thus advertised, the country people with whom I am now dealing look upon us in America as being an excitable, rather untrustworthy people, holding nothing sacred, and with little personal pride or elevated patriotism.

If there is a difference in the alertness of the people, there is also, it must be admitted, a difference in their leaders, who would, and who do, consider it disgraceful to advertise themselves at the expense of the blunders, or even the sins, of their countrymen.

Though one may look askance at the political and educational condition of this class of the English populace, one can have little but admiration for the thousands of Englishmen who work away year in and year out at the details of local government in England.

The country Towns, Boroughs, and Districts, and Parishes, and all the machinery of their government, are entirely managed by the voluntary labors of those with the wealth, leisure, and ability to do so. They sit as Magistrates, they govern the towns as Councillors and Aldermen, they look after the roads, sanitation, water supply, lighting, schools, poor-houses, and are expected by the powers that be in Parliament to put into, and keep in working order, educational and licensing enactments; and recently, the whole reorganization of the territorial forces, or new Army Bill, and the putting into effect of the Small Holdings

Act, are to be largely entrusted to them for their successful operation. That they undertake all these duties, that they do them so well, and with so little — almost no — friction, and with so little dissatisfaction to those whom they thus govern, is, I am inclined to think, the most impressive feature of English life.

They are called "The Great Unpaid," and the name is truthful rather than humorous. They act as local commissioners, known as General or District Commissioners of Taxes, and collect the income tax, while quite independent of party and holding their appointments directly from Parliament. All Justices of the Peace are *ex-officio* commissioners. The land tax is also collected by unpaid commissioners. Of the County Councils having under their control lunatic asylums, bridges, main roads, which are responsible for the county rate, I have written. Chairmen of Quarter Sessions also try all cases not necessarily going before Judges of Assize, and also hear appeals from Justices of the Peace at Sessions.

More than an hundred hospitals in London and the country are administered by governors and committees, as are the British Museum, the National and Portrait Galleries, and many others.

Royal commissions and departmental committees do an immense amount of work. Lord Beaconsfield said: "The government of this country is considerably carried on by the aid of Royal Commissions. So great is the increase of public business that it would be probably impossible for a Minister to carry on affairs without this assistance." The London County Council demands and, fortunately for the nation, commands the most varied talents for the successful administration of the affairs of London. All of these men are unpaid in money and scarcely even receive very wide recognition, let alone applause. The School Committee alone in London spend nearly $18,000,000 a year, and have under their management some 750,000 children and 10,000 masters and mistresses. The managers of these schools give their services and in addition look after the schools of cookery, laundry work, manual training, gymnastics, swimming schools, home nursing, asylums for the mentally defective, blind schools, truant schools, pupil-teachers' schools and so on. No country in the world receives so much and such valuable service from its leisure classes, or rather its upper classes, since many of these men are already professionally engaged, or busy with large private affairs. The large landholdings, the concentration of wealth, the position and privilege accorded to birth and breeding are thus in some sort compensated for. The most superficial student realizes that these people would not countenance an idle, or a purely pleasure-loving aristocracy. Herein lies the secret of the permanence of the English classes in these days of rule by the masses. On the whole they pay, and pay with strenuous and honest service, for what they receive.

The chapter on "Who are the English?" outlined the historical forces, or genealogy, of this system of unpaid self-government. If the ownership of the land in a few hands, and the aggregation of wealth in a few hands are evils, this wonderful system of efficient unpaid local government goes some way to palliate them. The saving of expense to the taxpayer must be enormous, and it may well be set down as unquestionably true that the work is far better done than it could be by a paid staff of political servants. Administration, whether at home or abroad, is apparently the birthright of the well-trained Englishman. When one sees at close quarters how admirably he keeps his own house in order, one is the less surprised at his hitherto unparalelled success as a colonizer and administrator in other countries.

The application of law without common-sense

results in friction and chicanery unending; while common-sense without law becomes mere paternalism tempered by tyranny. The happy medium is the application of the law by common sense, and nowhere may this be seen to better advantage than here. Imagine the British Empire administered for a year by Frenchmen! If it were not for the horror of what would follow to innocent people, nothing could be more grotesquely ludicrous. The results to the humorist would be even more illuminating than should the English undertake to do the dressmaking and millinery work of the French. I venture to say that nothing in the whole realm of æstheticism could be more awful than that.

Even as complicated a measure as the new Small Holdings Act, which, roughly described, is a bill to enable persons without land in England and Wales to become possessed of a certain number of acres by proper payments, the land of course to be leased or purchased outright from the larger landowners, has been turned over to the County Councillors to work out. When one realizes the jealousies, and the jobbery, that such a taking and giving of property might entail, one must needs envy in a measure a nation where there is a competent body of unpaid workers willing to undertake so distasteful and so techni-

cally difficult a task. This very day there appears
in the *Morning Post* the following advertisement:

EMPIRE MOVEMENT

Ladies and Gentlemen of independent means are invited to
offer their *services gratis* for the promotion of the "Empire
Movement" at home and throughout the Empire. No expenses
paid. Formation of local permanent Committees, distribution
of literature, etc.—Address: Earl of Meath, 83, Lancaster Gate,
London, W.

The italics are the letter writer's.

To what extent this appeal in a morning paper
will be answered I have of course no means of
knowing, but it is a pertinent and timely proof
of what has been said in regard to the faith of the
Britisher in the existence and willingness of the
unpaid and unprofessional worker to take additional burdens upon his shoulders. At any rate
it will probably result in correspondence for the
noble lord that very few men would care to undertake gratuitously. They do not confine their
interest and their activities to official matters of
administration. In such semi-public matters
as hospitals, agricultural and flower shows, cricket,
and rowing, and football, and provident clubs,
golf, and here and there polo clubs, they not only
support and encourage, but they participate.
Their interests of this kind are even greater and

more varied than in the public work which is done under the law. It is this genuine and wholesome good-fellowship between all classes which tempers the strict social demarcations. There are classes to be sure, but the classes all belong, and take pride in making it evident that they do belong, to one all-powerful class, which is England.

The more prominent one is by birth, wealth or position, the more it is looked upon as incumbent upon such an one to take an active part in local and national affairs. The masses have grown to feel that they can depend upon the classes to lead, and to lead courageously and wisely. Though England has become perhaps more democratic in certain ways, it is still very evident that the Englishman likes a gentleman to lead him. I am told that in the army this is made unmistakably evident. It is not mere snobbery, though there may be a touch of it, but it is the centuries old instinct of the English to have faith in *noblesse oblige* as a real factor in life.

There died only lately a shy, awkward Englishman, of great name and great estates, to whom it was a kind of torture to speak in public, to whom it meant hours of drudgery to master problems of State. He became the most trusted of English statesmen. When people spoke of

"The Duke," it meant the Duke of Devonshire. He was never in the least shifty, or ingratiating, or amenable to even the lofty bribes of office or ambition. He held a brief for England, and made no fuss about it. He was typical of the class, which, numbering its thousands far less conspicuous than he, do the work of England because they consider it a duty. When England arrives at her Pass at Thermopylæ, this large class will have to be reckoned with, and I venture to prophecy that there will not be even one left to tell the news, if things go against them.

This sense of duty to England, when exercised by the English abroad, takes on an air of aggressiveness and superciliousness which have often been noted by foreigners. As a matter of fact they are unimaginative administrators, rather than supercilious. They look upon themselves as sentinels of a kind of Anglican Almighty whether at home or abroad, and the stiffness of their deportment should be forgiven them, rather than held up against them. A man who has India at arm's length and Ireland squealing at his feet, must needs be robust and matter of fact, rather than nervous and an idealist, if he is to sleep nights. As an example of devotion to duty I cite the case of an English gentleman of comfortable income who, finding when the South African war broke out that he had no military experience, enlisted and went out as a farrier or blacksmith. He had learnt horseshoeing as an amusement in his youth, and was, and is, an amateur in gold and silver and iron work. He shod horses until his value was recognized for other duties, and he came home a major, having been twice wounded. What can Ireland, or Germany, or other enemies do against a nation whose gentlemen are made of such stuff as that!

Of the smaller domestic social life in the town itself the variations are so many that it would be quite impossible to make an inclusive category without weariness to both writer and reader. There are musical, and debating, and mutual improvement societies, and these are becoming more and more common, and they flourish or not according to the talent available.

One marked difference between the English and the American town is the part played by the local churches in the American towns. They are often the centre of the amusements of the town. Around them grow the literary and musical and even the dramatic clubs. Church "sociables," and picnics, and suppers, are often part of the regular programme of church work. According as the local pastor is energetic and of varied talents, social and literary, these activities flourish. In England this is not the custom. The people in the town itself lunch and dine together, and on a much smaller scale keep the social ball rolling along much the same lines as their wealthier neighbors of greater social position. I well remember my astonishment at the first dinner given to some ten or a dozen neighbors who had been civil to us, to find in the hall where hats, coats, and wraps had been left, various rolls of music of different sizes and descriptions. I hastily informed the hostess of this discovery. Our duty-loving English guests had come prepared to do their share towards the general entertainment after dinner. This was before the days of bridge playing, and what happens now I know not. But at that time each one came prepared to sing or play for the edification of the others. Most amateur music in England, as elsewhere, my experience teaches, is not an aid to digestion; and to the ultra-sensitive it may even be a test of patience; but the English are duty-doing rather than artistic, and an amiable host forgets of course certain painful laryngeal exercises in his appreciation of the unselfish desire of a guest to do his, or her, share toward the general entertainment.

The English dinner party, in the provincial towns and cities at any rate, is a heavy, prolonged and rather lugubrious affair. One feels sometimes as though it would be neither surprising nor inappropriate should one suddenly hear a voice saying: "Brethren, let us pray!" In England, as elsewhere, little people give bad big dinners, and big people give nice little dinners.

It was considered proper in Northbridge to give rather pretentious dinners of many courses, with servants added to the staff for the evening. I have seen on more than one occasion the groom, in livery of belt, breeches, and boots, assisting at the service of the dinner. It must be added, however, that the dinners were given apparently as a social duty, and as a return for similar courtesies received during the year, rather than as an attempt at display. It adds something of both ludicrousness and lugubriousness to a dinner to hear the assistant of the local undertaker, who is serving as a waiter for the evening, whisper to your host, who has ordered your glass refilled with champagne: "There ain't no more, Sir!" Even if one be still thirsty, the incident is forgotten, however, in the knowledge that your host is doing his best in your honor.

There is little exuberance or elasticity in provincial hospitality, though it is as kindly and generous as anywhere in the world. They labor under the disadvantage of certain racial char-

acteristics, which, while it makes administrators
of the finest quality, does not produce entertainers. I can imagine that the Duke of Devonshire himself was probably not a scintillating
host, and no doubt England thanks God that he
was not, and with reason.

In the American town that I have in mind as a
contrast, there was no attempt, even by people of
similar means and position, to live up to any such
social standard as that of dinner-giving on any
scale whatever.

Strange as it seems, having in mind the small-
ness geographically of England and the ease with
which one may go from place to place, the English town is more an entity and less dependent
upon neighboring large towns and cities than is
the case in America. The people in Northbridge
keep within their own borders more, and depend
more upon themselves for such amusements, rec-
reations and social enjoyments as they have, than
would hold true of an American town. Here, as
elsewhere, they cultivate the faculty of being
sufficient unto themselves, and display that resourcefulness in small matters which distinguishes them in large affairs.

Here again, too, their climate influences their
way of living. I doubt if there was one man in a
hundred in Northbridge under seventy-five and

not a pauper who was not an active participant in some form of sport—hunting, shooting, cricket, tennis, golf, rowing—and many in addition interesting themselves in the local militia, volunteers, or yeomanry. Some part of every day in the year they can be, and are, out of doors. While in Bear's Cove more time is given to, and more interest taken in, novel or reading clubs; in Northbridge, out-door sport claims more time and keener interest. While from the economic point of view it may be regretted that the land is so unequally distributed, from the point of view of the inhabitants of a country town, it is a most agreeable and convenient arrangement. The land is all cultivated, and the fields, and woods, and country lanes are in and of themselves a vast park, open to all so long as there is no disturbance of the game and the cattle. And what a park it is! This soft, dreamy, drowsy, English countryside, in the summer months at least, is the fairest setting in the world for a holiday, and goes far to account for the English love of out-door life and for many of the differences between an American and an English country town.

Perhaps the main, the fundamental, difference between the two is after all that the English being less imaginative, and with fewer opportunities, and hence with less incentive to change their social or financial status, seem to the American to be more contented, more peaceable, and calm — the unsympathetic American might phrase it as duller, less enterprising. These country town people are seemingly striving to live as did their fathers and grandfathers; in America the restlessness is the result of the strife on the part of most people to have a portion of the wealth, the good fortune, the opportunities, of their grandchildren. The Englishman looks back for his standard, and makes tradition and precedent serve as guide; the American looks forward, scans eagerly the far horizon of the future, rebels against old customs, against the ways of the grandfathers, scoffs at caution, and lives as much as he can in the future. The Englishman lives upon his income knowing how hard it is to increase his capital; the American all too often lives upon his capital and looks upon the opportunity to participate in the enormous increase of natural wealth of his country as a more or less assured income. The Englishman prosaically tries to live upon what he has; the American lives upon what he thinks he deserves, upon what he expects. One can readily see how this fashions differently the setting of life. The one results in calm, in contentment, or, at any rate, a forced contentment which imitates the reality;

the other results in an attitude of expectancy, of constant striving and restless watchfulness. The American even in a country town is surrounded on all sides by the evidences of what twenty-five years of Future have done; the Englishman is surrounded, on the contrary, on all sides by what hundreds of years of Past have done. The American naturally enough leans forward; the Englishman leans back. We all know which is the more alert position of the two, and which is the more restful. The one is trying to keep what he has; the other is trying to wring what he can from the future. The one plays with what he has; the other gambles for what he wants. The one tries to make himself comfortable in last year's nest; the other is looking for the best place to build himself another nest, better and bigger than the old one.

The country town in England and in America differ accordingly. In the one they are making the best of what they have inherited; in the other they are mainly solicitous about what is to come. The house of the Englishman is being mellowed and smoothed down. More vines and roses grown on it every year. The house of the American is in a constant state of repair, of being added to, of being improved. Both to the eye and to all the other senses the one spells repose, quiet; the other advertises activity and restlessness. Each prefers his own. Fortunately it is no business of mine to decide between them. If I have come anywhere near accuracy in noting the differences, I have satisfied my own purposes.

IX

SOCIETY

IT is with some misgivings that I put the word "Society" as the heading for a chapter. The word has been so misused, and is so often supposed to apply only to that small knot of people who are the mere dregs of opulent idleness that one is inclined to apologize for its serious use. It is not for me to place the blame in any one quarter, upon the news and sensation-hungry press, upon the notoriety-loving wives, or upon the advertising husbands, but the trouble lies somewhere there. That the very word "Society" should call up visions of monkeys, madcaps, and mountebanks, reckless expenditure, gilded display — a company of men and women, in short, engaged in the fatuous activity of trying to mould pleasure out of idleness, a task as hopeless as to build an enduring monument out of mush — shows at once how false must be the standards which have lent this meaning to the word.

There is, none the less, and despite these loose vagaries of meaning, such a thing as Society in every capital and in every country, difficult as it is to define. It bears something of the resemblance to the rest of the community that the sunny side of a peach, upon which a monogram or the head of the King has been outlined by the sun, does to the rest of the peach. It has had more sun, more care and more money spent upon it. It implies first of all wealth, and after that certain subtle laws of cohesion which make this company of men and women known as Society, the acknowledged, significant, and socially powerful association of their day and generation. Such a company existed at Versailles, still exists in Vienna, is easily distinguishable in London, and in a more shadowy form in America.

Where there is a king and a court this company finds its centre there, and one knows where to go to look for it. Where there are none, the centre is shifting and evasive, and the boundaries indeterminate.

In other chapters it may be seen that the English do not take readily to either the social or political dictatorship of a king, nor have they ever been courtiers. Until within a comparatively few years the wealth of England has been the wealth of landholders and landlords. The members of this class have represented the nation politically and socially, both at home and abroad. From them have been drawn the members of Society. It is often said that anybody with money may become a member of Society in England, and this is with many limitations true, but it is not, as many people think, new. England has always been willing, not to say eager, to distinguish worth and wealth. James the First, needing money, created two hundred baronets at one thousand pounds apiece at Burleigh's suggestion. Charles the First insisted upon creating knights, whether the knighted liked it or not, in order to collect the fees.

The landowning or territorial aristocracy has been recruited again and again from the successful in other walks in life, either for good, bad, or indifferent reasons. In the last fifty years the wealth of the landowners has decreased enormously, and the wealth of the manufacturer, the banker, the builder, and those engaged in commerce of whatever description, has increased even more noticeably. As a result of this more people have been taken into this body in the last few years, but this has always been the custom in England. It marks no change, only a difference in quantity. It is, and always has been in England, from this class that Society emerges. It is the only class here from which any distinguished company could come.

As they have been also the governing class and as London is the seat of government, London has been the setting for all social activities of any importance. There is social life of course in Edinburgh, and in Birmingham, and in Dublin, and in Leicester, but Society meets in London. Society not only comes to London, but must come to London. There are no rivals, and there is nothing to call Society anywhere else. The body from which Society is drawn and the playground or meeting place in the season are fixed. This accounts in no small measure for the lack of advertising and notoriety about social matters here. In the season there is so much going on, so many political, social, and other affairs, that it is physically impossible for the newspapers to distinguish them all with head-lines and paragraphs, or to make sensations of them even were that the custom. Any one of a dozen functions, all in one day or night in London, would be meat and drink to the sensational press for columns of matter and days of comment in America. When it happens that a horse show, a church congress, a county cricket match, or a school or university cricket match, inter-regimental polo match, a regatta on the Thames, half a dozen balls, a political hostess's reception, an international exhibition, the Royal Academy picture exhibition, are all going at about the same time, the journalist is swamped by his material, and people and parties are left inconspicuously and happily alone by the very impossibility of sensationalizing everything. Where in New York or Washington there is one wedding, or one ball, or one football match, or one big dinner, London provides a half dozen of each day after day, and even the housemaid would be bored by an attempt so colossal to play upon her curiosity, her taste for high life, or her love of exciting gossip.

If every fellow in the play is a "noble Marquess" or a "belted Earl" one becomes surfeited, no matter how voracious the appetite. London for three months in the year absorbs the entertainers and entertainments of all England, and each and all are more or less lost in the maze of social doings. Court functions are officially noticed, but without comment; lists of names are given, and those who care to do so permit their gowns to be described. Any one who wishes may, on payment of a guinea, chronicle his arrival, departure, or whereabouts in the staid columns of the *Morning Post;* and a few people through their secretaries, or other paid agents, contrive to keep themselves more or less bepara-

graphed from time to time. But no body of
people, great or small, find it to their credit, or to
their advantage, to permit a minute advertisement of themselves along theatrical lines. London is so much bigger than anybody or anything
in London, that the very bulk of the place keeps
all more or less inconspicuous. No man or
woman can be interested or active along so many
social, political, and athletic lines, and as a consequence each is subdued to the color of his or her
own employment. There is no one centre for
the newspaper limelight to play upon, and its
distribution over such an enormous stage leaves
all the actors in a less glaring light.

Less easily explained, but none the less to be
noted, is that law by which Society, as well as
art, and literature, and politics, follows the
nation's centre of gravity. In the days of
Elizabeth, for example, the centre of gravity was
among the middle classes, and Drake and
Raleigh were great men. After the Restoration
the centre of gravity moved toward the aristocracy, and one has only to glance through Bishop
Burnet's history of the time, by the way, to discover for one's self how vastly improved are the
manners and morals of men and women since
those days of the foul and the filthy in Society and
the Court. There are few even professedly

pornographic writings containing such a list of bestial details and scandals as those enumerated, apparently with some gusto, in the first edition of this ecclesiastical worthy's History.

At about the beginning of the eighteenth century the centre of gravity, both social and political, became fixed in the great Whig families who had carried through the Revolution. The Society of London drawing-rooms then, and thereafter, maintained a vigorous influence both in politics and in literature. It is from these great territorial families, whether Whigs or Tories, that Society ever since has derived its sustenance, its traditions, and its power.

Such, roughly, is the pedigree and the background, as London is the meeting place, of English Society for three months in the year. It would be missing a chief characteristic of English social life not to bear in mind just here, that it is only for these two, or at most three, months that Society meets in London. The Englishman may have a house in London, but his home is always in the country. The best of them still love the land. It is at the country-houses, where for the greater part of the year the English are at home that one sees English Society in its natural and graceful setting. Even the clothes of the women are becoming, and the manners of both men and women appropriate and happy in these surroundings they love best of all. In their own homes in the country, doing the things they genuinely love to do, shooting, riding, fishing, looking after their estates, entertaining generously, surrounded only by those agreeable to them, with nothing to make them self-conscious; here at last the Englishman thaws, and becomes almost lovable! He has been criticized, this Englishman, in these pages, never with intentional unfairness, but in this setting of his own home in the country, there is not a word, except in praise — and I may add on my own behalf — in affection and admiration to be said. If you want him at his best, go and stay with him in his home in the country! There and then he is the best fellow imaginable, and you leave him and his home with respect, with affection, and with admiration. A third, and distinguishing feature, is that Society is dominated by masculine not by feminine influence.

The London season is from May till the grouse shooting begins in August. Why? asks every stranger who hits upon a dry and hot July in London. The reason is a very simple one: Men are shooting up to Christmas time, and then hunting after that. They will not live in London when sport is calling them to the country. In summer there is no shooting and no hunting, but there are Parliament, polo, and cricket in London. Society meekly adapts itself to the man's duties and diversions.

At the risk of vain repetition I may not emphasize too often this preëminence of the man in England. We have noted it in other places, but it comes to the fore again even here. Society is so patently, even impertinently, for the women in America, that to the American it is with some awe that he sees even social matters dominated by and adjusted to, the convenience and even to the whims of the men here. One may say humbly, and with apologies to his countrywomen, that this masculine dominance is not altogether a failure. It is perhaps old-fashioned, and due also to the refined feminine influences of one's past and present surroundings, but it never seems quite as though the social adjustment of things is right when woman becomes conspicuous, and certainly not right or wise when she becomes the target for the camera and the paragraph. It is my humble belief that a woman cannot become "well known" without becoming *ipso facto* too well known.

It seems that Dame Nature by an iron law ordained that the male bird should wear the brave and conspicuous plumage. Apparently when it is attempted to upset this world-old law of precedence, and the female is clothed in the plumage and perquisites of the male, she fails. She all too often becomes a cocotte in France, a divorcée in America. It somehow takes away from the fairest bloom of womanhood when she struts the stage of the world, when, *spectatum veniunt, veniunt spectentur ut ipsœ.* It is certainly not for their health, it may be doubted if it be for their happiness, to shift the burden of even social preëminence to the shoulders of women.

It has come about in America by easy and natural stages. We have amassed in a few years great wealth with no traditions behind it and no weight of responsibility upon it to keep it steady. It is too new to be left to take care of itself, and the energies of the men are devoted to keeping, controlling and adding to it. Very few of the men who have it, most of their fathers, and nearly all of their grandfathers, have, and had, no other resources. That is the only game they knew or know. But it must be spent. It cannot be said of us by our worst enemy that we Americans are misers. Palaces, and steam yachts, and motor cars, and equipages, clothes and pocket money are provided for, or should one be more accurate in saying, piled upon, the women of these opulent ones. Many of the women in consequence are forced into being idle spend-thrifts.

There is no such outlet for voluntary work in America as in England. We have written in another chapter of the amount of unpaid polit-ical, charitable, educational, and other work done here by the men of the leisure classes. Many of these opportunities are also open to, and are taken advantage of, by the women. The wife and daughters of a rich man in England, with the church, the schools, the poor in the neighborhood of his estate, may find their hands full of work. It is not resented here, it is expected. In Amer-ica, the schools, at any rate, are governed by the State, and idle ladies who should without tradi-tion and precedent behind them invade the pre-cincts of the State-paid schoolmaster or school-mistress would receive but a scant welcome. An idle man, whose thoughts and actions are continually driven back in and upon himself, is a pitiable object, and generally a physical and mental invalid before he is fifty. What of a woman under such circumstances? Is it to be wondered at that she shirks what might be her only salvation — motherhood, and becomes with satanic selfishness a peevish follower of her own whims?

The English woman knows that tradition, the law, and Society, demand of her that she shall make a home for a man; the American woman has been led astray by force of circumstances into thinking that her first duty is to make a place for herself. Far be it from one who owes much, if not all, to an American mother and an American wife, to offer these conclusions as an attack. They are meant as an explanation of the unfortunate doings and wasted lives of only a small, very small, knot of women in America, but a company so highly-colored, so vociferous, and so advertised that they stamp themselves upon the superficial foreigner as being typical, when as a matter of fact they are merely hysterical.

Wherever in the history of the world woman has assumed, or been accorded, this unfortunate and artificial prominence, it has meant decay. Aspasia was the tolling of the bell as manhood died in Greece; harlotry in France has now a recognized place, with privileges unknown, and certainly unrecognized, amongst the fighting nations of the world; and let us be quite frank and admit what all the world thinks, that men who cannot and will not fight are not men at all. Where the æsthetic is more cherished than the athletic, women may thrive but men decay.

In America this deprivation of woman's true function of the home keeper has been rudely and suddenly jarred and thrust on one side, but not, I believe, permanently, by the idleness which often comes with unexpected and untraditioned wealth.

> "It is not death, but life that slays:
> The night less mountainously lies
> Upon our lips, than foolish days'
> Importunate futilities."

It may be said that it is not entirely the fault of the women, or of the men, that this situation exists, and let me repeat that it applies only to a very small proportion of men and women in America, but we happen to be dealing for the moment with that small number. The American is too much occupied with affairs to have time to spare for much social recreation; nor has he cultivated that facility in sympathy, in expression, and in manner, which makes the artificiality of Society a comfortable relaxation for him. Our women are almost obliged to surround themselves, and to use, for social purposes, either very young or inferior men. This is not good for women. Nothing a woman tires of so soon in a man as her own virtues and vices; nothing she so soon learns to despise in a man as her own methods of conquest. One may say, without much fear of intelligent contradiction, from either my countrymen or my countrywomen, that the male drawing-room notabilities in America are not of the type that one would care to increase, or to exhibit to the world, as typical of American manhood. The men who have made America great at home, and respected abroad, would, alas, find little to interest them at our most widely advertised social functions.

To a very large extent this is not true of English Society. The ablest and the most notable men from all walks of political, financial, literary, artistic, and adventurous activity, find their way, at least from time to time, to English drawing-rooms and dinner tables. They go not only because they meet the fairest and most attractive women there, but because they meet men there of their own calibre. The women provide the soft stuff in which delicate things may be packed together without breakage, they serve as agreeable and sophisticated buffers when people of different tastes, pursuits, and aptitudes come together. The ideal host is a woman not a man, whose sympathy and trained perceptions put conflicting and uneasy talents together, and make them forget their antagonisms. No man can do this as can a woman, and no woman learns the art who

only deals with women or with inferior men.
Men add a difficulty to social life, which improves
it when it is overcome.

Perhaps the most outstanding feature of social
as of other phases of life in England to an American is the fact that it is the man's code of ethics
which obtains and not the woman's. A woman
cannot claim a divorce on the ground of adultery
alone. The offence must be accompanied by
cruelty, or be committed so openly and frequently as to mean cruelty, before it becomes
cause for separation or divorce. Divorce indeed
is only for the rich, for those who can afford a
prolonged and expensive legal battle. It is not
for discussion here whether this is good or bad,
but one may say as an American that the flings at
American methods in such matters are hardly
warranted.

"In Divorce Court procedure there is now
one law for the rich and another for the poor."
From Sir J. Gorell Barnes's speech to Liverpool law students, February 5.

"It is the serious reproach of our existing
divorce laws that the relief they grant is practically out of the reach of the working classes
in this country, by reason of expense and the
absence of local courts empowered to grant it."
From the judgment of Lord Justice Fletcher

Moulton in the case of Harriman *v.* Harriman,
February 9.

Under the Summary Jurisdiction (Married
Women) Act of 1895 there were granted up to the
end of 1906, 72,537 separation orders. Seven
thousand separations a year amongst this small
population, or one to about every 540 of the
population, is not a showing that would tempt
any but the ignorant or the unthinking to hold up
hands in pharisaic horror where other nations are
concerned.

The Englishman looks at the whole matter,
not from a logical or a highly ethical point of
view, but from his usual makeshift common-
sense point of view. He holds that a lapse from
fidelity in a man does not destroy his usefulness,
neither is it irretrievable; in a woman it may on
the contrary interfere irretrievably with the rights
of all others he holds most dear, the rights of
succession and property. Failure to keep his
word or his contract, whether in gambling or
commerce, he refuses to forgive and punishes
swiftly and surely both socially and legally, but
infidelity he looks upon as unfortunate but
not criminal. There have been many instances
of politicians and statesmen notoriously un-
chaste, whose status in the service of the State
and whose usefulness have not been in the least

interfered with by that fact. One recalls the
episode of poor King George, whose wife on her
deathbed said to him: "You will marry again."
"Oh, no," whimpered the monarch, "J'aurai
des maîtresses!" "Mais ca n'empêche pas,"
replied the Queen. "Depend upon it," said a
French lady of the old régime, "God Almighty
thinks twice before he condemns persons of
quality!" One is led to suspect that the great
English church dignitaries, and other English
moralists, have something of the same feeling.
I find it hard to believe that the Archbishop of
Canterbury would openly rebuke the reigning
sovereign, or the heir to the throne, even though
he were notoriously unfaithful. It must be with
some sense of discomfiture, if not of shame, that
the clergy, paid as they are by the State, rebuke
gambling and unchastity amongst the lower
orders, but never whisper disapproval of these
vices among the great. Even the great Churchmen are apparently believers in the doctrine of
compromise. They preach that cautious Christianity which holds up an ideal for all, but applies it as a rule only for some, and those the least
conspicuous and the most amenable. These parsons are on the side of the angels doubtless, but
they seem very loath to do the devil any harm,
when he appears in the garb and with the man-

ners of a gentleman. Logic, as we have seen, is not applied to life. They have discovered that it is not workable. They hold that the Decalogue, for example, is in ten different parts, and though one part be broken the rest may still be intact. Morals are not a jug, which if it have one hole is useless to carry water, but rather a platter, which though it be chipped and scratched may still serve to pass the loaf. They recognize that the bread of life itself is served on, and eaten from, some very disfigured platters, and that the world would starve even spiritually and morally if it were required that all platters should be without spot or nick.

So long as such matters do not become the subject of public scandal, so long as a man is not dragged through the courts, little attention is paid to that phase of his private life. It is known to everybody; it is mentioned in public by nobody. It is not considered prejudicial to a man's usefulness, and were a political opponent to use such weapons against a man he himself in all probability would be the sufferer.

I need hardly call attention to the abysmal difference in this particular between the masculine code which applies in England and the feminine code which applies in America. One of the ablest and most useful chief magistrates we have had in America since Lincoln was nearly defeated when he was first a candidate for the Presidency by noxious stories about his private morals, and at that time he was a bachelor. His life and services proved beyond peradventure how foolish and contemptible was the application of such standards of judgment. The American politician of the small fry order has, however, played the cards of domesticity and a certain namby-pamby sentimentalism to the utmost limit of fancifulness. Behind the noise and confusion made about the seventh commandment the politician and political hanger-on have accomplished the most variegated and daring assaults upon the eighth commandment known to political history. The "Thou shalt not" in the seventh is so vociferous that it is scarcely an audible whisper to the political conscience when it is pronounced in the eighth.

Society, in the large sense and in the more restricted meaning of the word, is learning that a much advertised domestic felicity may be the home and hiding place of a set of burglar's tools. A man ought, of course, to be both clean in his private life and honest in his public life, but it is a pity to be fooled into such over-emphasis of the one that the other is forgotten. A chaste thief is no better than a rake. There are probably more of the former, and fewer of the latter, in American than in English social and political life.

It is not our business here, or the purpose of these pages, to enter upon an ethical discussion, or to approve or to disapprove of either the English or the American code of morals, but merely to note the application and the differences, and if possible to offer some explanation of the whys and wherefores.

It should be kept in mind that Society in England has a status of its own, is outlined in the Constitution itself, is prayed for by the priests of the National Church each Sunday, and that, therefore, a large number of persons are in Society by the law of the land and may not lightly be set aside even on account of moral delinquencies.

It is, I believe, a popular notion that rules of precedence are trivial regulations of temporary officials or chamberlains framed somewhat to suit their fancy. On the contrary, the law of precedence in England is as good a law as any other in Westminster Hall, and is *established* by *Act of Parliament*. The "Act for Placing the Lords" was passed by Parliament in the reign of Henry the Eighth, and even as early as 1399 there was a regulation entitled "The Order of all Estates and Gentry of England."

The English scale of precedence is curiously ungallant in excluding the ladies. The wife of the Archbishop of Canterbury or of York or of a bishop has no place, possibly due to the fact that rules of precedence date from a time when Churchmen did not marry. It seems more than Britishly illogical and irrational in more ways than one that the wife of a saint should not receive her compensating reward in this world! But the same holds good of the wives of the Prime Minister, Lord Chancellor, the Speaker, Secretary of State, Privy Councillors, Chief Justices, and Judges — they none of them have any position guaranteed to them in the laws of precedence. Another curious inconsistency is the fact that the eldest son of a younger son of a peer has a place, while the eldest son of the eldest son of a peer has no place.

In Sir Roger de Coverley occurs the passage: "I have known my friend Sir Roger de Coverley's dinner almost cold before the company could adjust the ceremonials of precedence and be prevailed upon to sit down to table."

A woman who has acquired a dignity by marriage loses that dignity on contracting a second marriage with a commoner. She may retain the title by the courtesy of Society, but she loses it by law. Indeed this particular phase of the law of precedence was carried into the courts by a certain titled lady who contracted a second marriage with a commoner, and was finally settled in the House of Lords, judgment being given against her.

In a word, Society in one sense in England is part and parcel of the law of the land. "Precedence is not regulated by mere conventional arrangements; it is no fluctuating practice of fashionable life, the results of voluntary compacts in Society; but on the contrary is part and parcel of the law of England," to quote from Dod.

The Sovereign and the members of the Royal Family are the apex, not only of the Constitutional, but also of the social, structure of English Society. Next comes the Archibishop of Canterbury, then the Lord Chancellor, then the Archbishop of York. The Lord Chancellor's position between the two, is a compromise arranged after the days when the Lord Chancellor ceased to be a priest. The Lord High Treasurer, if he be a noble of high rank, follows after the Archbishops, so, too, the Lord President of the Council, the Lord Privy Seal, the Lord High Constable, the Lord Steward of the Household, and several other high officials, take precedence of the other dukes of England, provided they are dukes themselves, by virtue of their office, but if they are not dukes then they only take their place at the head of other peers of the same degree as their own. With the exceptions of the two Archbishops and the Lord Chancellor, the table of English precedence is one of personal not official rank. John Jones or Henry Brown may be Lord High Constable, or Lord Privy Seal, or the Lord Great Chamberlain, but none the less the last created peer would take precedence of him, though probably in a public procession there would be no scuffling to assert one's self. It is much too long and intricate a matter to describe in detail, and the table of precedency may easily be found in any English almanac or year book, should the reader care to investigate for himself. Suffice it to say that after those mentioned come the Dukes according to the patent of their creation; eldest sons of Dukes of blood royal; Marquesses in the same order as Dukes; Dukes' eldest sons; Earls in same order as Dukes; younger sons of Dukes of royal blood; Marquesses' eldest sons; Dukes' younger sons; Viscounts in same order as Dukes; Earls' eldest sons; Marquesses' younger sons; the Bishops; Barons in the same order as Dukes; Speaker of the House of Commons; Treasurer of the King's Household; Comptroller of the King's Household; Vice-Chamberlain of the

Household; Secretaries of State under the degree of Baron; Viscounts' eldest sons; Earls' younger sons; Barons' eldest sons; and so on, and so on, down to "Naval, Military, and other Esquires by office."

As we have shown, women take the same rank as their husbands, or as their elder brothers. Daughters of peers rank next immediately after the wives of their elder brothers, and before their younger brothers' wives. The daughter of a duke marrying a baron degrades to the rank of baroness only, while her sisters married to commoners retain their rank and take precedence of the baroness. On occasion an hostess might well require to have a brain of a high mathematical order, and much quickness and astuteness, to marshal her guests in and out of the dining-room, with due regard to their social and official rights.

The outline of these matters given here is merely to impress upon the reader that there is a mould in England for social life. There is a certain class which dominates by right of birth, tradition, and wealth, and there are certain fixed rules of the game which are as much the law of the land as any other law. To the American at any rate, this puts another face on the problem. He must look at it with these differences well in mind, and interpret it according to its own rules and precedents. The wayward and vague criticism of ignorance, or the parochial methods of those who apply the standard of a limited experience to social affairs totally different from anything they know, only bring discontent, bitterness and teach nothing.

Radicalism in England, whether social, political, or literary, was for a long time only a costume and a way of wearing the hair; it is now a philosophy with considerable political and some social power. It is not, however, of the integral tone and temper of the English people. America, on the other hand, has been from the first an experiment in radicalism. Not to be a radical is not to be an American. One may be by birth an American, but still not be in any patriotic or political sense an American. The American is not merely watching, he is, or ought to be, taking part in the attempt of a people to govern themselves, and to give big and little, high and low, educated and uneducated, as nearly as may be equal opportunities.

It becomes a simple matter to mark off the differences which should distinguish such a Society, whether we take the word as meaning the whole people or accept the narrower meaning thereof, from Society under monarchical rules and customs.

Simplicity, not ostentation, must be the supreme virtue in such a community. In England men of wealth and position feel it incumbent upon them to emphasize their position by a certain splendor of living. In America, to emphasize such things is to controvert and deny the value of the main lines of growth of American civilization. The Englishman hands down from father to son a position and a setting which each feels it incumbent upon him not as a fashion but as a duty to maintain. It may be said to their credit that in the main this has been an aristocracy born to duties first, to privileges afterwards, and it is because, with of course the black sheep exceptions, they have lived up to this standard that they still hold the place and power they do.

But the American who surrounds himself with a superfluity of uniformed menials with bulging calves and powdered heads is simply framing a picture of life entirely inappropriate to the history, precedents, and *raison d'être* of his country.

The recent discussions about more money for our ambassadors seem to omit the pith of the problem, which is, that our ambassadors are not in Europe to play up to a king or to an aristocracy, but to represent the American people. When our ambassadors need a score of flunkies to make a setting for their diplomatic mission, they no longer represent America. Franklin, Jay, Bayard, Lowell, and Choate impressed these sensible English people more, and be it said some of them did far more for their country's honor, peace and prosperity than any millionaire ambassador could do. A big house does not represent America, but sturdy simplicity, ability, and the good manners of a kind heart do, and so far as my experience goes, we have been fortunate thus far in being represented by men of that type in England. At the time of this writing, America is honored in the persons of her present ambassador and his chief of staff by their representation of the very best qualities of America's best type of citizen.

In noting these differences, and in calling attention to the fact that there is a constitutional framework bolted together by the laws of the land itself, for the reception and the moulding of society, it must not be understood for a moment that this is Society. There are Dukes and Dukes, Marquesses and Marquesses, Earls and Earls, and they are no more all alike, or all of the same social or political position, or importance, than are the same number of butchers and bakers. That an Englishman by right of birth and hereditary dignity is a part of the social framework, does not mean that he plays a part

in Society, or is even admitted within its portals.
His birth and title give him a distinct advantage,
but they are by no means open sesame.

On the contrary, the outstanding social figure
of the early part of the last century was a man
whose grandmother was a lady's maid, whose
mother was reputed to have been Lord North's
mistress, and who made his mark in the Society
of the day by patronizing royalty, bullying the
nobility, and insulting his equals. It must have
been rather a dull Society which suffered Beau
Brummel for any length of time. It always has
been rather an easily amused Society, and is so
to-day. The men are out-door men, many of
them hungry and tired by eight P. M., preferring
physical rather than mental sensations. The two
popular stage sensations of the late season, much
discussed even by serious men, and patronized by
both the smart and the great, were two unclothed
women, one interpreting Chopin with her legs,
the other representing Buddha with her hips.
They were curiously enough both Americans,
and I could not help thinking that they must both
have died of laughter had they been provided
with sleeves to laugh in. To see an English
Prime Minister assiduously offering his social patronage to a provider of this quality of entertainment is a feature of English life which leaves the

Frenchman, the American, and the German with a bewildering sense that he is either mad or blind.

There is, however, a feature of English social life which makes it interesting even despite itself. England is an Empire. She has men fighting, travelling, exploring, governing and acting as her diplomatic agents in every corner of the world. These men come and go through London, and it is a rare dinner party, or drawing-room function where one or more men are not present who offer variety and interest as a mere result of their experiences. They supply the something new and fresh, without which any Society becomes a very dull meeting of the same people over the same bowl of gossip.

As in other walks in life here, competition is keen. Lady A., or Lady B., or Mrs. Jones, or Mrs. White, could neither attract nor compel people to their houses night after night to meet over and over again a few men and women drawn always from the same knot of playmates. Just to be seen at Lady A.'s, or at Mrs. Jones's would tempt nobody after a certain time. London is far too full of interesting things to do, lively people to meet, and an unending variety of social and other amusements, to make it worth anybody's while to be entertained always in the same way by the same small knot of people.

He must be very difficult to amuse or interest
who finds time hanging heavy upon his hands in
London. Of a morning he may ride or watch
the riders in Hyde Park. Sunday after church
he may see a procession of all the social notabilities of the season again in Hyde Park. Sunday afternoon he may stroll about Tattersall's
and see English men and women in their worship
of the Horse. With a taxi-cab he may get to a
different golf-course every day for a month, and
none of them bad. There is cricket at Lord's
and the Oval. There is polo at Ranelagh, Roe-
hampton and Hurlingham. There are num-
berless excursions on the Thames in an electric
launch, or he may wield the oars or punt himself.
He may have the box seat, or, if he be proficient
with the reins, take the cushion himself for a
drive on the coach to half a dozen or more
different places.

There is lawn tennis at the Queen's Club, and
real tennis there and at Prince's, and he must
be friendless indeed if he have not a friend to
introduce him at one or the other or both of these
clubs. The English clubs are friendliness itself,
and again he may find any one of half a dozen
open to him if he prove himself a clubable person.

If he cares for more serious things, I defy him
to find more courtesy anywhere than will be his

portion as a guest of the powers that be at the British Museum, where quiet, capable servants, and one of the great libraries of the world are put at his disposal. The Tate Gallery, the Wallace Collection, the National Gallery, and the National Portrait Gallery are delightful places to idle in and to recreate one's belief in English art after an hour at the Royal Academy — at any rate the Royal Academy of the last two years. He can hardly stay long in England without making friends, and then he may see many of the private collections of pictures, porcelains, and historical treasures in some of the great houses in and about London. If he cares to see the law courts, the police courts, or to visit the great universities, or the House of Commons, or the House of Lords I can only say from personal experience that there will be no lack of hospitality shown him, and nothing spared to satisfy any legitimate curiosity or interest.

On one of my own frequent visits to the House of Commons, the member who introduced me carried his hospitality to the limit of himself "heckling" a Cabinet Minister, and then making a half-hour speech, whether solely for my entertainment or not I cannot say.

I have often hunted from London, and very comfortably too; and if one cares for racing, there is scarcely a day during the racing season when one may not travel down to a race meeting, and be back in time for dinner. The National Sporting Club has capital sparring exhibitions every Monday night of its season, and sometimes oftener.

Indeed, a man must go out of his way to choose an amusement or an interest that may not be his for the asking. It must have been an effeminate American who remarked that all good Americans go to Paris when they die. Paris may be a good place to go if one is dead or decrepit, or if one loves no more virile exercise than that taken on the cushions of an automobile, but men who are alive and well would prefer London. It is not to be wondered at then that if these be a few of the interests open to the stranger the Londoner finds too many distractions to permit any tread-mill social requirements to curtail his comings and goings.

Although snubbing and climbing, jealousy and malice, play their part here as elsewhere, the social status of many is so assured that they need not, and do not, attend much to what is brought them, or taken from them by their social com-panions. There is an ease of manner, a sim-plicity of speech and bearing, a lack of effort, which are, I take it, the result of this social

stability. But this is only true of the best and
the highest placed classes in England. America
is not alone the home of social awkwardness.
The laborious gentility, the careful speech, the
pose of being at home, *ses nonchalances qui sont
les plus grands artifices*, are painfully apparent
amongst English men and women, who are striving to appear what they are not, or who are out
and out "bounders." The natural shyness, and
slowness, and lack of adaptability of the race
come out with mortifying distinctness when the
English undertake to play a social part which is
a bit above their station.

Those who have suffered socially, financially,
or morally, the frayed, the failed, and the flayed,
are more horribly conspicuous in their efforts to
appear at ease here than anywhere else. The
others appear all the more serene and confident
by comparison. These latter worry very little over
questions of whether they profit or not by being
seen in this company or that, and as a consequence the same general law which welcomes
prowess wherever it appears in England applies
to that microcosm of life called Society. Ability,
success, wealth, provided they be amenable to
the manners, speech, and to that curious categorical imperative of the etiquette of the day and
generation, go where they please and outdistance

easily the mere holders of titles, no matter what they be. I have all through these pages made it a law not to mention names, or to refer to personal experiences, otherwise one might easily offer instance after instance, and example after example, of the truth of this. Every Englishman knows — the American must accept it without proof — members of the nobility, from dukes down, who are hopelessly left out in social matters. The genuine democratic instinct of the people makes itself felt even in the limited companies of which we are writing. Not even the King himself can assure the election of a "bounder" to a club or reëstablish a damaged duke or earl, or demand and be accorded entrance and entertainment in certain great houses for his friends. No Englishman living knows the English, however, better than the present occupant of the throne, and he rarely makes blunders of a social or diplomatic description. Indeed, no ruler in Europe, or anywhere else, makes so few. While of the Queen, one is not exaggerating, or mawkish, in saying that she is not only popular but the darling of the people, high and low alike.

Even in Society a man must do something, be something, to hold his place or to get a footing. It begins at school where the boys must devote themselves to one or another game. It is not a matter of choice. They are impelled to it, not only by the authorities, but by the even more rigorous laws of the boys themselves. One must be a "wet-bob" or a "dry-bob." One must row, or play cricket, or foot-ball, one or the other, but play and play hard they must. They believe in concentration and hardness. "*Virescit vulnere virtus*" is the motto of both masters and boys. This education, like life, is terrible for the feeble, but splendid for the strong. Nicholson, Burton, Palmer, Gordon, Cromer, Kitchener, Curzon, Milner, Rhodes, Roberts, and hundreds more, less conspicuous, but all heroic servants of England are the result of this policy — even the stranger knows their names and their services. Lord Roberts, an old man then, and grieving for the loss of his only son, when asked to go to Africa replied: "I have been keeping myself fit in case of such an emergency!"

This training in their youth has much to do, I believe, with the almost universal reticence of manner and of speech among the better classes. Boasting, "bucking" as they call it, talking of one's self, of what one has, of what one has done, is seldom or never heard. It is with much difficulty that you can get even an account of first-rate deeds out of first-rate men. Men never wear buttons or orders or advertise their distinctions. They hate uniforms, and shed them as though they carried disease whenever their duties no longer require them.

We are a more voluble and peacocky people. We spread such tails as we have, rather too often perhaps. Men of merely formal rank love the titles of "General" or "Colonel" or "Captain." Others adorn their buttonholes with orders of foreign wars, or other conflicts, who have never left their native shores and never seen a gun fired in actual warfare. These are trifling displays of a certain sort of theatrical vanity that do little harm, but the lack of self-control, the lack of personal dignity which such small vanities imply may in larger matters do great harm.

A certain Cabinet Minister, after the death of the late Prime Minister, made a deplorable speech in the House of Lords. The poor man was evidently, but quite unknown to his colleagues, on the verge of a mental collapse. No word of that scene was heard outside the chamber. No reporter, no servant, no member, betrayed the lamentable breakdown of the offender. What splendid magnanimity, and courtesy, that implied. Can any people be the better if in the evening every newspaper in the land is shouting the details of such an incident through the streets by the raucous voices of its distributers?

Liberty I would have, yes, and light upon dark places where plots against the people are hatched, but I would have justice and courteous reticence too. One of the great defenders of the American people in their days of infancy, Burke, wrote: "Wherever a separation is made between liberty and justice neither is in my opinion safe." It is never just to be cruel. It is the weak the uncontrolled men in any community, in any country, who through vanity or love of notoriety throw their own and other people's dignity to the winds.

It is a strange word, and I know little of its etymological ancestry, but it conveys so definite a personality to my mind, that I shall use it in the hope that my contemporaries appreciate the nice shades of meaning it conveys. The word is Nincompoop. There is no place for this creature in either English life, or in that particular essence of English life — English Society. Bad men there are, and women of the type of that acquaintance of Boswell of whom Dr. Johnson said: "Sir, I think your lady is very fit for a brothel." The rules and the curiosities of the laws of Society are as strange and as difficult to define here as elsewhere. They call the chessboard white, they call it black, as Browning says, but why, no man knows.

But be they bad or good, no man is suffered

long, no man holds his place, who does not do
something. Even Beau Brummel was the most
finished social bully of his day. Even the
English themselves scarce realize how often they
ask the question, "What has he done?" The
women ask it, the men ask it. One would expect
that question in a democracy rather than here.
"Who was his father?" or "Whom did he marry?" or "How did he make his money?" are
familiar questions asked about newcomers in
America. This English society still intuitively
and instinctively asks the question, the answer
to which throughout their history, has been the
key to unlock every door, whether political or
social. Above all things, if the new man has
done something for England, his place is assured,
and his reward little short of munificent. And if
a man be born to a high social position all the
more is expected of him, and if he does not live
up to the standard, he is even more an outcast
than is one whose social birthright is accompanied by few responsibilities. Their great
nobles are great by reason of their duties and
responsibilities. An idle, or a vicious bearer of a
great name, is more conspicuously ignored than a
commoner of the same calibre.

It goes almost without saying that much of
the talk about Society here or in America is

purely fantastic and imaginary. Much of the writing about Society in America is merely silly, when it is not of the *Fireside Companion* quality, adopted by the socialist to advertise his wares. Society in America is awkward, but it is not vicious. Many rich people do not know what to do with their money, just as the yokel in the drawing-room does not know what to do with his hands. As Clement of Alexandria phrased it nearly two thousand years ago, so the situation is not new: "Riches wriggling in the grasp of the inexperienced."

The most obvious thing about Society, whether English or American, is that its behavior is so correct, its morals so good. When one remembers that Society, at any rate in America, is so largely composed of the unemployed rich, with money, leisure, and constant temptation, Society compares very favorably indeed with any other section of the population. That the wealthy leisure class is no worse than the hard-working poorer classes is surprising after all. There is less drunkenness, less wife-beating, less murder and assault in the West End than in the East End, and when one realizes that money and idleness are more common in the West End than in the East, this is a matter for congratulation. It is the cheaper newspapers, not the people themselves, who are bad. The thousands of readers who pore over the doings of Society would mob the newspaper offices if they knew how dull and commonplace are the heroes and heroines of the comedy, and how bored they often are with themselves and one another. The sins of Society are only the sins of the slums gilded. Adultery, stealing, drunkenness, sycophancy, are much alike and seldom romantic, wherever we find them. Society is used by the newspapers as a sort of continuous side show. The Bearded Lady, the Skeleton Man, the Giant, and the Dwarf are really impostures, but the gullible public are kept in the dark, and not allowed to know that the Wild Man of Borneo is only a tattooed medical student, who will return, in due time, to resume his chosen studies. If Society were really occupied in hard drinking, in participation in voluptuous entertainments, in orgies of expenditure, in the suppression of child-birth, and at the same time indulging amongst one another in the desultory amativeness of Australian rabbits, Society would be rather exciting — which of all things it is not. The newspapers, and a few irresponsible writers, are the self-instituted proprietors of this collection of freaks which they call Society, and by means of cheap paper and the extraordinary development of the printing press, they give exhibitions daily in every city, town, and hamlet in America. They know very well that the Bearded Lady's beard, and the Wild Man from Borneo's skin, cannot be inspected closely by the audience, and so they riot fearlessly in their descriptions. But there has been nothing in heaven or earth, or the waters under the earth, since Barnum died, which at all resembles what they picture.

Of our ninety millions of people, the large majority are hard workers, clean in their living, economical in expenditure, and scrupulously honest in their dealings. The newspapers amuse them with pictures of a pronounced melodramatic order labelled Society. All the things they do not do, and do not have, are represented to be the daily provender of these morally amorphous beings. To them, it is inferred, dollars are as doughnuts, champagne is as well-water, and when they are not being fined for the excessive speed of their motor cars in one court, they are being divorced in another, or buying up bucolic magistrates, to remarry them in another.

It is only where intelligent people treat such humbug seriously that harm is done, or when an official, or a writer, for revenue or for advertisement, pretends to believe these tales and makes capital out of them, that class may be set against class, and real trouble follow. The only effective criticism that can be passed upon people, is to be better than they are. Exploiting the weaknesses, and exaggerating the foibles of any class of one's countrymen is not a man's task. It is easy to play upon the credulity of a simple people, and simple people living far from this madding crowd may be excused for being deceived; but our more intelligent and more experienced people at home and the same class in England must be dubbed stupid when they accept such descriptions and, alas, *mit der Dummheit kämpfen Götter selbst vergebens.*

It is necessarily true that in a country, as in England, where social functions may be said to be, some of them at least, a part of the machinery of government, and where many others are avowedly for political purposes, the ends and aims of Society's doings are more clear and more dignified than in a Society, as in America — outside of the political doings of Society in Washington — where apparently the end is amusement only and the aim diversion.

Lady Palmerston was a great political hostess, and credited even with keeping her husband in power. The great nobles with great houses in London who entertain the King of Spain at a ball, or the colonial visitors at a reception, or the

Church Congress at a reception, do so as a public duty. No one in London imagines for a moment that such entertainments are given to enhance their social standing, or that such entertainments can be other than rather tiresome functions to the host and hostess, however smiling and amiable they may appear when you make your bow to them. Such entertainments are undertaken as a patriotic duty. Until comparatively recent years, the House of Commons was rightly named the best club in London. Its members were drawn largely from the same class from which the members of Society are drawn. Though this has greatly changed, noticeably so since the last general election, there is still a pronounced flavor of politics in Society, and of Society in politics. This gives Society a certain consistency, a certain seriousness, a certain excuse for being. All sets, the "smart," the "fashionable," the "conservative," the artistic and literary — and Society divides into groups along these general lines — are, from the very fact that their members and their families and friends are of the official governing class, interested in politics. Indeed one might say that while Society's vocation is amusement, its avocation is politics. Here again the fact that politics, domestic and Imperial, are concentrated in London during a few months in the

year explains to the American how this can be so.
This political — using the word in a broad sense
— atmosphere of social life in England is a very
marked feature to an American. At luncheons,
at dinners, during a call at tea-time, even at garden parties, the interest is either sport or politics
or both.

Racing in England is a veritable obsession.
It not only engrosses the entire attention of many
distinguishedly "smart" members of Society, it
is one of the serious occupations of a number of
the great nobles of the country, and the betting
side of it permeates to every hole and corner of
English life. One need not be an over observant
student of Engish life to note that a lion and a
horse with a horn on its forehead uphold the
English shield — and that St. George of England, though he was a pork butcher, is astride a
horse as he kills the dragon. One may say with
some truth that "smart" Society in England
revolves around the King and the horse. There
is, however, a conservative, wealthy, tradition-
loving section of Society, represented, let us say,
by the Duchess of Buccleuch, which, though
representing Society as much as others, have little
more in common with those above-mentioned
than has the Bishop of London with the secretary
of the Jockey Club.

There is a difference between threads which interlace and threads which tie together, and this may serve as illustrating the relations of the different groups of English Society to one another. They all interlace, but they do not all tie together. They cross but they do not knot.

I have no mandate, and no taste, for the task of cataloguing names, of retailing scandal, of hinting at rumors. No one can live among friendly people without hearing, and seeing, and knowing what it must be a point of honor not to reveal. The broad outlines are quite enough to teach all that it can profit others to learn. The squalid, foul-mouthed, and mean-spirited chronicling of the weaknesses of men and women, whether they be placed low or high in social rank, can never be the business of one who studies other countries, or loves his own.

"To be honest, to be kind — to earn a little and to spend a little less, to make upon the whole a family happier for his presence, to renounce when that shall be necessary and not to be embittered, to keep a few friends, but these without capitulation — above all, on the same grim condition, to keep friends with himself — here is a task for all that a man has of fortitude and delicacy. . . . In his own life then a man is not to expect happiness, only to profit by it gladly when it shall arise; he is on duty here; he knows not how or why, and does not need to know; he knows not for what hire, and must not ask. Somehow or other, though he does not know what goodness is, he must try to be good; somehow or other, though he cannot tell what will do it, he must try to give happiness to others." An Englishman wrote that, and from the days of Sir Philip Sidney all through the years till now, there have been Englishmen who have faced life in that way. The names of many of those gentlemen we know, and their deeds and their fame we know, and we, English and Americans alike, cherish their memories as a joint heritage. There are many such in both countries to-day. Society is not composed entirely of such here or elsewhere, but it is not altogether lacking in either men or women who wear the amulet of chivalry, even in these prosaic days.

X

CONCLUSION

IT will be a disappointing miscarriage of the
author's intention if these pages merely
serve to ruffle the feelings of the English,
and to make Americans more carelessly confident.
Both nations have something to learn of one
another, and England being so much the older
country her experiments, her failures, and her
successes have the advantage of the searching
test of time — and certainly time is either the
father or mother of truth.   One is loath to accept
new social or political policies too readily; one
is equally loath to discard methods that have
endured the strain of centuries.

The American who learns nothing from a
study of the English people cannot be said to aid
much in the solution of his own country's problems.

First I put their respect for the law, their law-
abidingness, and their hearty approval of swift
justice, illustrated over and over again in the
foregoing pages.   In a country where political

assassins, financial buccaneers, and wealthy law-breakers generally, may, and sometimes do, thread the courts of justice as in a maze, till patience is exhausted and escape all too often made possible, there is still something to learn from the English. He is either blind, or a traitor to his country, who does not see this and proclaim it.

That we have many races to deal with makes the situation more difficult, but should not in the least interfere with our aim and our steady progress toward reform.

The reticence, the self-control, the even temper of the English, high and low alike, irritate the American often enough, when they should, on the contrary, teach him the value of these things.

The homogeneity of the people, and the result-ant good feeling and fairness on both sides; the wholeness of the nation, the interlacing of the classes, which result in the sturdiest kind of patriotism, verging though it does at times to the side of commercial selfishness, are well worth imitating.

The enormous amount of unpaid and voluntary service to the State, and to one's neighbors, in England, results in the solution of one of the most harassing problems of every wealthy nation, it arms the leisure classes with something worthy, something important to do. Not only their willingness to accept, but their insistence upon, the duty owed to the nation by the rich and the educated has, I believe, more than anything else, given them the long lead in national predominance that they have held until lately. When a man has made wealth and leisure for himself, or inherited them from others, he is deemed a renegade if he does not promptly offer them as a willing sacrifice upon the altar of his country's welfare. There is no blinking the truth that these people have not only an unequalled training for governing, which begins as far back as the Sixth form of their public schools, but they have an instinct for it. The sober, slow, even temper fits them for the task. They govern relentlessly, but confidently and fairly. They govern by law, not by autocratic methods, and they govern always with the aim of increasing, not decreasing, the personal freedom of the governed. They govern to the glory of England, not to exploit themselves. They know that the long years of expatriation and obscurity, if crowned by success, will be amply, even splendidly, rewarded.

England dangles the costliest prizes that are given to men anywhere in the world before the eyes of her citizens. High rank and great fortunes are offered to any man who distinguishes himself in her service. What England would have given Washington, and Franklin, and Hamilton, and Grant, and Lee, and Jackson, and Sherman, and Lincoln, and Cleveland, Taft, and Magoon, and others, had they been servants of hers, one hesitates for fear of exaggeration to say. The head of their church, the Archbishop of Canterbury, is paid $75,000 a year; the Archbishop of York, $50,000; the Bishop of London, $50,000; the Lord High Chancellor, $50,000; the Lord Lieutenant of Ireland, $100,-000; the Lord Mayor of London, $50,000; the Head Masters of their great Public Schools are said to make, if they have a house, as much as from $25,000 to $40,000; their ambassadors to the great Powers receive the equivalent of $50,000; and the men who conquer and control for them in their colonies are rewarded as we have seen. Bear in mind, too, that any man may come to the front in England, whatever his origin. Kitchener and Roberts worked their way up from the bottom. Chamberlain and Asquith, Lloyd George, Haldane and others — do not belong by birth to the governing class, and the same may be said of hundreds more, now conspicuous in England's service. These prizes are not for a select few. They are impartially distributed. There you have the soundest philosophy, and the most generous and fairest practice of democracy in the world to-day. Their method is not to pull every man down to a barren equality, but to push every man up to a brave ideal.

Ill-gotten wealth, misused power, a weakly wielded inheritance, receive little homage in England. We sometimes make mistakes about them in that matter, and call them snobs. It is true they love a lord, and cringe to wealth and power, but this homage is widespread and a part of the national character, because at bottom they expect much, and have so often received much, from rank, and wealth, and power.

There were fifteen hundred Etonians serving in the Boer war, and one hundred and fifty of them lost their lives. Probably a nearly similar proportion was furnished from other schools according to their size, Eton being the largest public school in England. There is somthing to be said even for their love of a lord if they receive fair value for their loyalty, and it must be said that when the pinch comes the Engish noble and the English gentleman have always lived up to their obligations.

This accounts for the fact that in this country of constitutionally fixed class distinctions there is so little class feeling. The Russian noble, instigating a war to save a commercial concession and accompanied to the battlefield by champagne and mistresses, has no parallel here. They have their faults and their black sheep, but their faults and weaknesses are not those of feline effeminacy.

The hundred years of republican government in France and America, diversified in France by autocracy and monarchy, have had little effect upon them. Indeed, monarchy was never more popular in England than to-day. Even the new temper, which is pushing the State on to become a grandmotherly guardian of the people makes but slow progress. Shorter hours for labor, a minimum wage, State insurance, the pensioning of the aged, the free feeding of school children, and the taxing of incomes upon a scale upwards, are new to England.

In spite of the demagogue — and the demagogue is having his day in England just now — the people seem to have a stability of common-sense which is even more valuable than a training in economics. Leisure, which shorter hours imply, has no value in and of itself. More people misuse it than profit by it, to whatever class they belong. Leisure is the tag of the classes—of the rich, of the great—so foolish people think at least, and therefore they demand it as one of the perquisites of equality. Leisure in reality is nothing of the kind. Leisure is the residuum of economy. All men may have it, and all economical men, whatever their work, do have it. Leisure is, and always has been, the reward of economical men. Many idle men never have it. Shorter hours do not produce it, pensions do not produce it. The only thing that produces leisure is work, and hard, painful work at that. You cannot dodge pain as part of the heritage of mankind—you may perhaps change the kind. It would make us all soft if you could. Some men will always have to have their legs cut off as a result of unavoidable accident, or as a result of courage that could not be denied; all you can do is to discover, and to use anæsthetics and to some extent relieve the pain of the operation, but no State controlled by mortal man will ever make accidents, disease, and suffering impossible. The permanent destiny of mankind is to work, and to some extent to suffer, and the less work the more suffering.

It is the ghastly portent of the time that social and political forces are demanding that men should work less instead of planning to make it wholesome for them to work more. Work, and nothing else and nothing less, is man's salvation.

It is easy to see how this new doctrine has arisen. As the belief in the supernatural, or to put it in the common parlance of the street, the belief in God, has grown less strong, there has come a preposterous belief in man, a deification of men. Men have transferred their allegiance and their thoughts from God to man. The Channing school of Unitarianism in New England, which revolted from the exaggerated orthodoxy of Jonathan Edwards, and the philosophy of Comte in France, are organized illustrations of the better side of this change. But this refinement has percolated down through the masses in the coarse form of a mere vulgar and frankly selfish socialism. Man is to be the god, and as such is to be worshipped, provided for, and exalted. The fundamental philosophy underlying all forms of socialism, disguise it as you will, is the worship of man. The pandering to this new doctrine in the name of Christian socialism is simply loose-mindedness. The pith of Christianity and the pith of socialism are as the poles apart. But the pulpit has its demagogues, and its opportunists, no less than the forum. This diluted Christianity, which accepts the doctrines whilst waiving the obligations, is nowadays dubbed manly. Manly merely because it sides with man against God, but could anything be less so ? It sugars the penalties, softens the warnings, emasculates the commandments, and all to please the mob; not to harden them, not to inspire them, not to lift them, but to throw their thoughts back upon themselves. Christianity is at least virile enough to crucify its God, and to announce that pain points the way to salvation. This new god is to be fed and educated for nothing as a child; is to work only eight hours a day as an adult; is to be pensioned at seventy, and never to bear a cross, much less be nailed upon one, if by any means it can be avoided.

We in America are only just recovering from an epigram which held that labor should not be crucified. The only labor that counts for anything in the world has always been, and always will be, born of pain. That is its glory. The nearer labor comes to being a sacrifice of self, the nearer the laborer comes to being a hero and a saint. Labor is dignified only when it ceases to watch the clock, and when duty calls is willing to bear a cross. Wherever and whenever the individual, or any class in the community, whether rich or poor, balks at labor, at pain, at sacrifice, at the cross in short, you have in that individual and in that class a menace to the community and to the State. And it is this very individual, and this same class, that the professional philanthropist, the political and economic sentimentalist, is doing his best to encourage. There is no surer, no shorter way to murder the State than to keep such as these alive. This new doctrine, that at all hazards men must live, is a pagan doctrine, and bad morality and bad economics as well. It was a French judge who met the issue as it should be met. The prisoner before him charged with stealing bread said: "Ma foi, il faut vivre!" "Je ne vois pas la necessité!" replied the judge.

I have no intention of sermonizing, or of straying from the subject. I have tried briefly to describe a prevalent philosophy of the day which enlists demagogues, opportunists, and, in the case of France at any rate, practically dominates the situation. There can be no question of her decadence as a result of this, which shows itself clearly in the departments of industry, and of commercial and mercantile enterprise. It is said by an authority on the subject that this is the fundamental evil, viz., "the colossally disproportionate proportion of the number of officials *maintained by the State*." This develops a mentality characterizing not only the whole official world, but those connected with officials, and those who hope to become officials. Their minds become torpid, they are exhausted by the least effort on their own behalf. In a word they are emasculated. All these superfluous officials instead of being citizens who produce, are parasites and consumers. At the end of the Empire these people numbered less than two hundred and fifty thousand. Between January first, 1906, and January first, 1907, they have increased by two hundred thousand, and before long they will number a million, out of the total population of France of 38,000,000. One man out of every thirty-eight, counting men, women and children, in France a "torpid," "emasculated" dependent upon the State. That is socialism as nearly as any State has adopted it thus far, and who applauds it? This is the system of coddling men into the Kingdom of Heaven, and who regards the France of to-day as in the least resembling that locality?

Even the casual reader will have noticed in these pages reference to the large sums spent in support of an ever increasing number of paupers. It looks on the surface as though here in England, too, there is a tendency to lean unduly upon the State. The generous, not to say affectionate interest in her poorer population by England arises, however, from quite another source. I still believe, though at the present writing the signs of the times do not perhaps warrant it, that the English have no taste for the bureaucratic socialism I have outlined. It is because they are English, not because there is any general feeling that they have a right to be supported by the

State, that there is in England this generous largesse for the poor and the unfortunate. There is a wide difference between the kindly doles of a friend, and the assumption of a right to pick his purse. England's million paupers are not such a drag upon the State, not such a numbing influence upon others, not such an example of unenterprising feeders at the public crib, as are the million petty officials of the State in France. At least, nobody in England strives and studies to become a pauper, as his end and aim in life; while thousands in France prepare themselves to pass the examinations entitling them to become pensioners of the State, to be drugged to torpidity by petty duties for the rest of their lives. There is a possible political and domestic salvation for the pauper, there is none for the petty employé of the State.

He has studied England in vain if he has not convinced himself that the core of their vigor and enterprise is their independence, their individualism, their willingness and their ability to take care of themselves under all circumstances. This socialistic condition of national life produces men of ignoble economies and timorous patriotism. What boots it that the Bank of France to-day has a horde of over $700,000,000 in gold, more than any other country at the moment, if she cannot breed men to defend it, men to use it in her own industries and commercial enterprises, and if at any moment Germany may march again across her frontiers to take another *milliard* and another of her departments? What are such economies worth to the people of France?

We have remarked more than once in these pages that there were here and there signs of decadence in England, that perhaps we may be looking on at the parting of the ways in the history of this colossal Empire. If this be true, we have put our finger on the sore spot. Their history, their traditions and precedents, all point away from this modern tendency to lean upon the State.

The suffrage is new in England, the newly made electorate is still uneducated, still comparatively little interested in larger political affairs. Even now the great majority of the English are only — as they always have been — keen to be well governed, they show no signs of artificial political excitement looking toward an active participation for themselves. They still prefer to be let alone as they did a thousand years ago. It is a novelty to them to find that they can coerce the State into taking care of them. For the moment the novelty of the situation stirs a certain number of them, and there are self-appointed leaders in plenty to urge them on. But not until the Saxon ceases to be a Saxon will he really take to this kindly and eagerly. If that time ever comes then indeed the British Empire will crumble fast enough.

These days of new commercial rivals, and of intense commercial competition, have had a serious effect upon English life as we have seen, and it is folly for the Englishman to ignore them, or to pooh-pooh them. It is, however, folly worse confounded to turn from his virile lineage of individual independence to the weak alternative of petty State interference at every turn as a refuge or a remedy. Grant that one in forty of the inhabitants is a domestic servant, that one in every forty-four is a pauper, that one in every eleven in Ireland is living on the rates, that lunacy is increasing, that the birth-rate is steadily declining, that 30.7 per cent. of the population of London is in poverty, that the entire middle and upper class in London number only 17.8 per cent. of the population, and all this is true, does the solution of these and other problems lie in any scheme for making men less independent, more timorous, more ignobly cautious, readier to trust to the State rather than to themselves to extricate the nation from this slough of despond ? It may be so, but as I study them and their history, I try in vain to make myself see it.

Whether as individuals, or as nations, we co-operate valiantly in bringing upon ourselves our own unhappiness. England has been steadily increasing her taxation, steadily increasing the toll upon large fortunes of late, flirting in short with the theory that the curbing of wealth means distribution to the poor, and now she is aghast at the number of the unemployed, and at the decrease in her export and import trade. Just why capital should continue to offer itself upon the altar of taxation indefinitely it is hard to see, and yet without capital, and capital encouraged and protected, there can be no employment of labor, and no increasing commerce and industry.

We have in America the largest aggregations of wealth under one control in the world. We have one man with more money than any man in history has ever had. We have also a population of nearly ninety millions, increasing of late years at the rate of a million a year, and we cannot get men enough in years of average prosperity to do our work, and we pay the highest wages, and our people live in the greatest average comfort. There may be, and there has been undoubtedly, misuse of wealth, but wealth *qua* wealth is a blessing to everybody. Because one strong man commits murder no one would set out to legislate so that no man shall be strong. Any legislation looking toward the curbing of the competent and the plundering of the thrifty can end in but one way.

When one sees evidences of such intentions in England it is quite within bounds to prophesy evil days to come. England of all nations has made her way in the world by giving her citizens, and protecting her citizens in, the largest liberty compatible with fair play to all. When she shows signs of hampering her strong men, of curtailing their enterprise, and of withholding part of the prizes they win, she is turning her back on her whole history, and interfering with the best and the unique qualities of her people.

I know of not one but several English fortunes, and there are no doubt many more, which have been lodged in Switzerland, where there is no taxation upon foreign securities. The books are kept there, the control is there, and this is done on the ground that taxation in England is becoming confiscatory. This means taking the very blood out of the veins of the body politic. At the same time the Prime Minister is announcing officially, as a result of a recent unfortunate and leaky interview with the German Emperor, that England proposes to maintain the two-power standard of her fleet. The two-power standard means, that her fighting force at sea is to be kept equal to that of any two other powers plus ten per cent. These are brave words, but it is almost laughable to think what would happen should America and Germany start to build ships against her. England would be bankrupt in ten years, her population would emigrate to Canada, South Africa, Australia, and the United States, and the lonely island would become a fourth-rate power used principally as a play-ground by Americans.

Though we Americans may not like the English, we are of the same race, and at bottom I, and most of my countrymen, would not like to see the old man downed. There are several things that may happen to divert destiny. Should England go to war now with Germany she would probably win and would badly damage her most serious and most irritating rival, and give her shipping, her industries, and her commerce a new lease of life. Her premier securities, which, by the way, have declined in value enormously in the last ten years, would go up, and there would be a wave of enterprise and revived hope through-out the Empire. That may happen, and if it is to happen, the sooner the better for England. The Germans since 1870 have taken the place of the English as the boors of Europe, and there would be few tears shed in any capital in Christendom were they chastened.

A political and commercial federation of this great Empire is a second possibility, the result of which would necessarily put England in a very powerful position. Wheat, coal, iron-ore, cattle, sugar, oil, all the sinews of national life, are there, waiting to be organized for offence and defence, while England still smiles superciliously upon her colonies. Canada alone could feed her. Canada alone has a wealth of lumber, coal, iron, limestone and good harbors where ships could be built, with all the materials for the complete building almost within a stone's throw of the docks. An Imperial Parliament, with the natural resources of the great Empire behind it, and the revived energy of a splendid race behind that, and the unhampered capital of the bankers of the world behind that, and unimpaired credit to boot, would solve the problem swiftly enough.

Still another possibility of a renewal of the national life lies in the Englishman's way of working through shifty compromises, till he reaches a practicable hypothesis to go upon. He may be doing that now. These things that we are enumerating as symptoms of a mortal disease may be merely the various phases of recovery. England's agriculture was nearly taxed out of existence by the number of her paupers in the forties, but drastic methods saved her. She has endured fire, and plague, and famine, and escaped, and this may happen again. She has two precious assets to help her. The one is the independence of her best and most powerful citizens, men who despise popularity for its own sake — men like Cleveland, President Eliot, Choate and Root in our own country — the very mainstays of their country wherever they be. There is nothing shifty or selfish about them, and they dare tell the mob that the honey of the demagogue is in reality poison. Such a man was Lord Salisbury, such another is Grey, the present Secretary of State, and there are many more. When matters come to the worst, the Saxon races have always been able to produce their own saviors in this type of man. The Cromwells and the Lincolns are not all dead yet.

The English people, too, are not a chattering race. He who has lived in Spain, in Italy, in France, realizes that one of the chief differences between those countries and the northern nations

is that the people in the former live in the streets,
the people of the latter live in their houses.
Every barber's shop, café, and street corner in
Madrid, or in Florence, and even to some extent in Paris, is a loafing place, a debating club,
and a political and social meeting place. Men
do not think, they talk! London may be
gloomy, New York and Chicago deserted after
sunset, but Madrid, Rome, and Paris are
alive with swarming, gesticulating, chattering
thousands. The climate may have much to do
with this, but for the moment I have nothing
to say to that; the fact remains. The doers and
the governors of the world to-day are not spending their leisure chattering in the streets. One
may laugh at the moroseness, the dulness, the
heaviness; one may make epigrams to the effect
that we take our pleasures sadly, but somehow
we feel that after all the laugh is with us, for
though we may take our pleasures sadly, we have
taken a grim grip upon much the most and the
best of the world, and the sinewy Saxon hand
shows only slight signs of relaxing.

This independence of the few, and this silent
steadiness of the many, must be reckoned
with as the unknown quantities always in abey-
ance in England, and of enormous potential
force.

I note these three contingencies, war, an Imperial Federation, and the steadiness of the people and the independence of their governing class, as likely, any one of them, to change the present trend of things. The last is, of course, the serious and valuable asset. For a thousand years these people have held to the same general lines of progress. Let the best govern, let the rest alone, and give us a workable not a theoretical lead over our fences.

They will see some day, one hopes, that the present day doctrines we have described are not suited to their race. If they were not so parochial, if they did not so confidently believe, as Doctor Johnson once said, and as some of their statesmen have broadly hinted many times since, that "all foreigners are mostly fools," they would be much nearer a realization of this than they are now. The ignorance of their masses, which is complete, and even of their governors and gentlemen, of the political and social and economic methods of other countries is extraordinary. Of what the very doctrines they are now tampering with have done in France, in Germany, and even in their own colonies, they are blandly oblivious. They seem to be constitutionally unable to learn anything from the blows other nations have received, or are now receiving, they must be hit, and hit hard, before they awake to the fact that there is any danger. That is one reason why it is so difficult to visualize to one's self what will happen. They are being hit, and hit hard, just now. One mailed fist is sometimes shaken perilously near the British nose. What they will do when once they are well awake to the situation, I for one decline to prophesy. Those who have read these pages may perhaps be able to come to a conclusion more satisfactory to them than mine would be.

Whatever may be the outcome of the commercial and industrial ferment which has brought to the fore new problems, not only for England, but for other nations, England has taught, and still teaches, mankind the art of governing other races, and has worked out along common-sense lines the only feasible method of securing peace and prosperity under a democratic form of government. Barring America, I should say that the masses in England are still to-day, in spite of much poverty, in spite of the suffering contingent upon the re-adjustment of industrial methods, the most contented, the least nervous about the final outcome, and the most confident in Europe. Personally I am deeply in debt to the English for many delightful friendships, for generous and unstinted hospitality, and for teaching me much that I have tried in these pages to pass on to my own countrymen.

" Were my heart as some men's are, thy errors would not move
    me!
But thy faults I curious find, and speak because I love thee!
Patience is a thing divine: and far, I grant, above me!

Foes sometimes befriend us more, our blacker deeds objecting,
Than th' obsequious bosom guest, with false respect affecting.
Friendship is the Glass of Truth, our hidden stains detecting.

Hidden mischief to conceal in State or Love is treason!"